DOWN TO EARTH

Reykjavík 26/11/20
~~For~~ Paul,
With kind regards.
Árni

40-3, 45, 46-7
131-2, 137-8, 140-1
151-3, 161-2, 165, 206-7
217-8, 221

BEFORE YOU START TO READ THIS BOOK, take this moment to think about making a donation to punctum books, an independent non-profit press,

@ https://punctumbooks.com/support/

If you're reading the e-book, you can click on the image below to go directly to our donations site. Any amount, no matter the size, is appreciated and will help us to keep our ship of fools afloat. Contributions from dedicated readers will also help us to keep our commons open and to cultivate new work that can't find a welcoming port elsewhere. Our adventure is not possible without your support.

Vive la Open Access.

Fig. 1. Hieronymus Bosch, *Ship of Fools* (1490–1500)

DOWN TO EARTH: A MEMOIR. Copyright © 2020 by Gísli Pálsson. This work carries a Creative Commons BY-NC-SA 4.0 International license, which means that you are free to copy and redistribute the material in any medium or format, and you may also remix, transform and build upon the material, as long as you clearly attribute the work to the authors (but not in a way that suggests the authors or punctum books endorses you and your work), you do not use this work for commercial gain in any form whatsoever, and that for any remixing and transformation, you distribute your rebuild under the same license. http://creativecommons.org/licenses/by-nc-sa/4.0/

First published in 2020 by punctum books, Earth, Milky Way.
https://punctumbooks.com

ISBN-13: 978-1-953035-16-5 (print)
ISBN-13: 978-1-953035-17-2 (ePDF)

DOI: 10.21983/P3.0306.1.00

LCCN: 2020947754
Library of Congress Cataloging Data is available from the Library of Congress

Copy Editing: Rachel Katz
Book Design: Vincent W.J. van Gerven Oei
Cover Photograph: A "time-lapse" photo taken during the Heimaey eruption, 1973. Courtesy of the Science Institute, University of Iceland.

spontaneous acts of scholarly combustion

HIC SVNT MONSTRA

GÍSLI PÁLSSON
DOWN TO EARTH

Translated by Anna Yates &
Katrina Downs-Rose

Contents

Habitat · 19

On Top of Glowing Magma · 31

The Mountain Erupts · 67

The Battle for Heimaey · 117

Epilogue · 203

. . .

Timeline · 223

Bibliography · 227

Acknowledgments

The environmental challenge that accompanies the Anthropocene, the Age of Humans, is the greatest problem that humankind has faced, and it is important that it is discussed frankly and in language that people understand. This book, about living through a natural disaster, has its own long history. The idea was born some years ago, shortly before I revisited the library in Manchester to look for that first news article about the Heimaey eruption, but its content and emphasis have changed over the following years.

My experience of volcanic eruptions where I grew up in the Westman Islands is the catalyst for the autobiographical anecdotes that are recalled here in a wider context, with reference to eruptions elsewhere in Iceland and abroad, as well as other natural disasters. The content, however, has to do with the subject matter that I have worked with as an anthropologist over the decades. I have long been interested in the ideas of people in different societies and different times, about the relationship between humanity and nature, science and science history, and connections between the world of experience, society, and environment. Most of this is encompassed within the field of environmental anthropology, in which comparisons and direct experience in the field are important research tools.

Here, my many disparate fields of interest — personal experience, nature, and society — have coalesced in my approach of what I have called geosocialities. I thank Marianne Elisabeth

Lien and the residential research group that she convened for rewarding and creative collaboration—not least Marisol de la Cadena, John Law, Andrew Mathews, Benjamin Orlove, Hugh Raffles, Heather Anne Swanson, and Sverker Sörlin. My collaboration with Heather Anne on "geosociality" was particularly stimulating and productive.

I am most grateful to numerous friends and colleagues. My research assistants, Björgvin Agnarsson and Sigurður Örn Guðbjörnsson, gathered historical sources and took some of the interviews that I make use of, and Kristín Harðardóttir dealt with applications and reports. Hjalti Elíasson generously lent me the substantial collection of newspaper reports that his mother, Liljan Þórarinsdóttir, had conscientiously collected during the Heimaey eruption. Magnús Bjarnason granted me access to his unpublished memoirs ("Privatissimo") from the time of the Heimaey eruption, a real boon. He says there that although his story is very ordinary, he had to retrace it "if only to add flesh to the big story that will undoubtedly later be told." I hope that this book can become part of that big story, and part of an even larger one as well.

Many other people have been helpful, including colleagues, writers, and specialists in the field of sociology, philosophy, and geoscience. Some who have provided me with informative interviews and others with good advice include: Aðalbjörg Jóhanna Bernódusdóttir, Ari Trausti Guðmundsson, Arnar Sigurmundsson, Atli Ásmundsson, Ásdís Jónsdóttir, Björn Bergsson, Dominic Boyer, Einar Gylfi Jónsson, Einar Örn Stefánsson, Guðmundur Karlsson, Gunnlaugur Ástgeirsson, Helga Hallbergsdóttir, Cymene Howe, Ingibergur Óskarsson, Jóhanna Helena Weihe, Jóhanna Ýr Jónsdóttir, Júlía Andersen, Karl Sigurbjörnsson, Kolbrún A. Sigurgeirsdóttir, Kristinn Hermannsson, Kristín Jóhannsdóttir, Kristín Vogfjörd, Kristján Stefánsson, Leó Kristjánsson, Páll Einarsson, Páll Zóphóníasson, Ragnar Baldvinsson, Sigríður H. Theodórsdóttir, Sigrún Inga Sigurgeirsdóttir, Sigurður Högni Hauksson, Sigurður Þ. Jónsson, Steindór J. Erlingsson, Svala Hauksdóttir, Svavar Steingrímsson, Sveinbjörn Björnsson, Sverrir Magnússon, Valdimar K. Jónsson, Valdimar

Leifsson, Þorsteinn Vilhjálmsson, Þórður Tómasson, and Þórir Ólafsson. I thank Kári Bjarnason and Sigurgeir Jónasson especially for their assistance in searching for photographs in the latter's vast collection. Various financial and moral support must be mentioned, especially from the University of Iceland Research Fund, the Westman Islands culture center Safnahús Vestmannaeyja, and the Center for Advanced Study (CAS) in Oslo. My sister Auðbjörg read over a draft of the manuscript and made several comments, and my late brother Karl joined me on mountainous walks and assisted with scanning photos. I thank Guðný Guðbjörnsdóttir, Helgi Bernódusson, and Sigurður Óskarsson for lively discussions about the project, its scope, and content. Helgi and Sigurður Örn Guðbjörnsson studiously read drafts, tactfully indicated potential improvements, and directed me to important sources. My sincere thanks go to my editor Guðrún Sigfúsdóttir at *Forlagið* in Reykjavík and her colleagues who patiently and creatively nurtured this work from the beginning, and to Katrina Downs-Rose and Anna Yates who skillfully translated the Icelandic text. My friend and independent editor Nancy Marie Brown did a fantastic job critically revising the English manuscript, ensuring a much smoother flow and sharper focus. Last but not least, I thank Eileen A. Joy, Vincent W.J. van Gerven Oei, Dan Rudmann, Rachel Katz, and their colleagues at punctum books for taking interest in my book and for pulling it through the production process.

*In the memory
of my brothers,
Sigurður Þór (1953–1971)
and
Karl (1961–2017)*

Novels are no use at all on days like these, they deal with people and their relationships, […] with society, etc., as if the place for these things were assured, the earth for all time earth, the sea level fixed for all time.
— Max Frisch, *Man in the Holocene* (1980)

The words are eruptions within him, magma that has to come out.
— Jón Kalman, *Eitthvað á stærð við alheiminn* [*Something the Size of the Universe*] (2015)

You ask of my companions. Hills, sir, and the sundown, and a dog large as myself. […] They are better than beings because they know, but do not tell: and the noise in the pool at noon excels my piano.
— Emily Dickinson, Letter to Mr. Higginson (1862)

HABITAT

BÓLSTAÐUR

The haunts of my youth have vanished, in two senses — they rest under layers of mental debris, accumulated along life's way, and under the lava that flowed from the flanks of Mount Helgafell, "Holy Mountain," in Iceland's Westman Islands in 1973. These facts evoke in me both pure curiosity and a poignant sense of loss. Where is my home? As have so many others throughout history, I long for a world that is no more, for a place of belonging that can never be regained. Can I have something in common with a lava field? Can I identify with a mountain, or connect with a contemporary event in the geological history of the Earth, the way other people identify with their generation, genetic fingerprint, or zodiac sign? In the terms of the Christian burial ceremony, what is this earth, these ashes and dust, from which we come and to which we return?

For most people, the place where they live is significant; it defines and shapes them. Birth certificates, passports, and official reports require an address, a village, a country. But place, as a word, rings rather flat, referring to geographical coordinates, to two-dimensional space. *Habitat* implies something deeper: a three-dimensional home supplying roots and groundedness, an intrinsic bond between a person and the earth. In a sense, con-

Fig. 1. Heimagata, Westman Islands, in 1942, Bólstaður is down to the left.

sciously or unconsciously, where you live becomes your habitat, the center of your universe, your vantage point.

My first habitat was a small, wooden house on the isle of Heimaey in the Westman Islands, forty-nine square meters in size and built on bare rock that thousands of years ago had been hot lava, welling from deep below the Earth's surface. The house had the name of Bólstaður. I have always thought Bólstaður a fine name, literally meaning "habitat." As my habitat, Bólstaður was a microcosm of Heimaey, whose name means "Home Island." Bólstaður was a place where the future was certain.

One of the oldest pictures of me is from Bólstaður (fig. 1), at number 18 on Heimagata, "Home Street." I am leaning against the south side of the house in bright sunshine, next to the steps that many generations of people had climbed on all kinds of errands since this worker's cottage was built under the Danish monarchy in the early twentieth century. That little boy was probably mischievous, maybe shy and a bit of a loner, although there was no lack of good company (fig. 2). Perhaps he wondered what he would be when he grew up.

Fig. 2. The author at Bólstaður.

Bólstaður succumbed to glowing lava in the middle of the eruption of 1973. I was not there, nor were my parents or siblings. I was a graduate student in England, while they had moved to the mainland four years before. We were not among the five thousand refugees fleeing the eruption that night. I did not see Bólstaður destroyed. But I came across a picture, the final photo of my birthplace, around the time that I began writing this book. I was startled to see it. When I showed it to my siblings and our mother, they reacted the same way I did: shocked and silent. Nothing has outmatched Nature here. A light westerly breeze carries off the clouds of steam rising from the lava, giving the photographer a clear view of what once was Bólstaður. The advancing lava has already buried one end wall of the house where my mother "birthed me in the bed," as she put it. The other end wall has been thrust forward, and the lava has set the house on fire; flames lick the roof and windows (fig. 3). In the heat, the sheet asbestos of the roof has exploded into white flakes, which

Fig. 3. Bólstaður on fire, April 2, 1973. Photo by Eiríkur Þ. Einarsson.

flutter down like snow onto the black volcanic ash that has settled around the house.

The bulky television aerial on the roof of Bólstaður is still standing. It presumably still picks up a signal from the mainland, but there is no one home to receive it. I gaze at the photo for a long time, my eye drawn again and again to that aerial. Is it a metaphor for the present day? A reminder of our feeble attempts to respond to terrifying natural disasters? Of the indifference of people here and abroad, despite unequivocal knowledge of the state of the world? Although the Earth is everything to us, we take it for granted until it reminds us uncomfortably of its existence. The eruption of Mount Helgafell in 1973 was one such reminder. The destruction of my home, Bólstaður, while the Westman Islanders battled with lava on the village's doorstep, now seems to me a warning.

When I was born, in the middle of the last century, humankind seemed capable of anything and progress seemed evident in most fields. Now our habitat is faced by problems greater than ever before — the temperatures are rising and the glaciers are melting. Storms, floods, and fire wreak havoc and many creatures, including humans, must flee their homes. And these problems are largely manmade. I was just over a week old when the Age of Humans began. No wonder I find the subject has a hold on me. The Age of Humans, or Anthropocene which comes from the same root as anthropology, the study of humans, is a new geological epoch characterized by profound, possibly irreversible, human impacts on the Earth. These human impacts, like the traces of earlier epochs in geological history, are recorded in the Earth itself, and manifest in a variety of ways, one being an increase in volcanic eruptions. Guided by Earth scientists, I choose to take the view that this new age commenced in the middle of the twentieth century, with the harnessing of atomic energy, which left its chemical imprint in glacial ice and lake bottom sediments. Geologists like round numbers, so I choose as a start date 1950, even though the first atomic bomb was deployed in 1945. Sometimes this new age is dated from the beginning of industrialization in the eighteenth century, from the founding of the oldest nations, or from the first attempts to make and harness fire around 400,000 years ago. In any case, it is only a very small period in the history of the Earth, the solar system or the universe, which is over twelve billion years old.

Awareness of the Age of Humans is even newer. Irrespective of its exact start-date, the concept was not coined until the twenty-first century. I first wrote about it, from an anthropologist's point-of-view, in 2013. Like most of those who have spoken up about it, the idea that humans are changing the Earth somewhat alarms me. I wonder how it will affect me, how it will affect my habitat, here in Iceland, in the vicinity of volcanoes. The answers I have found are not comforting. Studies of ice cores from the glaciers in neighboring Greenland have helped trace human impacts on the environment, including the rise in global temperature. This warming is causing glaciers around the world to melt, reducing the pressure on the Earth's crust, which leads to increased volcanic activity and more frequent earthquakes. Iceland has many glaciers. Research here has shed light on this link between global warming and earthquakes. As summarized by the British newspaper *The Guardian*: "Climate change is lifting

Iceland—and it could mean more volcanic eruptions."[1] Some media have described the Icelandic crust to be like a trampoline, in constant motion. Iceland is thus like the island of Heimaey, my "Home Island," which floated, unaware, on top of a pool of glowing magma for a decade before the eruption came that destroyed my home, my first habitat, Bólstaður.

How does one deal with such knowledge of impending doom? Some Icelanders, reading the media reports of the new research, joked that the new times could create new opportunities for our tourist industry. For visitors in search of adventure, the message could be: "Welcome to the trampoline! Jump on!" But I am an anthropologist. My response was not a new joke, but a new perspective. I began to rethink those tired binaries—nature versus nurture, nature versus culture, human versus environment—that separate us from the Earth. I began to think of myself as part of the earth.

It is not as strange as it sounds. Think of eating. Eating links your body to the soil in which crops are grown, as well as to the histories of farming, fertilizer, property ownership, and the process of soil formation. People are made of the same elements as our planet (hydrogen, carbon, sulfur, etc.), and cannot survive without them. As Russian chemist Vladimir I. Vernadsky put it, "the material of Earth's crust has been packaged into myriad moving beings whose reproduction and growth build and break down matter on a global scale. [...] *We are walking, talking minerals.*"[2]

This new way of thinking challenges the very definition of "alive." To me, for instance, as an Icelander, few things are more alive than the volcanic activity I have witnessed. Volcanoes are full of life, even though they may lie dormant for long or short periods, and people rightly speak of "their" volcano with due respect.

---

1 Suzanne Goldenberg, "Climate Change Is Lifting Iceland," *The Guardian*, January 30, 2015, https://www.theguardian.com/environment/2015/jan/30/climate-change-lifting-iceland-volcanic-eruptions.

2 Lynn Margulis and Dorion Sagan, *What Is Life?* (Berkeley: University of California Press, 1995), 49.

EYJAFJALLAJÖKULL [eiːjafjatlajœːkvtl]

From Heimaey, my "Home Island," just south of the Icelandic mainland, the Eyjafjöll mountains are entrancing and beautiful, with their shining white icecap all year round. The name means "mountains opposite the islands," and some of my ancestors came from the farms at their feet. The eruption of Eyjafjallajökull, named with *jökull* meaning "glacier," in 2010, and the subsequent turmoil, made me write this book. I was prompted to turn my passion for anthropology towards "firmer" topics than usual, towards the Earth itself, its ash, ice, floods, fire, and lava. As I began to write, the loss of my childhood home and my life lived almost entirely in the vicinity of volcanoes coalesced in a way that I found challenging.

Although I have not lived on Heimaey for many years, this glacier-topped volcano, Eyjafjallajökull, touches me as closely as it does those who live nearby and observe it daily. It didn't escape my notice when the historic eruption began. About midnight on March 20, 2010, a harmless little eruption began on the rocky pass that separates the glacier from a much larger icecap to the east. Countless tremors had heralded this eruption. They had begun late the previous year, gradually intensifying until the earth opened. One day, I drove towards Eyjafjallajökull in the winter twilight, stopping where the road ended and the volcanic plume could be seen. A group of people had gathered to watch. The eruption was impressive even from this distance. People called it a "tourist eruption," an ironic term for an eruption that is spectacular enough to attract sightseers while posing no threat to life or property. About fifteen thousand people went onto the glacier to stand within half a kilometer of the glowing crater.

After a brief hiatus, on April 18, the volcano began a second phase, this time erupting close to the middle of the glacier. Now about 800 people in South Iceland had to evacuate their homes, as the eruption covered the land with ash and melted the ice. Icebergs in the floodwater destroyed roads and bridges. At my home in Reykjavík, Iceland's capital, 150 kilometers west, I experienced for myself some effects of this second, more powerful phase of the eruption: the volcanic gases, falling ash, and accompanying anxiety. Would everything be buried once again, and toxic fumes pollute the senses? I put a white dish out on the balcony to monitor the ash fall and bought masks and protective goggles in case the ash and fumes exceeded safe limits.

The eruption became a globally significant event. It was compared to the Laki eruption of 1783, the most catastrophic volcanic eruption in Icelandic history, when ash and fumes spread across the world—although that was not understood until much later. As ash from Laki fell on fields and meadows and a dark haze drifted across the heavens, no one at the time knew why. Some say that the French Revolution of 1789 was caused by crop failure and famine due to the Laki eruption. Millions of people in India, Egypt, and Japan starved to death. But this time, in 2010, thanks to satellite technology, the progress of an eruption in Iceland could be watched live around the world. Soon Iceland was on everyone's lips, this time not because of famine and revolution. Eyjafjallajökull closed airports across Europe. It had a considerable impact on daily life and travel for ten million air passengers and their families all over the world, far from the actual volcano.

When the eruption of Eyjafjallajökull was at its peak, people wanting to travel to and from Iceland had to seize an opportunity to fly. Since volcanic ash can cause engine failure, planes could only fly when the wind direction was favorable. I set off for a conference in northern Norway on May 7, expecting to return two days later. But the wind changed, and my flight home from Oslo was cancelled. A day later I was on my way, but flew first to Scotland, where a special facility had been set up to receive planes that had had to change their flight plans, and from there we flew on to Akureyri, in North Iceland, one of the few Icelandic villages to have an airstrip long enough for our plane to land. Next came an overnight coach journey to Reykjavík. We stopped briefly at a service station, so that people could eat, stretch their legs, and use the facilities. The coach

Fig. 4. Under Eyjafjallajökull, 2010. Photo by Ragnar Th. Sigurðsson.

reached the city at about nine the next morning. The passengers, feeling slightly high after all their wandering, compared notes and admired the morning sun. The surreal journey home from Norway had taken 26 hours, instead of the usual three. A similar experience must have inspired the French comedy film, *Eyjafjallajökull* (2013), which chronicles the trials of a divorced couple who, when their flights were cancelled, were forced to drive together, willy-nilly, across Europe to get to their daughter's wedding in Greece.

At the farm directly below the glacier, the eruption's consequences were not comedic. Ash, possibly toxic, buried the sprouting crops and covered the meadows. It reached the point where the family had to pack up and leave. Farmer Ólafur Eggertsson took what he expected were the last photographs of his farm, Þorvaldseyri, images of huge, roiling clouds of ash enveloping the fields and houses. His pictures appeared widely on the internet and helped establish Iceland and the glacier in the minds of millions of people around the world (fig. 4). On social media, people who knew no Icelandic competed to spell and pronounce the glacier's tongue-twister of a name, sometimes with the help of the standard phonetic alphabet. When the eruption was over, tourists began pouring into Iceland as never before. Many headed straight for Þorvaldseyri, where Ólafur and his family have now built a visitors' center for curious guests. There they can gaze towards the glacier, enjoy a documentary film about the eruption, buy a vial of ash or a T-shirt, and remember the dark days of 2010. The volcanic activity that drove Ólafur's family away is now an important source of their income. The ash from Eyjafjallajökull, it turns out, was not toxic, as it had been when Laki erupted in 1783. The meadows at Þorvaldseyri are greener than before the eruption.

Some volcanoes, like Eyjafjallajökull or Mount Helgafell on Heimaey, lie dormant for hundreds or thousands of years, believed to be extinct, then wake suddenly from their slumbers. They don't bother the same people twice. Others erupt every few years, and the threat looms over the local people throughout their lives. Mount Etna on Sicily, for example, one of the world's most active volcanoes, is almost constantly at work. Many other natural disasters, such as floods, fires, and storms, assault people generation after generation. Should they not make us think about the close connection between humanity and the earth?

In our schools, for generations, no one was taught to think that way. Anthropologists like me were taught to study humanity. Anthropology and the other social sciences established themselves in the wake of industrialization, a little later than the earth sciences, and placed themselves on the opposite side of the scholarly tectonic plate boundary. Social scientists embraced daily life but ignored the earth, except for the thin surface visible from day to day. Conflicts in societies and geological upheavals, we thought, had nothing in common.

Lately, with the rising awareness of the scale of environmental change, more and more scholars are now daring to cross these borders in the academic world. Even these daring boundary-crossers, however, often persist in sidelining their own personal experience when writing about the Earth, when it should instead be examined and used systematically. Messages from the depths of the earth, recorded in tangible form as seismograms, can be preserved in archives — although the seismogram that bore the clearest message of the eruption which destroyed my first habitat, Bólstaður, recorded at Skammadalshóll on January 22, 1973 was lost. It was sent to be copied, and nothing is known of it since. But it is harder to grasp what has been written in the flesh and bone and cerebral cortex of a human being. Sometimes it is best to forget. There were Westman Islanders who had been through difficult times as children who, unlike me, rejoiced, in their heart of hearts, when their home vanished under ash or lava. They wanted to forget the building and what happened there, but memory does not always obey our orders.

Even when we think we have a cast-iron memory of certain events, it is not necessarily so. British neurologist Oliver Sacks, author of popular books such as *The Man Who Mistook His Wife for a Hat* (1985) that explored the human brain, nerve impulses, and memory, spoke from experience.[3] In London during World War II, Sacks experienced German air raids; he believed he had a memory of a large bomb falling behind the family's house and setting buildings on fire. But his brother, who was five years older, knew better. Oliver had in fact been evacuated to safety by that time, so he could not have seen or experienced the event. Yet he "remembered" it as if it had happened yesterday. "It is startling," he wrote, "to realize that some of our most cherished memories may never have happened — or may have happened to someone else."[4]

Although many of the secrets of the past will never be unearthed, we can sometimes shed light on them by reflecting, by conversing with ourselves or others, or by archaeological excavations using diggers and drills. Much of what I have written in this book draws on my own experience or has been brought to light with help from others. It was important to me to go

---

[3] Oliver Sacks, *The Man Who Mistook His Wife for a Hat* (New York: Touchstone, 1985).
[4] Oliver Sacks, "Speak, Memory," *The New York Review of Books*, February 21, 2013, https://www.nybooks.com/articles/2013/02/21/speak-memory/.

to the locations in the story, talk to people, seek out significant documents and images, display respect for memories, and give them space. A narrative of any kind is inconceivable without a point of view, and all who compose texts must explain who they are and where they stand. Without such transparency the reader cannot trust what is being presented or assess the influence of the author's connections and vested interests. So, let me be clear: A personal "partial" account is not a weakness but a strength. It is essential that I, the person tapping at this keyboard, the author Gísli Pálsson (sometimes called "Gísli from Bólstaður"), say something about myself and step, quite literally, down to earth.

ON TOP OF GLOWING MAGMA

DANCING ON ICE

I came into the world on a dark winter's day in 1949, not far from an old volcano, Mount Helgafell, in the Westman Islands off the south coast of Iceland. On Thursday December 22, at four in the morning, my mother, Bára Sigurðardóttir, woke up, just as though an eruption had begun. She was in labor. When her water broke, she woke her mother, Auðbjörg, head of the household at Bólstaður. The women decided to ask Ketill Brandsson, who rented a room from my grandmother, to get the midwife. Ketill-the-netmaker was part of the household, kind and good with children, and joined in evening games of whist on weekends and holidays. It was impossible to call out to anybody else. My father, Páll Gíslason, was at sea on a fishing trawler, grandfather Sigurður was dead, and my older sister, Auðbjörg, was only eleven months old. Just before seven o'clock Ketill hurried out into the dark and walked up the road towards the volcano. The street lighting was sparse, but the light glinted off the road.

The road was slick with ice, and a little water trickled across the surface. Ketill knocked on the door of midwife Guðrún Ólafsdóttir's house, who got ready in a hurry, and they walked down to Bólstaður. They held hands in the icy conditions, even though they had little in common other than an intention of aiding Bára at Bólstaður; they slipped and slid back and forth on the mirrored road and took turns supporting one another. The bag containing Guðrún's midwifery instruments, catheter, scissors, and so on, swung around in the gloom. An observer who did not notice the big leather bag might have thought the couple were lovers, but the windows were unlit and there were no witnesses. Ketill was fifty-three years old, Guðrún twenty-nine. They said later that they would have liked to have had a film of their lively dance down the icy road on the way to Bólstaður. Their pas-de-deux would have been worthy of Hollywood.

When they reached Bólstaður, "I [had] already birthed you in the bed," my mother told me much later. Grandma helped, and all went well. I was born at 7 a.m. on the shortest day of the year—my mother was in a hurry. Two days after I was born Dad came ashore for Christmas. He tried to act pleased, but two children born in the same year was a bit much. Those were hard times and many struggled to find work. More than six decades after my birth, on a visit to an old people's home in Reykjavík, I bumped into a woman from the Westman Islands. We struck up a conversation, and she asked me who my family was. I told her that I was Páll and Bára's son. "Oh, yes," she said, and smiled, "didn't they have two in the same year!" Children arrive uninvited, just like volcanic eruptions.

Mother Earth

In 1949 there were many volcanic eruptions around the world, including Mt. Puracé in Colombia, Villarrica in Chile, Cumbre Vieja in the Canary Islands, and Ngāuruhoe in New Zealand. Seventeen people died in the Colombian eruption and the island that erupted in the Canary Islands broke up and part of it vanished into the sea.

In the human world, the Cold War raged; it had begun not long before. On my birthday the front page of Reykjavík's morning paper reported on the US president Harry Truman and Soviet Union leader Joseph Stalin. The day before, Truman had delivered a speech in memory of those who gave their lives in World War II. "If man could achieve self-government and kinship with his God throughout the world," he said, "peace would not tremble in the constant dread of war." That same day, Stalin the shoemaker's son had, according to the newspaper, celebrated his seventieth birthday. Flags had been raised all over the Soviet Union, Eastern Europe, and parts of China, but the birthday was not mentioned in either the Vatican or in Belgrade, capital of Marshal Tito's Yugoslavia.

Why, in writing of these "social" events, do I separate them from the natural world? Why do I create, on our single home planet, two separate worlds? Indeed, Mother Earth is one all-encompassing ecosystem, according to the Gaia hypothesis, and humans are part of it.

Gaia is derived from Ancient Greek, referring to Mother Earth as the source of everything: the heavens, oceans, humanity, gods, and giants. The word is closely related to *geo,* from *gē,* which means earth, the root of the modern term *geoscience.* When British chemist James Lovelock and American biologist Lynn Margolis first advanced the Gaia hypothesis in the 1960s, some called it pseudo-science, informed by romantic new-age thinking, but now it is seen as a chilling herald of the Age of Humans. Lovelock's book, *Gaia: A New Look at Life on Earth,* published in 1979, urged people to see the Earth as a kind of living organism. It has had a dramatic impact. Astronomer David Grinspoon believes that the Gaia hypothesis has been fully vindicated in recent years. People now recognize the profound impact of organisms, including themselves, on the planet itself. Grinspoon writes, "Earth is a biologically modulated planet through and through. In a nontrivial way, it is a living planet."[1]

The idea that the Earth is alive is not new. It may, in fact, be as old an idea as humankind itself. Not until the industrial revolution and the rise of modern science were people convinced that the Earth was inanimate and immune to human influence. Although its interior continued for a time to be described in terms

---

[1] See David Grinspoon, "Why Most Planets Will Either Be Lush or Dead," *Nautilus — Cosmos,* December 2016, http://cosmos.nautil.us/short/73/why-most-planets-will-either-be-lush-or-dead.

of arteries and entrails, all in frenzied motion, these were just remnants of ancient ideas, empty metaphors. Life and the Earth became two separate worlds, while the underworld became a resource for the human world above. Scientists began to view the Earth from a distance and jostled to establish their impartiality. The Earth died, it has been said, when humans harnessed nature, armed with science and technology.

However, just when the Western world had concluded that technology and science could solve every problem, storm clouds began to gather. Around the middle of the last century — around the time of my birth — a lively debate began about the planet's limitations. Still, no one spoke of a new era until 1988, when environmental historian Donald Worster published *The Ends of the Earth*. Worster suggested humanity was "approaching a grand ritualistic climax." He wrote, "It is irresistible to ask whether we are passing from one era into another, from what we have called 'modern history' into something different and altogether unpredictable."[2] That "something different" is the Age of Humans.

The label that seems to have been adopted for this age is not above criticism, and no doubt people will argue about it for a long time. Doomsday predictions have a long history and now, as before, it is right to be wary. Some people believe it is more correct to talk about the Age of Capitalism than the Age of Humans. Many also express surprise that people still see a need to grant recognition and respect to *Homo sapiens* by naming the current age after ourselves, as the Age of Humans. It is certainly food for thought: Precisely when the idea gains traction that humanity is an integral part of nature, not something outside of it, when all divisions between nature and society, or between the natural sciences and the social sciences, are being challenged, why do we persist in defining the Earth's problem as a human problem?

---

2 Donald Worster, *The Ends of the Earth: Perspectives on Environmental History* (Cambridge: Cambridge University Press, 1988), 4.

Whatever we think of the name, semantics must not overshadow the real issue. Whatever we call this strange epoch, characterized by the measurable and harmful influence of humankind on the Earth, we must face the fact that it is the start of something new, calling for a new way of thinking.

The Voices of Stones

If the Earth is alive, and volcanoes are alive, are stones alive too? Many people believe they are, and this idea is not at all new. In myths and folklore of many cultures, stones have special powers that rank them with humans. The medieval Icelandic sagas refer to rock-men, who are the personal guardians of powerful humans, and protective wights, who live in rocks and mountains. Sometimes these stories reflect the tension between Christianity and older pagan beliefs. As *The Book of the Icelanders,* the story of the Icelanders' conversion around 1000 CE, recounts:

> Þorvaldr asked his father to be baptized, but he was slow to respond. At Giljá there stood a stone to which he and his kinsmen used to sacrifice, and they claimed that their guardian spirit lived in it. Koðrán said that he would not have himself baptized until he knew who was more powerful, the bishop or the spirit in the stone. After that, the bishop went to the stone and chanted over it until the stone broke apart. Then Koðrán thought he understood that the spirit had been overcome. Koðrán then had himself and his whole household baptized, except that his son Ormr did not wish to accept the faith.[3]

The story, written down in about 1240, is said to relate to a large, apparently intact rock that can still be seen by the farm of Giljá in northern Iceland. Icelandic folktales collected in the nineteenth century make frequent reference to "hidden people" who

---

3 Ari Þorgilsson, *The Book of the Icelanders — The Story of the Conversion,* trans. Siân Grønlie (London: University College London, 2006), chap. 2, 35–36.

are the guardians of rocks and mountains, with some of these concepts still currently used.

Author Þórbergur Þórðarson (1888–1974) wrote entertainingly and passionately about stones and their meaning for him when he was growing up on the farm of Hali in southeast Iceland early in the last century. In his book *The Stones Speak*, first published in 1956, he treats the rocks in the mountain towering above the farm as if they were living characters. "Until finally, after all these years," writes Þórbergur about one stone, "it had succeeded in freeing itself from the bondage of the mountain and hurtled down here to our slopes so that it could live as a free individual." In Þórbergur's mind the rocks were his friends. They "gave a homely life to the slopes in the same way folk give life to the farmstead," he writes: "Of all 'dead things', I felt the rocks and stones to be the most alive. This was because they were the most natural and definitely had the longest memories."[4] Sometimes Þórbergur pressed his ear against the stones and listened, "to hear if they were telling [him] something."

Þórbergur himself continues to speak although he is long gone. In the winter of 2018, I drove to Hali where a center has been established in his name to honor his extensive and somewhat eccentric contribution to Icelandic literature. The journey from the capital took about seven hours, driving counterclockwise around the island, with the rising Atlantic Ocean on the right and the melting glaciers on the left. The center was celebrating Þórbergur's 130th anniversary with a literary festival, and I had agreed to give a talk on the subject "The Stones Speak, at Last." I had in mind the predicament of the modern age, as products of human activities, such as plastic and the fallout from nuclear tests, were increasingly fossilized among geological strata, and the continued, if not escalating, relevance of Þórbergur Þórðarson's ideas about stones.

---

[4] Þórbergur Þórðarson, *The Stones Speak,* trans. Julian Meldon D'Arcy (Reykjavík: Mál og menning, 2012), 236–39. See also Soffía Auður Birgisdóttir, *Ég skapa þess vegna er ég: Um skrif Þórbergs Þórðarsonar* (Reykjavík: Opna, 2015). For a medieval Icelandic perspective, see Viðar Hreinsson, *Jón lærði: Náttúrur náttúrunnar* (Reykjavík: Forlagið, 2016).

Fig. 5. The stone that spoke at Hali. Photo by the author.

The next morning, a couple of hours before the festival was to begin, the news spread that a huge stone had fallen from the mountain above Hali (fig. 5). I rushed to the scene to take photographs. The stone had landed neatly in the middle of the main road, halting traffic in both directions, as if it were making a point — perhaps to urge people to stop and reflect on their life's journey. I was puzzled and a little scared. A small group of travelers had stopped to examine the magnificent stone's colors and shape. Some gently touched it. Some gazed at the mountain above to imagine where it had spent its earlier life and the route it had taken. The Road and Coastal Administration in the nearby village of Höfn had been notified and soon a worker arrived on a tractor to move the stone and clear the remaining debris off the road. He gently nudged the stone off the road and further down the hill towards the ocean, as if to complete its journey. A few months later, the stone was moved to its "home" at Hali for permanent residence.

The hillside above Hali is littered with stones that have fallen over the centuries, forming a kind of parliament of liberated, enlightened stones. Þórbergur imagined in his book that before they made their escape, for thousands of years their perspective had been constricted and one-dimensional, but as they descended, they faced a bright and open vista. But no stone of that size had fallen at Hali for decades, least of all to land in the middle of the main road. The festival was genuinely affected, moods were high and the program was slightly derailed. Speakers and audience members from the neighboring farms and the nearest village mingled and laughed. As I began my talk, I wondered if the stone had spoken at last. If so, what did it have to say? The question seemed pertinent. If we imagine humanity as a future fossil, engraved in the geological strata of the Age of Humans along with plastic and other human products, what happens to our voice? What will we say?

The ideas Þórbergur entertained are not confined to Iceland; on the contrary, they are quite common. British anthropologist Hugh Raffles asks: "What can a stone do?" The answer, his work shows, is quite a lot: "A stone can endure, it can change, it can harm, it can heal. [...] It can open and close the gates of philosophy."[5] The voices of stones are now being heard better than before. As we acknowledge the escalation of environmental problems, the hard, material world is gaining a new meaning, coming to life and intruding on people's lives.

We've long known that humans are social animals, that "no man is an island," and that we are shaped by our relationships with other people. When we lose someone close to us, we are tangibly reminded of the fact that we are not indifferent. Part of us is gone, and at the same time still present in some way. Social scientists have emphasized this idea of an individual's social awareness, including it in their criticism of the idea that each of us is autonomous. Now many feel as though this view is too narrow, and that we are also made up of organic and mineral ingredients, and without them humans would be quite different. It makes little sense to look on the Earth simply as the setting for human life, as the stage on which a play is performed for a

---

[5] Hugh Raffles, "Twenty-Five Years Is a Long Time," *Cultural Anthropology* 27, no. 3 (2012): 526–34, at 527. See also Hugh Raffles, *The Book of Uncomformities: Speculations on Lost Time* (New York: Pantheon, 2020).

while. The drama cannot be separated from the stage — and the stage has its own history.

"A Single Volcanic Furnace"

In his book *Mundus Subterraneus,* published in 1665, the German Jesuit priest and polymath Athanasius Kircher described the malevolent beings one would meet climbing down into a volcanic crater. A hundred-some years later, Alexander von Humboldt (1769–1859), a pioneer of the earth sciences, argued that "a single volcanic furnace" was behind all the volcanic activity on the planet.[6] The first geological map was produced in 1815. One spring day in 2017, I stood in front of this historic map in a museum at Cambridge University in England. It is less spectacular than might be expected for a map that changed the world. On it the underworld looks merely decorative. The mapmaker was William Smith, a self-educated geologist from London, who, alone and in great detail, located the coal, ores, and other resources beneath the surface of Great Britain, and thus laid the foundations both for great advances in geology and the life sciences, and for extensive mining.

Gradually, other scientists added earthquakes, volcanoes, and geological strata to this scientific map of the world. They asked once again: What caused eruptions? To some, the answer seemed obvious once the theory of continental drift was advanced by German meteorologist Alfred Wegener in 1912. Continental drift, now called plate tectonics, postulates that the Earth's crust consists of thick plates that are in slow but constant motion above the furnace at the center of the Earth. They move apart or together, or slide under one another. Where the Earth opens between plates, it gives rise to ridges and volcanoes. Iceland is one of the places on Earth where a ridge rises out of the ocean, and eruptions, consequently, are frequent here. Interestingly, however, while Wegener visited Iceland three times,

---

6   Andrea Wulf, *The Invention of Nature: The Adventures of Alexander von Humboldt* (London: John Murray, 2015), 197.

he did not associate the volcanic activity in the country with continental drift.

Around the mid-1960s, the theory of plate tectonics became a widely accepted truth. However, it was not until the 1990s that people could monitor continental drift directly. With the help of satellites, it became possible to detect Earth movements from space. Although Earth scientists are still unable to travel far beneath the surface of the Earth, they can now look into our dynamic planet. With the assistance of supercomputers and mathematics, they can scan the interior of the Earth as though it were a human body and monitor long-distance magma movements deep beneath the surface.

Plate tectonics and the Gaia hypothesis harmonize better than might be expected. Planetary science indicates that for a very long time, living creatures have influenced the deeper subterranean realms of Earth, lubricating plate tectonic movements. One of the architects of the theory of plate tectonics, Norm Sleep, now suggests that life is deeply implicated in the physical dynamics of Earth.[7]

The drive to understand the causes of eruptions is not new. Testimony to this are the 36,000-year-old paintings in the caves at Chauvet-Pont d'Arch in France. In these, apparently one of the oldest known eruption pictures, painted about the time that *Homo sapiens* were colonizing Europe, it looks as though the eruption plume is squirting upwards from an aerosol can.[8] At the same time the paintings reflect the shapely volcano, the lowlands around, and perhaps its mysterious underworld too. It is known that about the time that the cave dwellers created their paintings, an eruption occurred in a nearby mountain.

The first people to settle in Iceland, in about 870 CE, had active volcanoes on their doorsteps, too. They witnessed earth-

---

[7] See David Grinspoon, *Earth in Human Hands: Shaping Our Planet's Future* (New York: Grand Central Publishing, 2016).

[8] Sébastien Nomade et al., "A 36,000-Year-Old Volcanic Eruption Depicted in the Chauvet-Pont d'Arc Cave (Ardèche, France)?" *Plos One,* January 8, 2016.

quakes and eruptions that caused major damage — several lava fields have been dated to the settlement period — and they were probably no less puzzled by them than the first painters in France. Reference is often made to an account in the *Saga of Christianity* of an eruption that occurred while Iceland's chieftains were meeting in the parliament at Thingvellir, in the year 1000, to decide if the country should convert to the new faith. The saga relates:

> The whole assembly was at the Law Rock. Hjalti and his men had burning incense, the scent could be smelt as strongly upwind as downwind. Hjalti and Gizzur then announced their mission outstandingly well. And people were amazed by how eloquent they were and how well they spoke, and such great fear came with their words that none of their enemies dared speak against them. But what happened there was that one man after another named witnesses and each side, the Christians and the heathens, declared itself under separate laws from the other.
>
> Then a man came running up and said that there had been a volcanic eruption at Ölfus and it was about to engulf the homestead of Þóroddur goði. Then the heathens spoke up: "It is no wonder the gods are enraged by such talk."
>
> Then Snorri goði said: "What were the gods enraged by when the lava we are standing on here and now was burning?"
>
> After that people left the Law Rock.[9]

Chieftain Snorri and his contemporaries in the tenth century, and the saga authors in the thirteenth century, had never heard of plate tectonics or the Gaia hypothesis, but some of them believed that events in Earth's history, large and small, were connected to the world of humans and gods. In the Icelandic sagas, natural disasters are rarely, if ever, natural events, in the modern

---

9 Þorgilsson, *The Book of the Icelanders*, chap. 12, 48–49.

narrow understanding of the term. They are most often brought on by the gods or by human sorcery.

The early Norse and Celtic settlers coming to Iceland could hardly have experienced volcanic eruptions before they arrived on the island in the ninth century. Even earthquakes were almost unknown in Scandinavia and the British Isles in the Middle Ages. But little is written about such events in Iceland's extensive medieval literature. The silence about volcanic eruptions in the other sagas seems strange.[10] Although the *Book of Settlements* and some forty sagas chronicle the first two hundred years of Icelandic society, as there were no indigenous people living on the island when the settlers arrived, examples of earthquakes and eruptions in these engaging works by master storytellers are rare and can be counted on the fingers of one hand.

Yet the author of the *Saga of Christianity* was clearly aware that the parliamentary site at Thingvellir stands on lava that came from an eruption. Recently, geoscientists have suggested that a major eruption in Eldgjá, "Fire Gorge," in South Iceland from 939–940, about seventy years after the settlement of Iceland began, may have driven the adoption of Christianity, fueling fears of retribution in the fires of Hell.[11] The scientists' claim, based on measurements from the Greenlandic ice cap, invites a new reading of the apocalyptic poem *Völuspá*, "The Prophesy of the Seeress," one of Iceland's most celebrated poems, with its reference to flames flying "against heaven itself."

In 1625, Þorsteinn Magnússon, the prior at a monastery in south Iceland, chronicled another major eruption, of Mount Katla. His, with the exception of Pliny the Younger's description of the eruption of Vesuvius in 79 CE, may be the oldest reliable contemporary account of an eruption anywhere in the world. Þorsteinn describes the eruption every day for the twelve days

---

10 Oren Falk, "The Vanishing Volcanoes: Fragments of Fourteenth-Century Icelandic Folklore," *Folklore* 118 (2007): 1–22.
11 Clive Oppenheimer et al., "The Eldgjá Eruption: Timing, Long Range Impacts and Influence on the Christianisation of Iceland," *Climate Change* 3, no. 4 (2018): 369–81.

that it lasted. He says, "We later became so accustomed to these wonders that they were given little attention [...] thus proving the proverb that anything bad can become so commonplace that it seems good."[12]

Were the saga authors in the Middle Ages silent about Iceland's eruptions because they were accustomed to these wonders? Because they were so commonplace as to demand little attention? Þorsteinn is defining, in a way, the attitude we now call "earthquake culture": Those of us in disaster zones simply learn to live with it. We try to mitigate the major consequences of earthquakes, eruptions, or other natural disasters. We try to react sensibly to the risk. But people learn from experience. Inevitably, our natural surroundings make their mark on our lives. As for myself, I am moulded by a volcanic island. My life is shaped by rocks and magma.

BURNING HEART

The volcanoes that erupted in 1949, the year of my birth — Mount Puracé in Colombia, Villarrica in Chile, Cumbre Vieja in the Canary Islands, and Ngāuruhoe in New Zealand — matter to me, but they are too distant to be cherished. The only volcano on the mainland of Iceland that is roughly my age is Mount Hekla, the entrance to Hell, as people used to call it in the Middle Ages. Hekla erupted on March 29, 1947, with an eruption of thirteen months, after being dormant for over a century. About an hour after the eruption began, the ash drifted over to the Westman Islands, where Bára and Páll at Bólstaður had fallen in love. A description by one of the geologists who observed the eruption is apposite:

> In front of the middle of the crater's back wall [...] a small promontory of clinker jutted into the well of magma, and in the mouth of the crater the lava channel narrowed. The

---
12 See Sigurður Þórarinsson, "Þorsteinn Magnússon og Kötlugosið 1625," *Árbók (Landsbókasafns Íslands)* 1975, no. 1 (1976): 5–9.

source was thus shaped like a heart. There were no margins to the magma; the burning heart filled the crater bottom from wall to wall.[13]

The ash from that eruption of Hekla has become part of me and my four siblings, part of our constitution.

Guðmundur Einarsson, a renowned Icelandic writer and artist and a keen outdoorsman, made a trip to Hekla in 1947 as soon as the eruption began, and observed it for the first few days. He wrote in a magazine article that year:

> You might say that the famous mountain has taken a dramatic approach, so many events happened simultaneously, on a grand scale. The mountain erupted compressed gases, ash, pumice, rock, and lava spatters. Floods of water cascaded down the slopes and an earthquake occurred in which the mountain tore open lengthwise, as often before and reported in the annals.[14]

"Most of Hekla's neighbors are fond of 'their mountain,'" says Guðmundur in the final words of his article. Reading it many years later I realize how close I am to my "kinswoman" Hekla, despite the fact that she has long been linked to Hell. In Icelandic we have a saying: "Everyone finds their own bird fair." Perhaps this needs revising to: "Everyone finds their own mountain fair."

Like many Icelanders today, I own a flat in the city and a cottage out in the countryside. Hekla is visible from the window of my holiday home. She is majestic and snow-covered, and sometimes shyly veils herself in clouds. Geologists have identified lavas from eighteen eruptions of Hekla in the last millennium, the oldest from 1158. These lavas tell the life history of Hekla, or at least part of it. Younger flows of lava engulf older ones. One of

---

13 Guðmundur Kjartansson, qtd. in Elín Pálmadóttir, "Hekla vaknaði 1947 af aldarsvefni," *Morgunblaðið*, March 27, 1997, 30.
14 Guðmundur Einarsson, "Heklugosið 1947," *Eimreiðin* 53, no. 2 (1949): 84–94, at 84.

them, from 1510, is completely hidden by lava that flowed in a later eruption. The volcano eradicates its own history as fast as it creates it.

For many years I had intended to climb Hekla and to cross the lava that is about the same age as I am, but for some reason it did not happen until 2016. One summer day, I drove with my wife Guðný, my siblings, and their spouses to the farm of Næfurholt at the foot of the mountain. My brother Karl, an expert on the local terrain, was our guide. One of the residents at Næfurholt was in the yard, so I rolled down the window and asked for directions. I told the man that we were looking for my lava from 1947. He responded kindly, smiling to himself, and advised us to follow the track that went up from the farmyard towards a large valley surrounded by mountains. At its end rose a shapely crater, Rauðöldur, with open arms toward the west. Opposite it was Axlargígar, "Shoulder Craters," and shoulders could certainly be seen in the landscape, rising from the lava field. I wondered if all volcanoes had shoulders, and where that idea came from. People have probably always personified volcanoes, imagining the cone that erupts as a capricious human head, and below it shoulders on which the mountain's cloak rests.

The clouds hung low and it rained on and off. Finally, we spotted the lava wall from 1947. We walked up onto it, but it was slow going, as the lava was covered with prickly lumps of scoria that shifted at every footstep. It was as if the ungrateful lava were hissing at me, with no regard for our family ties. I stumbled and drew a little blood when I rested a hand on a sharp stone. I became a bit worried, although I didn't say so. Hekla had last erupted sixty years ago, and geologists had issued warnings about the mountain being ready to erupt again. I turned back with the hissing of the scoria lumps in my ears and a souvenir from the rock pile in my pocket. Stones that are the same age as a person have a special place in the heart, compared to rocks that date back hundreds, thousands, or millions of years.

Island and Mainland

The Westman Islands are easily seen from the slopes of Mount Hekla. Hekla and Heimaey belong to the same geological rift zone, characterized by tectonic movement and volcanic activity. The settlers of the ninth century seem to have realized that the island was formed by volcanism. A manuscript dating from the fourteenth century, *The Book of Haukur,* part of *The Book of Settlement,* states that the first settler on Heimaey, Herjólfur Bárðarson, lived at Herjolf's Valley on the west coast of the island "where fires had brought lava."[15] As a child, I didn't give much thought to the formation of the island and I don't remember discussing the issue until geology became part of my school curriculum. But the towering cone of the volcano Helgafell, south of the village, was always a clear reminder of spectacular eruptions in the distant past.

Volcanic activity not only gave birth to the Westman Islands but also to their fertile fishing grounds — shaping the contours of the sea bottom around the island and directing the currents of marine life and water passing through — not to mention the big natural harbor on the north side of Heimaey, nicely protected from heavy seas by rocks and mountains. The harbor must have appealed to the early settlers who used the island as a fishing station, as the fishing grounds were some of the most bountiful off the Icelandic coast. Also, cliffs and mountains were teaming with birdlife feeding on the fishing grounds, which became an important source for subsistence.

The only inhabited island, Heimaey, was 11.2 square kilometers, covered by pastures, lava, and mountains. One of the earliest registers, from 1507, lists fifteen lots or farms, scattered near the hills of Mount Helgafell and around the harbor. The Westman Islands were, for many years, not subject to the same regulatory environment as other parts of Iceland. Official documents referred to Iceland and the Westman Islands as separate entities. For eight centuries the islands were domains of the king

---

15 Finnur Jónsson, ed., *Landnámabók I–III.* (Copenhagen: Det Kongelige Nordiske Oldskrift-Selskab, 1900), 105.

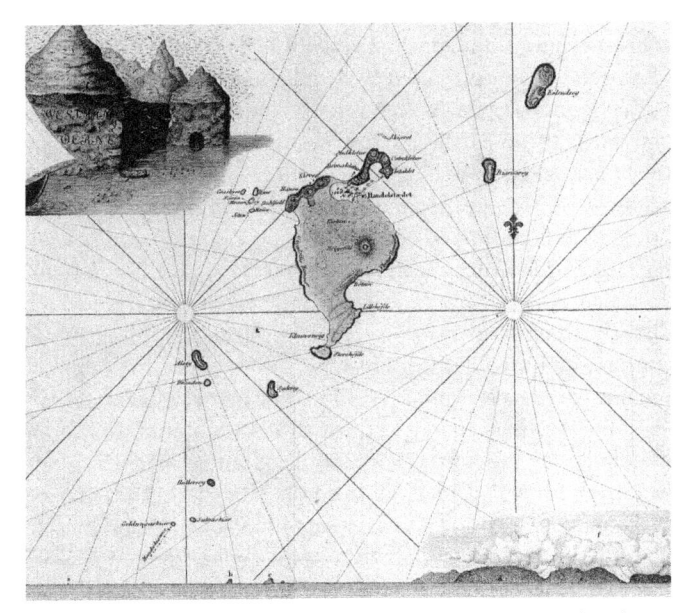

Fig. 6. One of the oldest printed maps of Heimaey. From *Beskrivelse over den islandske kyst* (Copenhagen 1788–1822).

of Norway or Denmark, Iceland's overlord from the thirteenth century until the twentieth. Access to them was so strictly controlled that the Westman Islanders themselves lived in grinding poverty. The inhabitants were tenants without rights. The population grew erratically over the centuries, depending on subsistence, colonial politics, and plagues.

But at the start of the twentieth century all restrictions were lifted. The advent of motorized fishing boats and access to the fishing grounds led to the development of a flourishing fishing village and an important port, also called Heimaey. When I was growing up, the expanding village around the harbor had four to five thousand inhabitants, three large fishing plants and a rapidly expanding fleet with large and small boats. Heimaey landed and processed more fish than any other port, largely during the winter season, the spawning time for cod, the most important species. Many boats, crew, and laborers from other parts of the country would come for the season. The dark winter days were often quite lively, with intensive work and festivities.

My grandparents, Auðbjörg and Sigurður, married in 1909 and moved from Eyjafjöll to the Westman Islands. They bought the house called Bólstaður, which had been built in 1906. Bólstaður was listed in the land register as a worker's cottage — a house with no farmland, the home of people who were neither farming in their own right, nor contracted to work on a farm. This had been a key concept in nineteenth-century society, distinguishing farmers, who then controlled everything in the country, along with the Danish Kingdom, from the laborers moving to coastal towns and villages. Life in the workers' cottages on the Westman Islands in the early days of motorized fishing held hope for the future. For a while, Grandpa had a fishing-ketch, the *Fortuna*, and a one-third share in another vessel.

Grandpa was twenty-seven years older than Grandma. He had a mustache and usually drank his coffee from an imposing mustache cup. He always kept a bottle of *brennivín*, Icelandic schnapps, in the bottom drawer of the chest of drawers and although he did not drink himself, he poured his friends a measure in a special shot glass when they visited the Westman Islands each spring to sell their products and buy fish in return. According to my mother, with his young wife, Sigurður was tight-fisted. She blamed it on the driftwood incident at Eyjafjöll. In the 1890s he had become embroiled in a bitter dispute between the county magistrate and the farmers. The magistrate interrogated Grandpa about a supposed theft of driftwood, one piece of timber, thirteen years earlier and found him guilty, locking him up for a few days. In barren Iceland, timber had been scarce for centuries and driftwood originating in distant lands was subjected to strict regulations and property rights.

In the property evaluation of 1916, Bólstaður and its assets were described thus:

> 2 apartments, 7 rooms in all. Stoves 2, cookers 2. Concrete basement, equal in size to the house, for dwelling or storage [...] The house has electric lighting [...] Plot 440 m², with a

wood and wire fence, cultivated vegetable garden [...] Fishstore in Skipasund [...] Vegetable garden at Flatir.[16]

Three men attested that this evaluation had been conducted with "assiduity and conscientiousness"; their signatures were accompanied by the following solemn words: "So help us God and His Divine Word." There was no mention of its being 1500 meters from the crater of an active volcano, for everyone thought Mount Helgafell was long extinct.

What I remember most about Bólstaður was being given the responsibility of lighting the furnace that provided heat for the house during the day. It wasn't deemed wise to keep it lit overnight, even though it was cold at night and the house was poorly insulated. On cold winter mornings, when Dad was not at home, it was my duty to creep downstairs in the darkness to the cellar, turn on the paraffin, dip the wick in oil, and light it. It was a huge responsibility for a boy. You had to be very careful with a naked flame and oil in the basement of a wooden house, as there could be a downdraught from the flue, and the furnace could explode, causing a disaster.

The world of my neighborhood was tiny. "Red Cross" parcels, ceremoniously presented in primary school, hinted at something bigger, something both mysterious and exotic. The parcels were a sort of Christmas present from Americans, intended for poor nations during the Cold War. From the parcels came a distinctive fragrance that was difficult to identify, as well as small toys: yoyos, whistles, and other things. Sweet rock candy indicated something even bigger, colonial times and a global connectivity, although that generally passed the young people by. Then, as was the custom throughout Iceland, I was sent to spend the summer on a relative's farm. I went to the mainland, to the farm of Skíðbakki in Landeyjar on the southern coast. My world expanded. The cliffs of the islands were left behind, and sand plains, meadows, and marshes took over.

---

16 Fasteignamat Vestmannaeyjasýslu, Westman Island Archives, November 5, 1916.

The Landeyjar area was surrounded by water, as its name, "Land Islands," suggests. The marshes were a fascinating world teeming with birdlife, but difficult to traverse and sometimes frightening. Since settlement times, Icelanders had struggled with such boggy areas, avoiding them or adapting them to their needs, harvesting from them peat, bog iron, and animal fodder. In the Icelandic sagas the marshes are usually described as hard to cross. Now the farmers of Landeyjar, and many other marshlands in Iceland and around the world, were enthusiastically draining them. In summer, big diggers slashed their way across the land, excavating ditches and flinging the soil to the side. The fields became like a grid, with straight lines and ninety-degree corners. Rural Iceland was being remade. Icelanders were convinced that this was progress, making it easier to get about and increasing productivity and profit. We had entered the Age of Humans, which had yet to be labelled by this name, where nature was an engineering project. The ditches sometimes became an objective in themselves under Icelandic agricultural policy, a symptom of the modern age.

The Icelanders belatedly understood that, although already beautiful to look at, the marshes had an important role to play in nature by cleansing the land, described as kidneys by some, and by harnessing greenhouse gases. The bogs and meadows at Landeyjar were my friends, sparking an interest in the natural environment which has been with me ever since. I collected birds' eggs, blew out the contents and took the shells home to the Westman Islands in straw and cardboard boxes that stayed with me for years. It was probably the smallest natural history museum in the country, but I loved it, and it had pride of place on the bookshelves at home.

The Neighborhood
In the urban plans drawn up in 1939 for the growing village on Heimaey island, Bólstaður was given the street address of number 18 Heimagata, "Home Street." A town square was planned, east of Bólstaður, where two streets met, and plots were tailored to fit. High stone walls or fences usually separated plots of land

in the Westman Islands, and people loved their little spaces; it was probably a relic of the time of the workers' cottages, in a society that was opposed to them.

The cottage of Bólstaður now acquired a cosmopolitan air, registered next to a square and a street, and with a house number. A chapter on "lost streets" in a local history book includes the following:

> Above Gilsbakki stood Bólstaður, a small, friendly house. Brynjólfur, father of Jóhannes [...] who was later manager of the Westman Island Ice Company, built Bólstaður [...] For many years it was the home of Sigurður Ólafsson and his wife Auðbjörg, parents of fishing vessel owner and accountant Óskar.[17]

Óskar was Sigurður and Auðbjörg's first child, born in 1910. There is no mention here of my mother, Bára, who lived at Bólstaður longer than anyone, with the exception of her own mother. In public discourse women were less visible than men well into the twentieth century, both in the Westman Islands and in the rest of Iceland, somewhat like "hidden people."

In the garden around Bólstaður the grown-ups grew potatoes and rhubarb, hung up washing, and cut the grass, and then left the scene to take care of other business. We kids played ball there, trying the patience of the neighbors. By the eastern gable there was a slight slope which was fun when it snowed and froze. Then we barreled down it on sledges, skates, or patent leather shoes. Further away was a playground, with sandboxes, swings, and seesaws. Here we made friendships far beyond our own home turf. In summer, as we grew older, the games moved out onto the nearby streets.

On the other side of the square was the YMCA, where people talked about Jesus at boys' meetings on Monday nights, sang, read from religious books, and held slideshows, while the girls

---

17 Guðjón Ármann Eyjólfsson, *Vestmannaeyjar: Byggð og eldgos* (Reykjavík: Ísafoldarprentsmiðja, 1973), 196–97.

had separate meetings. Apart from that, my world was bounded by the six or seven homes around Bólstaður. My mother had "grown up with the people" in these houses, she said. All of the houses had a name, a common custom in Icelandic towns and villages at the time. I was often at the house called Kalmanstjörn, "Kalman's Pond." On the ground floor lived Ólafur and Sigrún and their children. There was a lot of visiting between "Rúna at Kalmó," as Sigrún was called, and my mother and grandmother at Bólstaður; coffee and doughnuts once a week, as I recall. Children were always welcome and there was a special warmth in the air that was not just from the coal stove that was always burning. Rúna and Óli proved themselves good friends to my parents. Sometimes it was impossible to make ends meet at Bólstad, when Dad was unwell and there was no work to be had, when the income was insufficient for the expenditures, or when wages were paid late. It was then that the couple at Kalmó came to the rescue. Repayment could be delayed, and the interest was zero.

The relationship between my grandmother, Auðjörg, and her sister Gudda at the house called Sandprýði, "Pride of the Sand," was another special aspect of the Bólstaður family network. Gudda, who was two years older than Grandma, was a daily guest at Bólstaður for many years. Although I don't recall her, as I was only two when she died, I remember my father's graphic account of the sisters' visits, with the much-reciprocated "accompanying home" at the end. When Gudda came to visit she stopped for a good while, then Grandma had to accompany her home to Sandprýði, about three hundred meters away, then Gudda had to accompany Grandma back, and so it continued until one of them was left at her home, nourished in spirit but exhausted by the walk.

Dad exaggerated. He often saw the funny side of life, including his own, and invented things if necessary, pondering them and telling his stories with dramatic flourishes. Sometimes he was too quick off the mark. One of Gudda's grandchildren is Helgi Bernódusson, my classmate and good friend. One evening Dad was driving his truck past where Helgi was playing with some other kids in the center of the village. My cousin and I looked alike then, slim and lanky. Dad jumped out of the lorry, grabbed Helgi by the shoulder and exclaimed: "You should get yourself home, lad. You know you aren't allowed out so late." But when Helgi turned around, Dad realized that this boy was not his at all. Then his face changed to one big grin and he said: "No! Is it you, Helgi!" and pinched his nose. He jumped back into his truck, waved to Helgi with a smile, and drove away.

The sisters from Bólstaður and Sandprýði were very pious. They said their prayers and read the Bible, and always upheld Christian commandments and prohibitions in a way that we children found neither obvious nor reasonable. Whistling was not allowed, except in an emergency, as it was entertainment for the Devil. Yet Grandma and Gudda had lively conversations, often over cards, and told rude stories despite all their Lutheran morality, or so I was told long after they had both passed away. They "were quite free-spoken," said Mum as she roared with laughter.

For many of the elders, the neighborhood included Hidden People, or elves. Grandma often spoke about them, as if they were part of a segregated community. In 1962, my parents moved from Bólstaður into a modern brick house they had built on Nýjabæjarbraut, "New Town Street," where they lived until they left for Reykjavík in 1968. A small rock in front of that house was said to be inhabited by a family of Hidden People. Some local people always felt that there "was something there," as they said, and sensed that the rock, called Friður, "Peace," must be respected. Once, when Dad came home from work, Grandma Auðbjörg was standing out in the yard looking at Friður, only a few meters away. He greeted her but she did not answer; she seemed to be in a trance. Dad went in, took off his coat, and then came back out to look after Grandma. He laid his hand on her shoulder and asked what was wrong. She finally replied that she was watching a wedding at Friður; there were elves dressed in their best clothes, going in and out of the rock.

A Fatal Voyage

Dad and his sister Mæja grew up in eastern Iceland, although not always under the same roof. Their mother, Þórunn, could trace her roots to the Faroe Islands. When Þórunn died, the large family of children was split up, but all remained in the same area, Norðfjörður, "North Fjord." Dad and Mæja were always very close. They were remarkably similar, both in temperament and appearance. Somehow or other they thought about things in exactly the same way. They were easygoing and did not allow the worries of the world to concern them too much. Although not literally true, Mæja sometimes said that they were twins.

At seventeen, along with a whole ship's crew, Dad set off for the southwest of Iceland for the winter fishing season. He had been hired at half the adult rate of pay. The following season he joined the crew of a boat based in Norðfjörður, now as a full crew member, and narrowly escaped a watery grave. Halfway through the 1942 autumn fishing season Dad and his cousin Jói decided to take a break and go to the Westman Islands. They intended to visit their people in the islands and stay with their sisters. Dad had never been to the Westman Islands, but Mæja had urged him to come, writing to him in the east that it was time he came for a visit.

That autumn Dad was on a fourteen-ton boat, the *Gandur*, which carried a crew of five. They came into harbor in lovely weather, landed the catch, and were not in any hurry. They were not going to set out again until about four in the morning, to avoid the risk posed by many unexploded mines drifting around the sea, laid by the Allied forces that had occupied Iceland during World War II. At first the fishermen were terrified, but they were becoming immune to the risk, although somebody always had to keep an eye out. They were to go out fishing one more time, and then the season would be over. This is the way Dad told it during our conversation, in his characteristic rapid-fire narrative:

> So, we have finished getting the boat and everything ready—and now there is just the next morning left. Then

a man comes running along the jetty, and it's my cousin Jói, who reminds me about going to the Westman Islands. I ask him when we can leave, and he says that the coaster *Súðin* is leaving at six the next morning. I say I don't fancy the idea. Jói nags me: "Talk to Skipper Valdi and see if you can get off!" Valdi says it's fine; he'll get his father-in-law to stand in for me. So that's that. We leave on the *Súðin*, in the same calm weather as there has been for the preceding few days and anchor briefly off the coast by Hornafjörður. We are situated offshore just east of Meðalland by evening and the bell has rung for dinner, and we have come up into the mess about the time that the evening news was beginning. And the first news we hear is that the *Gandur* has gone down.

The news was a terrible shock for my father, and he lost his appetite completely. He had gotten a man to take his place on the boat and now that man had died. The two-week visit to the Westman Islands was a distressing time. The accident threw a pall over everything.

It was quite common for boats to go down in winter weather — like volcanic eruptions it was something Icelanders learned to live with — but judging from the debris that was found a few days later on the fishing grounds, it seemed that the boat was shattered by a wartime mine. The tragedy raised questions for Dad that, naturally enough, were quite different from those the Marine Accident Investigation Board had to answer. Why was he saved from the *Gandur*'s last trip? Why was it the *Gandur* that had to go down? Might the *Gandur* have been saved if he had been on board? Similar existential questions occurred to me when Dad first told me about the *Gandur*'s last voyage. Would I even exist if Uncle Jói had not urged Dad to take a holiday? If Aunt Mæja hadn't insisted he visit? What would the story be then?

Later, Dad went back to the Westman Islands for a whole fishing season and stayed with his sister Mæja. He met a girl at a dance one weekend; they chatted together and took a turn on the dance floor. It was my mother, Bára from Bólstaður. One

Fig. 7. Mom and Dad, Bára and Páll.

day, not long afterwards, he asked his sister to go to Bólstaður and ask Bára to meet him. Mæja complied, and the two women walked back to Mæja's house, where Páll waited. After a long talk, Bára and Páll announced that they were destined to be together, and from then on, they were inseparable (fig. 7). Dad set about things briskly, he "went all-out," as my mother said. When Mæja was asked about it just before she died, she smiled sweetly and shrugged her shoulders, in the way the whole family did.

LANDSCAPES

I practiced running on slippery rocks on Heimaey with the other kids. The trick was not to focus on individual stones, but to sense the space as a whole and to let oneself flow across the rocks. Otherwise things could end badly. In our world, kids and boulders belonged to the same space, society and nature flowed together as one. Learned people spoke of the Gestalt theory of

Fig. 8. Nature exploration on Heimaey. Photo by Eiríkur Þ. Einarsson.

visual perception, but we had no idea about this, and it didn't matter. The rocks punished you if you did not do things right. You tripped, were injured, or fell into the sea. Most kids did fall into the sea now and then, so it was just as well they learned to swim. The sea water in the swimming pool on the Westman Islands was freezing cold, and it was necessary to throw buckets of water over us kids standing on the side, to get us used to it before we were ordered into the pool.

Sometimes we took a break from running around on the slippery rocks to look at bugs and small fish trapped in pools between the stones. There were birds everywhere you looked, as well as seaweed and kelp on the beach, and various grasses and flowers in the fields and meadows, all with their names to learn. We explored inland, sometimes with binoculars and a camera slung across our shoulders like budding naturalists (fig. 8). We climbed up and slid down screes, crags, and grassy slopes. Even the pit of the crater of Mount Helgafell was not off-limits — to us kids, it was a playground.

We also worked on our sprang technique, the traditional method of collecting sea birds and their eggs from cliffs. You would fling yourself off a cliff edge, holding onto the end of a rope, and bounce back and forth across the cliff face. The cliffs, all with their own names, varied in difficulty and danger. Strong, determined teenagers worked their way up the ladder of respect that the cliffs defined. It was both a rite of passage and preparation for the adult work of providing food for the family.

Our food was usually sought from the ocean — we ate a lot of fish — but seabirds and eggs from the cliffs were an important supplement. Like the sea, the cliffs took their toll. Many a young man fell when collecting eggs on Heimaey and the outer islands. News of accidents and deaths spread between houses like wildfire, and the village would fall silent. The risk that went with climbing and rappelling did not dampen our enthusiasm, though. Perhaps you could say we were bewitched by the threat and beauty of the cliffs and the slippery rocks below.

I personally felt a bond with the majestic Heimaklettur, "Home Cliff," a wild part of Heimaey that could be seen from our kitchen window at Bólstaður. Heimaklettur is a hyaloclastite tuff formation with scree slopes and a grassy cap. It rose from the sea about forty thousand years ago, around the time the Neanderthals were dying out, after an intimate coexistence with *Homo sapiens* that produced many offspring of mixed blood. To my childish eyes, Heimaklettur was a reliable neighbor, towering over the village and unaffected by everything, not even by pounding waves and wild tempests. It demanded my attention. Sitting at the kitchen table I drew countless pictures of "The Rock," which is in fact a 283-meter-high mountain. The Rock took on many guises, depending on the season and time of day, with a constantly changing interplay of light and shade that challenged me each time I tried.

Island Out of the Sea

On November 14, 1963, when I was thirteen, came news that an eruption had begun on the sea floor near a small rocky islet just southwest of Heimaey. My school announced a holiday so that we could watch this singular spectacle. The eruption plume rose high into the air, close to land. The eruption was accompanied by powerful tremors in the Earth, an entirely new experience for us young Westman Islanders. We learned to look up when we thought we felt an earthquake, to see if the ceiling light was swinging back and forth. The ash sometimes filled the rain gutters of the houses that were used to collect drinking water. Without wells or springs to provide a main water supply, we islanders were reliant on rainwater. Any blockages had to be cleared, otherwise the home water-tank, usually a concrete cistern in the yard, would dry up.

Three French journalists working for *Paris Match* were first to make landfall on the new island, three weeks after the eruption began. They discreetly made their way out to the Westman Islands, worried that they would be prevented from reaching the eruption site, or that other journalists would beat them to it. My father, who was a lorry driver then, took the Frenchmen and their rubber dinghy with its small outboard motor out to the southernmost point on Heimaey, where they launched the boat and sailed out to sea, towards the volcano. They invited Dad to go with them. He did not understand French but realized what they meant after an exchange of gestures and declined the invitation. It took them about an hour to cross; they turned the boat around on the new island's beach, so they could sail away in a hurry if need be, then stayed half an hour, planting the French flag and taking photographs. They had to retreat when the eruption intensified, and ash and rocks rained over them. Icelandic reporters who landed around the time that the French were starting their engine to return were astonished to see men on the new island before them.

Westman Islanders have a long-standing affection for the fourteen "out-islands" that, along with islets and skerries, surround Heimaey, our "Home Island." Each out-island has its profile, use, guardians, and history. Many stories are told of summer camping trips, egg collecting, bird hunting, and fun, and some rivalry between island factions. Now a new island had been added to the archipelago, the first since Iceland was settled. It is no wonder that people feel strong ties to it and argue about what it should be named. At first there was talk of Gosey, "Eruption Island," or Frakkaey, "Frenchmen's Island." The agreed upon name, Surtsey, was not suggested by Westman Islanders, and many were initially unhappy with it. The name means Surtur's Isle, after a fiery giant in Norse mythology who has been given a new lease on life as a character in comics and films about the superhero Þór.

At the eruption's height, in the early spring of 1964, I sailed out with a few friends on a small fishing boat, in pretty rough weather, to take a closer look. Such trips, despite the risks, were not uncommon, and they were truly thrilling. The captain went as close as he dared. We could hear the rumble of the volcano and see glowing lava flowing out of the crater and into the sea. About seventeen months later, in the summer of 1965, I landed on Surtsey with a group of people transporting supplies to build a hut for scientists to stay in. The island was still simmering then. Another new island, which had formed in the same submarine eruption, was visible too. It later sank into the sea, as did its two siblings, but Surtsey remained, about one-tenth the size of Heimaey. It was a privilege to make landfall on this brand-new island, a unique natural laboratory. The eruption prompted many questions. Ever since, biologists and geologists have closely monitored the beginnings of new plant and animal communities on lava that have formed from dead magma.

That summer, we were ferried to the island by a rubber dinghy and stayed until evening, walking around for a few hours and examining boiling-hot fractures and clefts with minerals in bright hues. Often, we got close to steaming lava, risking our rubber shoes. Colorful surfaces were a sign of excessive heat. Some of us took colorful stones home with us, but their color faded quickly. The stones were sensitive to being touched and tossed around, and their pretty sulfur deposits came off. One of

Fig. 9. On Surtsey, in the summer of 1965. Another island is being born nearby.

my friends at the scene picked up an old camera my father had lent me and took a picture of me (fig. 9). The picture encapsulates that connection between Westman Islanders and the islets that have grown up from the seafloor all around us. Standing there on the newly solidified lava, I am innocence itself, a long-legged boy en route to school on the mainland, ready to kick up my heels and try my luck.

Among my neighbors, however, there was anxiety and insomnia. The eruption weighed on people's minds. Many feared it presaged further earthly convulsions. The summer I went to Surtsey, I was working at building the reinforced concrete walls of a new hospital for the Westman Islands. Iron rebar had to be cut, tied together, and placed in the formwork so that the concrete would be strong enough to withstand the major earthquake that some feared was soon to come.

The Volcano in the Living Room

No doubt ever since the first settlers arrived on Heimaey, Mount Helgafell has been regarded with awe, as the name it was given means "Holy Mountain." Clearly the mountain was unusual in some way; the settlers realized it had erupted at some time in the past. By 930, the end of the settlement period, Icelanders had witnessed at least two large eruptions. They knew what a volcano looked like.

The year I was born, American environmentalist Aldo Leopold published an important book, *A Sand County Almanac,* calling for a "land ethic." It aroused little attention at first but is now considered a seminal work. Leopold urged people to "think like a mountain."[18] Are we capable of seeing things from a mountain's point of view? Can we imagine how Mount Helgafell feels or what it has in mind?

In the summer of 1972, on a visit to Heimaey, and with the recent Surtsey eruption in mind, geologist Sigurður Þórarinsson asked, "What if Helgafell were to erupt?"[19] The consequences could be horrendous, with the mountain right on the outskirts of a village with a population of five thousand. The village had been expanding for decades from the harbor towards the volcano. One of the symbols of the community was the impressive stone church Landakirkja, "Church of the Land," built at the edge of the town under the volcano, between 1774 and 1780). Next-door was the primary school and a little further to the north the hospital and the pharmacy, the center of village with its homes and services, and the fishing plants by the harbor.

An eruption in Helgafell must have seemed an unlikely event; people had been living beside the mountain for over a thousand years and it had never erupted. Mum grew up around "lava and Helgafell," as she put it, "but there was no geothermal heat or anything." If there had been, I wouldn't have had to light that dangerous oil burner in the basement, nor would I have had to learn to swim in a freezing pool, as many houses in Iceland are heated with geothermal hot water pumped right from the

---

18 Aldo Leopold, *A Sand County Almanac and Sketches Here and There* (New York: Oxford University Press, 1949), 129. See also Jeffrey Jerome Cohen, *Stone: An Ecology of the Inhuman* (Minneapolis: University of Minnesota Press, 2015), 2–3.

19 Guðjón Ármann Eyjólfsson, *Vestmannaeyjar: Byggð og eldgos* (Reykjavík: Ísafoldarprentsmiðja, 1973), 162.

ground and swimming pools throughout the country are also geothermally heated. Before she had me, Mum had often hiked down into the crater of Helgafell itself, just over half an hour's brisk walk from the village. Only once did she think, "What if the mountain started to erupt now!" she told me, long after the mountain did erupt, in 1973, destroying the house where I was born.

In autumn 2010, French artist Nelly Ben Hayoun placed a few manmade volcanoes in Londoners' living rooms. She had modelled her volcanoes on live examples: Mount St. Helens in the US and Ol Doinyo Lengai, named after the Masai for "Mountain of the Gods," in Tanzania. She inserted detonators and explosives from fireworks in the interiors of her volcano sculptures and had them erupt now and again. Volunteers took care of them at home for two weeks and became experimental subjects in the process. Ben Hayoun describes her installations on her website:

> These designed supra-natural objects are large, reaching almost to the ceiling, imposing, and extremely inconvenient, erupting dust and gloop into the living rooms of volunteers seemingly at random. [...] *The Other Volcano* imagines a love-hate relationship, a 'sleeping giant' in the corner of your domestic environment, with the power to provoke excitement with its rumblings, and also perhaps fear (if not for one's life in this case, then at least for the soft furnishings of one's clean and neat 'living' room).[20]

Ben Hayoun's experiment is about threatening the cozy space of the living room with the unpredictable performances of a heaving, living mountain. Rather like having an exotic foreigner in the house, it's a feeling that is normal to Icelanders.

Some people on Earth have a volcano in their lives, others don't. Among those of us who do, many need years to become reconciled to their volcano. The same can be said of those who

---

20 Nelly Ben Hayoun Studios, "The Other Volcano," 2015, https://nellyben.com/projects/the-other-volcano/.

have experienced other natural hazards, such as wildfires or avalanches, for example, that destroy people and communities.

Our choice of language draws attention to the nuances of nature that we think are important and preserves the experience of generations. In a sense, the term natural disaster is not appropriate at all. Such a disaster — an eruption or an earthquake, for instance — always involves the close relationship between humankind and the planet, which underscores the continuous connection between Earth and us.

Global heating is a giant volcano in the room. Humanity has established a dangerous intimate relationship with the planet since coal was first adopted as a fuel in the service of capitalism and industry. No one has failed to notice that coal from the depths of the Earth has had a big influence on humankind. But while we celebrate its positive effects, we close our eyes to the negative. Little by little, the Earth has been getting warmer, and signs of this can be seen widely. Climate change calls for coordinated and targeted actions worldwide to reduce greenhouse gas emissions. These are radical actions, requiring alterations in our ways of life, attitudes, and economic systems.

Perhaps it is possible to draw a lesson from Ben Hayoun's experiment, regarding life on the Westman Islands in the second half of the last century. Research on radioactive particles shows that the lava which came up in the 1973 eruption, destroying my first habitat of Bólstaður, came from the same magma source as the lava of the Surtsey eruption ten years before. In other words, Westman Islanders had had simmering magma beneath their feet for a whole decade. That had not been known prior to 1997, when the research was published. Some islanders were shocked when they learned that they had been sitting on top of a glowing pot of lava, completely oblivious for ten years. I find the thought disturbing myself, even though I had not sat on top of that pot for so very long. I went away to school at Laugarvatn, on the mainland, in the autumn of 1964, at the height of the Surtsey eruption, and only visited Heimaey during the summers and between terms. Then in December 1968 my parents and siblings moved to the mainland. Still, many of my relatives and friends remained on Heimaey, and I have always thought of the island as my home and Mount Helgafell as my volcano.

THE MOUNTAIN ERUPTS

UNDER THE STYLUS

Although most people need no intermediary to sense a powerful earthquake, the human body is not a very sensitive earthquake detector. In a tectonically active area this is a real disadvantage, and people have long sought ways to predict earthquakes and determine their origin and direction. About two thousand years ago a mechanism was developed in China which appears to have had the ability to indicate the intensity and direction of tremors, even those that were too small for humans to feel. According to a twentieth-century description based on ancient texts, the invention and the design of mathematician, astronomer, and geographer Zhang Heng (78–139 CE) consisted of "a vessel of fine bronze, resembling a wine-jar":

> It had a domed cover, and the outer surface was ornamented with antique seal-characters, and designs of mountains, tortoises, birds and animals. Inside there was a central column capable of lateral displacement along tracks [...] and so arranged (that it would operate) a closing and opening mechanism [...] Outside the vessel there were eight dragon heads, each one holding a bronze ball in its mouth, while round the base there sat eight (corresponding) toads with their mouths

open, ready to receive any ball which the dragons might drop. [...] When an earthquake occurred the dragon mechanism of the vessel was caused to vibrate so that a ball was vomited out of a dragon-mouth and caught by the toad underneath. At the same time instant a sharp sound was made which called the attention of the observers.[1]

You could call this the first seismometer, originating from the Greek word *seiō*, to shake or quake.

Seismometers remind us that the boundaries between us and the environment are indistinct and unstable. When anthropologist Gregory Bateson tried to put himself in the shoes of a visually impaired person, feeling his way forward with a white cane, he exclaimed: "Where do *I* start? Is my mental system bounded at the handle of the stick? Is it bounded by my skin? Does it start halfway up the stick? But these are nonsense questions."[2] Bateson pointed out that people are shaped by their environment, and that all our implements and tools are part of ourselves, like our fellow citizens and the ground beneath our feet. The white cane and the seismometer are related, both indicative of humanity's desire to sense the environment and adapt to it. We feel our way forward in the shifting and living land with all kinds of sensory aids.

Iceland is an extremely tectonically active area, straddling the boundary of two tectonic plates that are spreading apart. The first modern seismometer was installed here in 1909, for researchers from abroad, in the Navigation School in Reykjavík. The school's principal supervised its operations for six years, until readings ceased during World War I because the seismograms could no longer be sent to Strasbourg for processing.[3]

---

[1] Joseph Needham, *Science and Civilization in China, Volume 3: Mathematics and the Sciences of the Heavens and the Earth* (Cambridge: Cambridge University Press, 1959), 626–35, at 627.

[2] Gregory Bateson, *Steps to an Ecology of Mind* (Frogmore: Paladin, 1972), 459.

[3] Páll Einarsson and Sveinbjörn Björnsson, "Jarðskjálftamælingar á Raunvísindastofnun Háskólans," in *Í hlutarins eðli*, ed. Þorsteinn Ingi Sigfússon

Information about these early observations is limited (but in 1912 a big, magnitude 7 earthquake in South Iceland was conscientiously recorded). The seismometer introduced in Iceland in the 1970s had a large rotating cylinder covered with paper. It was arranged so that its mounting, or frame, faithfully followed the movements in the earth, just as a house and other buildings do. A flexible arm, attached to the frame, followed along when the Earth trembled. On the end of the arm was a stylus, which scratched a clear mark in the soot, or carbon, coating on the paper wrapped around the cylinder.

What was the meaning of the strange hieroglyphics produced by such machines? Most people in Iceland probably saw the earliest seismometers as an intriguing new toy which might be useful in teaching. Few suspected that they would go on to play a hugely important role in society — as the inhabitants of earthquake zones around the world now know so well — or that their paper seismograms would indisputably become part of the fabric of history. Reading seismograms was a tedious process, and there were so many other phenomena in nature which were just as interesting as the undulations of the Earth's crust.

The Surtsey eruption had an important influence on the course of seismology in Iceland. It was the longest uninterrupted eruption since Iceland was settled, beginning in November 1963 and not ending until June 1967. Here, for the first time, people had the opportunity to closely monitor a long series of major and minor earthquakes. Soon after the eruption, regular and systematic measurements of earthquakes began, particularly on the Reykjanes peninsula in southwest Iceland and in other high-temperature geothermal areas. Earthquakes and volcanoes were high on the agenda for some time. In autumn 1972, for example, the Icelandic newspaper *Vísir* published an article headlined "Predicting eruptions: No more surprise eruptions but 'false alarms' possible," in which it was pointed out that many of the world's big cities are in danger from volcanic eruptions. No one can predict exactly when an eruption will begin,

---

(Reykjavík: Menningarsjóður, 1987), 251–78.

the newspaper wrote, but with progress in reading the signs it is "to a large extent possible to reassure people with logic [...] People struggle with so much uncertainty in life that we do not need to lie awake over thoughts of a mega-eruption on the Reykjanes peninsula, never mind Esja or other mountains in urban areas."[4] The time of the seismometer appeared to have arrived.[5] It was inevitable that the Age of Humans, which was making itself at home, would call for instruments of this kind. The Earth demanded attention.

Among the students at Laugarvatn Menntaskóli Junior College on the mainland in south Iceland were quite a number of Westman Islanders, and most of them, me included, joined the science program. We studied physics, chemistry, and geology. We walked in the mountains with our teachers and explored important historical sites, studying their rock formations, fossils, and glacial moraines, among other features. In the dark winter evenings, we observed constellations. But it was only after I had graduated that Þórir Ólafsson, my physics teacher and later professor and rector of the Teachers Training College, was put in charge of a soot-seismometer. Þórir was a patient and painstaking educator who often took an innovative approach, using his talent for opening students' eyes to the wonders of nature, whether to the structure of atoms or the universe itself. He was well-versed in physics theory and laboratory methods, introducing experiments on gravity, light, electricity, and the like to the classroom.

Greek polymath Archimedes (circa 287–212 BCE) imagined looking at the Earth from afar with the eyes of the gods, from a place that has been named *Punctum Archimedes* in his honor. There was no opportunity here for an Archimedean viewpoint, from which it would be possible to objectively view the planet's earthquakes. Instead, the seismometer at the Laugarvatn school

---

4 Haukur Helgason, "Eldgos séð fyrir: Engin óvænt gos en kannski 'gabb'," *Vísir,* October 10, 1972, 6.

5 Takesi Minakami, "Fundamental Research for Predicting Volcanic Eruptions," *Bulletin of the Earthquake Research Institute* 38 (1960): 497–644.

was undeniably attached to the earth that it monitored and described, and danced faithfully in step with it, like everything else that shook on the plate boundary, and it was worth listening to for precisely that reason. The seismometer and the man who tended it were firmly grounded, completely down to earth.

In the Moment

Þórir's seismometer measured many sorts of movement as they happened. The seismometer's stylus was similar to those used in record-players. The paper strip was coated with tangible soot, into which the stylus cut grooves, so that it was possible to trace the path of the stylus as the movements in the Earth's crust shook the mechanism. Þórir had to insert new paper in the seismometer every day — having first coated it with soot so the stylus could make its mark — and ensure that the mechanism was working properly. If that was not done, vital news from the bowels of the Earth might be lost. The previous day's intriguing paper seismograms had to be dipped in a special solution and cleaned, so that the record they kept would not end up "blowing in the wind," as Bob Dylan had sung and recorded on vinyl at the time of the Surtsey eruption, about a decade before.

Those were the days of vinyl. Black vinyl, made from crude oil and salt, ultimately recorded all sorts of upheavals of the time, quite apart from the rhythms and tunes of the musicians: a whole range of happenings, cultural revolutions, political movements, and student revolts. During my years at Laugarvatn, our record-players were playing the music of Herb Alpert and the Tijuana Brass, mostly the album *What Now My Love*. The album cover shows the trumpeter with his instrument, with a beautiful woman leaning against him, while the musician himself gazes straight into the lens. The theme is repeated on the cover of Dylan's *The Freewheelin' Bob Dylan*, which I acquired later. They were cool dudes, and a symbol of the times.

The principal of Laugarvatn Menntaskóli, Jóhann S. Hannesson, had been curator of the Fiske Icelandic Collection at Cornell University, named after linguist Daniel Willard Fiske, who had built an extensive library of Icelandic literature. Jóhann had been summoned home to Iceland to deal with the challenges of disorderly rural youth. His addresses to the assembled students were memorable, speculating aloud with great inspiration and thundering over us teenagers about what matters in life. He urged us to make our dreams come true and to put ourselves first. We had never heard anything like it. My interest in social affairs was stirred. Everything important in life had to do with people's interactions and ideas, with equality and fraternity, meetings and protests, with building a new world; the Earth could look to itself, I thought.

In the summer of 1972, three years after I graduated, however, I was passing through a corridor of my old school, Laugarvatn High, when something made me pause: the soot-seismometer. I had never seen it, or any seismometer, before. It was set up in a glass cabinet so that the students and others could observe it at work. My interests were fixed on anthropology by now, but I couldn't not look at the Laugarvatn seismometer. I examined the instrument and the traces on paper and listened to the tick of the stylus. Perhaps this encounter laid the foundation for my later interest in instruments, equipment, and the natural sciences, but I don't suppose it occurred to me then that such research was relevant to an anthropologist. The opposites within the academic world, two companies arrayed on either side of a major divide, two tectonic plates drawing apart, the humanities on one side, the sciences on the other, were taken for granted, and mostly they still are, though tremors of change are felt sometimes, as elsewhere on Earth.

Sea Shells and Seismograms

Geophysicist Páll Einarsson, now, like me, a professor at the University of Iceland, was studying in the US from 1970 to 1975. It was he who built, with his colleagues in America, the seismometer I saw at Laugarvatn, and installed it in the school, in the care of my physics teacher, in 1972. Another seismometer was installed at Sigalda in the highlands of south Iceland, the location of a major hydroelectric power station. The third went

Fig. 10. Geophysicist Páll Einarsson standing next to a seismometer similar to those that he installed before the Heimaey eruption. Photo by the author.

to the farm of Skammadalshóll in the south, and was to play a vital part in the story of the Heimaey eruption (fig. 10).

A farmer may seem an unexpected choice to take charge of a scientific instrument like a seismometer, but was he? Páll Einarsson didn't think so. As a youngster, he had himself spent the summers on a farm in Hornafjörður, in southeast Iceland. From an early age he had displayed an interest in geology and zoology, and as a boy, during his summer in the country in 1958, he discovered a new species of mollusc, *Mya arenaria*, the softshell clam or sand gaper, which was colonizing Iceland's shores. The following summer the farmer at Skammadalshóll, Einar H. Einarsson, found an exemplar of the same species at the Dyrhólaós estuary, some distance west of Hornafjörður. Both Einar and Páll sent samples to a natural scientist in the capital, whose job it was to keep track of such discoveries. He filed official records of their findings. The softshell clam spread around Iceland's shores, to become known as "a mouthwatering newcomer" to Iceland.[6]

It was this little-known shared discovery of the softshell clam that ultimately brought Einar and Páll together to work with seismography and marked a turning-point in the earth sciences in Iceland and predicted the historic eruption on Heimaey in January 1973. At the age of 19, Páll made his way east by bus to pitch his tent next to the farmhouse at Skammadalshóll. Einar and his wife, Steinunn Stefánsdottir, were cattle farmers and, in addition, Einar was nationally known as a poet and painter. Einar welcomed his young visitor, and the two discussed molluscs and other mutual interests in the natural world. Some years later, when Páll returned to Iceland with his new soot-seismometers, he asked Einar to take responsibility for one of them. He was quite sure that Einar would take good care of the equipment and he felt that looking after the seismometer could readily be combined with work on the farm.

Einar agreed without hesitation. He was keen to take on the seismometer, having carried out his own studies of the geology of the Mýrdalur region surrounding his farm, sometimes in collaboration with volcanology professor Sigurður Þórarinsson and other professional geologists. Einar and Steinunn at Skammadalshóll took conscientious care of the seismometer for many years. It became so important to them that when they moved into an old people's home in 1990, they took it with them, like a cherished ornament. The instrument had become so much a part of their lives that they could not bear to leave it behind or to dispose of it, although by that time it had, of course, long become obsolete.[7] The original plan had been to return the three seismometers to New York in the fall, when the Icelandic ex-

---

6 Guðrún G. Þórarinsdóttir, Magnús Freyr Ólafsson, and Þórður Örn Kristjánsson, "Lostætur landnemi," *Náttúrufræðingurinn* 75, no. 1 (2007): 33–40.

7 Þórður Tómasson, "Minning: Einar H. Einarsson Skammadalshóli," *Morgunblaðið*, October 17, 1992.

periment was completed, but somehow that idea was conveniently "forgotten."

The seismometer at Skammadalshóll was highly sensitive and recorded various phenomena that had nothing to do with geology or the Westman Islands. Einar read all sorts of signals from his seismograms, such as when the milk truck passed through the district to pick up milk from the dairy farms. Sometimes he made an explanatory note on the strip of paper before he sent it to Reykjavík for analysis and storage. He mentioned, for example, "a storm," "holes in the road," and "horses" passing close by the farmstead.[8] At the Laugarvatn school, too, Þórir noted some earth-shaking events, such as "skiers 20 meters from the seismometer."

Such events registered as tremors, and while they are easily distinguished from bigger occurrences in geological history, the microhistories of the human world are most likely related to the larger strokes of geology. The custodians of these seismometers did not fail to notice real earthquake tremors or earthquake swarms either. Sometimes Einar made little sketches on a seismogram of an erupting volcano, for instance.

During the days preceding the Heimaey eruption, the seismometers at Skammadalshóll and Laugarvatn were functioning perfectly. The ever-vigilant mechanism traced out a line with historic significance. Einar and Þórir must have seized these seismograms as they emerged from under the stylus and scrutinized the lines with a magnifying glass. Reading and understanding a seismogram is a delicate skill that demands extensive training and experience. What is up? What is down? Where is the time axis? How can you tell a real swarm of earthquake tremors from the shocks caused by a herd of passing horses or a milk truck in a pothole?

After several months with the seismometers in their care, Einar and Þórir knew what they were doing, but they had never

---

8 Seismographs from Laugarvatn (box ER 099), National Archives of Iceland, January 1973; Seismographs from Skammadalshóll (box ER 144), National Archives of Iceland, January 1973.

before watched the build-up to an eruption by means of seismography. The drums rotated endlessly, and the delicate stylus cut a clear line though the layer of soot, but perhaps initially, as they observed the first tremors, they may not have been quite sure what they were seeing.

The Tales They Tell

Einar at Skammadalshóll kept a diary, in which he made notes about the weather and his daily activities. On occasion he writes about his tasks around the farm: "This evening I took about half a trailer of muck from the cowshed out to Eyri."[9] But, reading Einar's diaries, it's clear to me that he was far less interested in his work on the farm than in the natural sciences. "Didn't do much today," he writes. "Didn't get much done today"; "was lazy, walked up into the valley and around, and then guests arrived." Much more of the diary is devoted to observations and figures of various kinds.

On Sunday, January 21, 1973, two days before the eruption commenced on Heimaey, for example, Einar noted: "Calm weather, mostly dry in the early part of the day, then a stiff easterly breeze and showers in the afternoon. Temperature +3 +4 +2." In Celsius, of course, so a little above freezing. He continued: "In the valley I saw about 200 fulmars, two wrens, five redwings, and one blackbird. This evening at 20:19:50, a swarm of earthquakes began at a distance of about 60 kilometers."

In a later report, Einar wrote:

> Nothing happened for nearly an hour, but then the earthquakes recommenced with increasing intensity. That night I looked up a paper by Robert W. Decker about research on Kilauea, Hawaii in 1965 and other years. It seemed to me that the earthquake swarm we were experiencing was so similar to what he described that there could scarcely be any doubt that it presaged a volcanic eruption. I tried to count

---

9 Einar H. Einarsson, "Diaries of Einar H. Einarsson," Regional Archive of Skógar, 1973.

the tremors on the drum, but that is difficult, especially on a soot-seismometer when the paper strip is in place. I counted to about 250. But when I counted them again after the paper had been removed, it transpired that there had been more than 300.[10]

Robert W. Decker was a well-known volcanologist who established a Center for the Study of Active Volcanoes in Hawai'i and, with his wife, Barbara Decker, wrote many books about volcanoes.[11] Reading them was a favorite pastime of the farmer at Skammadalsholl, in between animal husbandry, monitoring the weather, and counting wild birds. It was clear to Einar that things were heating up. We know now that the red-hot magma was flowing gradually upwards from about 15 or 20 kilometers beneath the Earth's surface, impatient after ten years of inactivity since the Surtsey eruption — although in geological time ten years is just a fleeting moment.

The following day Einar wrote in his diary: "Spoke to Þórir today. His reading of the earthquake swarm was the same as mine [...]. The swarm that started yesterday evening went on until 9 this morning [...] it looks as if the main swarm starts 64 km away and ends 60 km away." After a long telephone conversation with Þórir, Einar wrote: "The focus is either on the west side of Eldgjá, or in the Westman Islands. We really need a third seismometer." The circles around Laugarvatn and Skammadalshóll, indicating the distance from the epicenter based on the seismometer readings, intersected at two points. But without a third reading the location could not be pinpointed by triangulation. Several more seismometers were in use in Iceland at the time, but those which might have provided the necessary

---

10 Einar H. Einarsson, "Eldgosið á Heimaey 1973: Afrit af köflum úr dagbók og aflestrarskýrslum af mæli á Skammadalshóli," Regional Archive of Skógar, 1973.
11 *Wikipedia*, s.v. "Robert W. Decker," https://en.wikipedia.org/wiki/Robert_W._Decker.

information were either malfunctioning, or their readings were not immediately accessible.

Over at Sigalda, the third soot-seismometer Páll Einarsson had set up was not, strictly speaking, out of order. Reynir Böðvarsson, now a professor of seismology at Uppsala University in Sweden, spoke to Einar and Þórir about their readings. In order to try to pinpoint the epicenter, in the late afternoon of January 22, Reynir called the person in charge of the seismometer at Sigalda, but was informed that it was not operating, because the ethanol supplied for it had run out.[12] Seismologists would later cynically remark that the seismometer at Sigalda consumed far more ethanol than the others. The stylus on the Sigalda machine could not be relied on and contributed nothing. Perhaps the human element had lost touch with the Earth.

Einar and Þórir were both convinced that an eruption was imminent. In the dark of evening Þórir made his way up the slopes of Mount Laugarvatnsfjall, looking out eastward to Eldgjá, while at Skammadalshóll Einar went out to look west, toward the Westman Islands. He could not see the islands from his farmhouse, but he did not have far to go and knew exactly where to find a lookout point. No doubt he had climbed up adjacent hills and mountains to observe the Surtsey eruption ten years earlier. Visibility was good, but neither Einar nor Þórir could discern any glow of volcanic activity. Yet they were right, all the same. Had Einar kept a lookout for a few hours longer that night, he would have witnessed the beginnings of the eruption he had predicted and seen an unforgettable sight: Iceland's first, and so far, only, volcanic eruption in the vicinity of an inhabited area was about to begin.

The seismometer at Skammadalshóll tended to malfunction, but Einar could usually keep it going, with help from various people. He wrote in his report: "Since the seismometer was not working properly — but could be kept going with care and attention — I stayed by it for most of the night, as I didn't want to miss anything it might detect. When it was getting on towards

---

12 Reynir Böðvarsson, email, October 4, 2016.

one that night (January 23), I was taken aback, because sometimes there were two tremors in the same minute. Somehow I had a feeling that something was happening, and that kept me awake." About an hour later Einar checked on the seismometer once again, and concluded that "something serious had happened, because at 01:56:07 there had been a very odd quake, clearly shallow — but it had continued at a constant intensity far longer than a quake of that magnitude would generally do."

Einar at Skammadalshóll could not get to sleep, even though he had hardly slept for several nights due to his attentions to the ailing seismometer. Should he and Þórir, and their colleagues in Reykjavík, make it known that an eruption could be expected, either at Eldgjá or in the Westman Islands? At around 3 a.m. a car pulled up at Skammadalshóll. Einar wrote in his report:

> Mount Helgafell in the Westman Islands had started to erupt just before 2 a.m. I was not entirely surprised, because after the tremors started again yesterday evening I was expecting an eruption in the night. We drove straight out to Litla-Hvammsklif, and it was a fearsome sight we saw on Heimaey island. We could not see the actual source of the eruption clearly, but there was a continuous wall of fire south of the summit of Helgafell, and it seemed to stretch northwards, and we could be quite sure that appalling things were happening there. Before long rain moved in and cut off our view of the islands, and so we went home.

Over the following days Einar and Þórir continued to confer by phone about the seismograms and the progress of the eruption.[13] Einar wrote in his report that the earthquake swarm that had commenced on the Sunday evening had presaged "this huge event." When he later read reports about readings from seismometers at Laugarvatn, Sigalda, and Skammadalshóll, sent to him by Páll Einarsson, he noticed that Páll had made a note of

---

13 Páll Einarsson, Þórir Ólafsson, and Sveinbjörn Björnsson, interview, 2015.

two earthquakes off the Westman Islands as far back as October. "And I think that taught us a lesson," Einar observes.

These events marked a turning point. In a 2013 book on natural disasters in Iceland, Ármann Höskuldsson and his coauthors maintain, with reference to the seismographic observations leading up to the Heimaey eruption, that it is hardly "possible to avoid the conclusion that these events predicted the eruption."[14] "That was the first time," they continue, "that an eruption was predicted on the basis of geological observations in Iceland." Attitudes toward predictions based on seismography would change in the years ahead, with research and development in the field making huge strides, including the advent of GPS technology. On February 26, 2000, for instance, the Icelandic Meteorological Office warned, correctly, that Mount Hekla would begin to erupt within twenty-five minutes.[15]

The Organist
While hundreds of tremors were picked up by Einar's and Þórir's seismometers in the days preceding the fateful night of the eruption on Heimaey (until about 10 p.m. on January 22), news of these events did not reach the Westman Islanders. No quakes were perceptible on the islands, because they took place at great depth. What difference might it have made if a read-out from a third seismometer had been available, and if the implications of those readings had been widely known?

Ironically enough, there had once been a seismometer on Heimaey itself, installed in December 1963 shortly after the Surtsey eruption began. It was a mechanism with an ink stylus, an older type than the soot-seismometer. The seismometer had been installed in order to monitor the risk that the eruption on

---

14 Ármann Hökuldsson et al., "Eldstöðvar í sjó," in *Náttúruvá á Íslandi: Eldgos og jarðskjálftar,* ed. Júlíus Sólnes (Reykjavík: Viðlagatrygging Íslands/ Háskólaútgáfan, 2013), 403–25.

15 Ari Trausti Guðmundsson and Ragnar Th. Sigurðsson, *Eldgos 1913–2004* (Reykjavík: Vaka-Helgafell, 2005), 136; Páll Einarsson, "Short-Term Seismic Precursors to Icelandic Eruptions 1973–2014," *Frontiers in Earth Science,* May 8, 2018.

the sea floor might spread to Heimaey. It soon transpired that the Surtsey eruption was unlikely to continue in the long term and posed no threat to Heimaey. Hence, the use of the seismometer was discontinued, as it appeared to be an unnecessary expense in view of the minimal risk.

A surveyor who worked on the newborn island of Surtsey while it was still erupting recounted a remarkable sight. He was standing up on a hill, looking toward the mainland of Iceland. The sun was shining, the sky was clear, and the distant mountains were a beautiful sight. He spotted three unusual puffs of cloud, in a straight line. He assumed that these were heat clouds. One was directly over Surtsey, one over Mount Hekla, and a third over Heimaey. Many years later, it transpired that magma from Surtsey had been slowly flowing towards Heimaey. Hekla erupted five years after those puffs of cloud appeared in a clear blue sky — and Heimaey eight years later.[16]

Organist Guðmundur H. Guðjónsson had been put in charge of the seismometer on Heimaey during the Surtsey eruption. He had to change the paper and observe the progress of the eruption. He had studied music in Germany, but now it was his job to monitor the dramatic rhythms of the Earth itself. What did he read from the seismograms? Symphonies of nature? Celestial psalms? The geologist who had entrusted the seismometer to the organist asked him to go to the outer part of the island from time to time, to observe what was happening on the nascent Surtsey island. The organist was to describe individual explosive events and note their exact timing and then correlate these with the timings recorded by the seismometer. In between, the musician did his usual day job, playing the organ in the eighteenth-century stone church, for funerals and other ceremonies.

In January 1973, a seismometer would have been useful on Heimaey. There would have been no room for doubt that the epicenter of the quakes was directly under the island. Had the radio news on January 22 reported, perhaps even within a few hours, that there was a great likelihood of an eruption on Hei-

---

16 Ágúst Guðmundsson, interview, 2016.

maey, the Westman Islanders and Icelandic Civil Defense would no doubt have taken action. There were, however, no precedents for such a situation. Would the predictions have been believed? And perhaps there would not have been enough time to act, in any case.

Today almost anyone can take part in measuring earthquakes: An app called MyShake that detects and identifies earth tremors is available for smartphones and tablets. The public can monitor the movements of the Earth's crust directly, using the phone in their pockets, and share their knowledge instantly on the internet. This is one more example of our closeness to the Earth in the Age of Humans. As I write this, I download the app on my phone. Soon it sends me messages about mild quakes in South Iceland. These are commonplace but I am sensitive to the Richter scale, only higher figures make me worried.

PREMONITIONS OF AN ERUPTION

What did people do in the absence of actual seismometers? My grandmother Auðbjörg experienced the "greatest earthquake disaster since the country was settled" in South Iceland in 1896, as it was reported in the Icelandic–Canadian newspaper *Lögberg* that year.[17] The youngest of thirteen siblings, Auðbjörg was only three years old when the tremors shook her family's farm, Túnga. Much later, she described the terror when the farmhouse, built of stone and turf, collapsed. Ravens had lured the children out to the meadow before the worst occurred, and thus saved them from being buried by the ruined farm. Icelandic folklore abounds in such tales of ravens saving humans from natural disasters. Judging by Grandmother's description, ravens functioned as natural seismometers.

It has often been said that domestic animals and livestock can sense coming eruptions. About two hours before Hekla erupted in 1947, a dog on the farm of Skarð became agitated. The inhabitants woke sometime after 2 a.m., without realizing what

---

17 "Landskjálptarnir," *Lögberg* 40 (October 15, 1896): 2, 6, at 2.

had woken them. Drawing upon interviews, geologist Sigurður Þórarinsson observed that

> the housewife goes into the kitchen [...] and when she turns on the light she sees that an old dog, which usually lay and slept at night in front of the kitchen's outside door, is standing on the floor there, and he seems to be terrified of something, and very glad to see his mistress. Then she says [...] that she is not the only one to be affected.[18]

In his account of the terrible Laki eruption in 1783, generally known as *The Book of Fires,* pastor Jón Steingrímsson tells of portents that preceded the cataclysm. Thus, "a great number of monsters of various shapes" were seen a few years earlier at a place that was later covered by lava.[19] Near one farm "fireballs lay in heaps like foxfire. A bolt of lightning struck the lamb shed [...], killing lambs and splitting one of the supports from end to end, leaving its inner sides blackened as if scorched by red-hot iron." Elsewhere "the noise of musical instruments underground and the sound of bells ringing in the air was reported by many reliable people. That same spring the rainstorms had been unusually heavy. Dark red, yellow, and black striped flying insects were also seen here, as long and thick around as the end-joint of a full-grown man's thumb."[20]

Although the Westman Islanders were not conscious of any tremors until just before the Heimaey eruption, many of them had noticed disturbances similar to the ravens in Túnga and the dog at Skarð. Afterwards, many recalled premonitions of a great natural disaster, although generally no more notice had been taken of them than of the seismometers on the mainland in January 1973, and sometimes they had not been spoken out

---

18 Sigurður Þórarinsson, *Heklueldar* (Reykjavík: Sögufélagið, 1968), 148.
19 Jón Steingrímsson, *Fires of the Earth: The Laki Eruption 1783–1784,* trans. Keneva Kunz (Reykjavík: University of Iceland Press, 1998), 21.
20 Ibid.

loud. Some of these prophecies had lengthy histories. They were like long-term forecasts.

Helgafell's Revenge

In the mid-twentieth century, Mount Helgafell had been the focus of environmental activism in the Westman Islands. Travel to and from the mainland had always been a problem; for centuries the sea was the only route. But at the end of World War II, air travel opened up new possibilities. A little airport was built on a strip of land just south of Helgafell. Construction and maintenance of the runway required quantities of gravel, and the only practical option appeared to be to quarry scoria from the slopes of Helgafell itself. Within a few years the mountainside was marred by a large and ugly scar which was clearly visible to every passenger who flew in or out. The quarry had deliberately been located on the south side of the mountain where it would not be visible from the village, in order not to offend local sensibilities.

The first major critique of the damage done to Helgafell appeared in an article by geologist Sigurður Þórarinsson, published in an Icelandic environmental journal in 1950:

> I believe that Westman Islanders should, for their own sakes, think twice before they disfigure the jewel of the island, Helgafell, any further [...]. Undoubtedly, the Westman Islands will become an important tourist destination [...]; Helgafell is the first mountain seen by most foreigners who come to Iceland by sea [...]. Slovenly treatment of it is therefore a disgrace not only to Westman Islanders but also the nation as a whole.[21]

The Westman Islanders did not fail to heed Sigurður Þórarinsson's warning. Some suggested Helgafell and its vicinity should become a national park.

---

21 Sigurður Þórarinsson, "Náttúruvernd," *Náttúrufræðingurinn* 20 (1950): 1–12.

Fig. 11. Demonstration for the protection of Helgafell, November 1971. Photo by Sigurgeir Jónasson.

I remember vigorous debate in the press about the wounded volcano during my teenage years, when I was home on Heimaey between terms at school. These were the first environmental controversies I encountered, although at the time I didn't think much about them. Grown-ups debated a lot of issues, usually on strict party lines, sometimes arguing for the sake of arguing. The subject was addressed in the spring of 1965 at a meeting of the local Environmental Committee, established in 1957. One of the members had this recorded in the minutes:

> Helgafell is the pride of the Islanders and many of us would be deeply saddened if this key pride of the Islands were to be destroyed or further damaged [...]. And surely the same will be true for future generations. The name of the mountain is indicative of the attitude of the generation that gave it its name.[22]

---

22 See Gísli Pálsson and Helgi Bernódusson, "Hefnd Helgafells," *Fylkir*, December 2017, 12–13, 15.

Fig. 12. Guðni A. Hermansen works on his painting *Helgafell's Revenge* (1971). Photo by Sigurgeir Jónasson.

It was a time for radical action.

On November 4, 1971, a group from the local art school organized a peaceful demonstration up on Helgafell, where cranes and trucks were extracting scoria for the airport (fig. 11). Waving placards demanding protection of the mountain and cessation of quarrying, they blocked the road for a while and stopped work on the site. After some shouting and negotiations, the trucks were turned away, empty. The truck drivers, friends and former colleagues of my father, were divided on the issue. Some supported the protesters, while others offered critical remarks. One of them wryly commented: "Are we into war now? Am I a prisoner of war? You must have learned this from the bloody TV!" The times they were a-changin'.

One of those who took part in the protest was Guðni A. Hermansen, a well-known artist and musician in the Westman Islands. He was a quiet, peaceful person, and this was probably his only protest. No doubt over the years the debates about Helgafell had a profound impact on the artist, who had painted a number of works that showcased Helgafell and its beautiful symmetry in varied light conditions. None of them showed the mountain erupting. Shortly after the protest of 1971, however, Guðni began to paint his masterpiece, *Helgafell's Revenge* (fig. 12). No one had ever witnessed an eruption of Helgafell, but he now felt compelled to give this extinct volcano new life on canvas with the mountain spewing glowing lava out of its belly in all directions. Was Guðni's work perhaps a prediction? He worked long and hard on his painting. Less than a year after he finished, the Heimaey eruption began.

Guðni's painting is not unlike the oldest pictures of eruptions that were painted in caves in southern France. Had the cave-dwellers, like Guðni, predicted a future eruption, vengeance for misdeeds, or despoiling of nature? Bearing in mind that the Age of Humans was gathering steam, maybe Guðni's work could just as well have been called "The Earth Strikes Back?" When the actual eruption came, however, some geologists said that Helgafell had in fact spared the village. Sigurður Þórarinsson remarked that the fissure was amazingly "well placed": "It is as though Helgafell has served as a barrier and a buffer, so that the fissure formed in its side and did not go straight through it. In fact it's a not-uncommon phenomenon."[23] The mountain tempered justice with mercy so the punishment was a mild one.

Helgafell's Revenge has been owned for many years by Jóhanna Hermannsdóttir, who lives in Whiting, New Jersey. She was born and raised in the Westman Islands and knew Guðni well. On a visit home to the islands the year before the eruption, she bought the painting and took it back with her to the US. In January 1973 she received a phone call and was told that Helgafell had in fact begun to erupt. Guðni's work gained a new significance, there on the living room wall in New Jersey. When Jóhanna and her friends looked at the painting more closely over the next few days it seemed as though it were weeping.[24] The canvas opened up and tiny drops poured out of it, as if the painting itself had begun to erupt. Jóhanna tried to dry the canvas carefully with a soft cloth. Then she consulted an expert. He said to her: "Jóhan-

---

23 "Eins og Helgafell hafi hlíft byggðinni," *Morgunblaðið,* January 24, 1973, 11.
24 Jóhanna Hermannsdóttir, interview, August 13, 2016.

na, are you sure that it shouldn't just be like that!?" Probably, he added, the canvas had not been sealed correctly. She phoned Guðni, who told her that this was completely wrong. He had finished the painting quite correctly. Then the canvas stopped weeping. Recently, some people admiring the painting have spotted an angel in the fumes and ashes above the crater.

The title of Guðni's painting, which has come to symbolize the Heimaey eruption, evokes the religious undertones in Pastor Jón Steingrímsson's account of the Laki eruption of 1783. Writing more than four years after the eruption ended, the pastor referred to "volcanic chastisement" and "God's angry fire." The eruptions from the numerous Laki craters, he wrote, "far exceed any others that we have records of, both in the extent of the destruction caused and the activity itself, in the form of earthquakes […] as well as the withering of grass, and an epidemic which caused the death of many a man and animals by the thousands."[25] Jón witnessed the eruption and described it as precisely as he could: "Oh, how fearsome it was to look upon such tokens and manifestations of God's wrath!"[26] Here geology and theology coalesce, with repeated reference to the Almighty, sacred scriptures, and human behavior.

Dreams and Déjà Vu

Guðjón Ármann Eyjólfsson, a writer from the Westman Islands, dreamed about the Heimaey eruption. In the early morning of January 23, as he was forced to evacuate, he suddenly broke the silence by saying, "I have experienced this before. The evacuation of all the Westman Islanders happened in a dream of mine long ago." Later, he wrote:

> I dreamed that the moon was above the Heimaklettur cliffs. The weather was calm, very similar to that on the eruption night. Then suddenly it's as though the moon explodes and shatters in all directions, and golden fragments are all across

---

25 Steingrímsson, *Fires of the Earth*, 13.
26 Ibid., 45.

the sky, as if a stone were thrown into a still, mirror-like pool, creating ripples. [...] I thought I could clearly hear the hoofbeats from riders on the village quay. Everyone was fleeing the island. The atmosphere in the dream was the same as I experienced on the night of the eruption.[27]

Guðjón Ármann said it was a dream. But perhaps it has something in common with *déjà vu,* that peculiar and intense feeling of having experienced the identical event some time previously, even though this could not possibly have happened.

Elderly people's recollections of the months before the eruption, according to Guðjón Ármann's interviews later that year, typically link the natural disaster with high seas and surf. Lovísa Gísladóttir, a 78-year-old woman who lived in the Westman Islands when the eruption happened, revealed that she had "imagined something spectacular would happen. It was a year with thirteen full moons, and she had noticed an unusual amount of surf and spray at Urðir [on the west coast] [...] in January."[28] Some people clearly feared volcanic activity in the islands, though even the oldest islanders had never heard of any such event, let alone witnessed an eruption.

Children's narratives were also seen as presaging an eruption. Shortly before Christmas, Klara Tryggvadóttir, aged eleven, dreamt that Helgafell was erupting. No one took any notice of her, and she was asked to kindly stop "this nonsense." In an interview she said she had been out below Helgafell, and had had a very strange experience:

> When Dad, Grandpa, and I went for a drive round Helgafell last Sunday, and he drove along the road above Þorbjörn's meadow at Kirkjubær farm [...] I was suddenly horribly afraid, just all of a sudden, and told Dad that he should be as quick as he could because Helgafell was erupting [...] He just laughed and said that I could run home if I wanted. And

---

27 Eyjólfsson, *Vestmannaeyjar*, 321.
28 Ibid., 236.

Grandpa didn't believe it either. He said I shouldn't talk nonsense.[29]

I heard about a similar story told by Sigríður H. Theodórsdóttir, an old friend of my younger brother Karl. I vaguely remembered her, a cheerful kid on the playground close to my second home on Heimaey and decided to interview her. She was ten years old when the eruption happened, living with her family on the east side of the village. Her experiences pre-eruption were unusually clear, and the events in January 1973 are still fresh in her mind, as if they happened yesterday.[30] One day, early in the month, before school had begun again after the Christmas break, she was sitting and reading newspapers at the kitchen table in her home. Her father Theodór was at sea, but her mother, Kristin, was at home.

Sigríður was suddenly overwhelmed, "something just comes over me," she said. She called her mother. "Mum, Mum, there's going to be an eruption!" She was very upset, sensing great danger was at hand and that it would be best to hurry to the mainland, as far away as possible, preferably to the remote West Fjords. She had delivered the daily newspaper to the eastern part of the village and knew the area like the back of her hand; she knew which people were at risk. She had not dreamed about this and she had not seen anything at all reminiscent of an eruption, but the feeling of danger was overwhelming. Nothing like this had ever happened to her before.

The next three weeks or so, until the eruption, were difficult for Sigríður. She cried all day. Her mother was very concerned about her and discussed Sigríður's state and behavior with older, more experienced people. She made an effort to talk with her and calm her and tried to convince her that there was no danger. When her father came home from the sea and heard Sigríður's story, he got angry and begged her not to talk about it: "Such

---

29 "Flýttu þér heim, pabbi — það er gos í Helgafelli," *Tíminn*, January 26, 1973. See also Eyjólfsson, *Vestmannaeyjar*, 324.
30 Sigríður H. Theodórsdóttir, interview, Reykjavík, March 2016.

nonsense scared people, no need to behave like that even if she did want a trip to the Icelandic mainland."

Sigríður actually preferred staying at home, and had no particular interest in travelling right then, but now she felt she had no option. She did not keep quiet about her experience, quite the opposite. She told people in the neighborhood and the kids at school when term began about the danger of the coming eruption. After school she usually hurried home with her school bag on her back and a knot in her stomach: Her family must get a move on and leave, before it was too late.

Normally Sigríður fell asleep easily, early in the evening. But the day before the eruption she absolutely refused to go to bed, even though she needed to rest before a history test first thing in the morning. This was not because of the test; she was conscientious and didn't worry about exams. The ceiling light in the living room swung back and forth, and the TV signal failed now and then. She did not connect it to the anticipated eruption though, and nobody mentioned earthquakes. It was just the bad weather.

In a way, Sigríður was relieved when the Heimaey eruption began. The fear was gone, and she was in no rush. She went to a house nearby, to wake a friend and her parents. The father of the family, Eiríkur, came to the door in his pajamas, with sleep in his eyes. Sigríður said to him, "You have to get out, the eruption has started!" He snorted and said this was the final straw; the girl had started walking in her sleep! Then he realized it was light outside — in the middle of the night.

What did Sigríður base her prediction on? Physicists have long argued about what they call "spooky action at a distance," distant events that might be expected to be unrelated, since they seem to have nothing obvious in common.[31] Sigríður's forebod-

---

31 See Jim Holt, "Something Faster Than Light? What Is It?" *New York Review of Books* (November 2016): 50–52, https://www.nybooks.com/articles/2016/11/10/something-faster-than-light-what-is-it/. Also, for an anthropological perspective, see Marisol de la Cadena, *Earth Beings: Ecologies of Practice across Andean Worlds* (Durham: Duke University Press, 2015).

ing was certainly peculiar. Sigríður, who later studied business administration, says that although she has always been "sensitive," she never again had such a feeling as on that January day when she emphatically predicted an eruption.

One Westman Islander, ship's engineer Jón Ó.E. Jónsson, appears to have foreseen the volcanic event a year before the eruption, and based his prediction on his own observations. After a heart attack he was unable to work, so he started reading geology books for pleasure, and thinking about nature on Heimaey island. More than a month before the eruption, Jón told a young friend that "something very strange was happening on the eastern side of the island."[32] A fracture was opening up, which ran northwest to southeast, and it seemed to him that "either a dyke was opening or it was the precursor of a big event — an eruption, for example." "I haven't told a soul about it," said Jón, "because they all say Jón Ó.E. is crazy and can't be bothered to work anymore."

Nowadays it is urgent to seek out all sorts of news from the Earth, whatever we call it: observations, insights, dreams, omens, or actions at a distance. It is no good disconnecting our sensory equipment just because we don't understand how it works.

THE EARTH SPEAKS

Andy Warhol, as he is frequently quoted, forecasted that in the future everyone would have their fifteen minutes of fame. Now the furnace in the basement of the Westman Islanders was ready for its fifteen minutes — or more.

Monday, January 22, 1973 was windy on the Westman Islands, with a howling gale from the southeast. The anemometers measuring wind-speed on the Stórhöfði headland went wild. People ran between houses in the dusk, with the storm in their faces. Some drove, even though it was such a short distance. In

---

[32] "Heimaklettur," *Facebook*, 2017, https://www.facebook.com/groups/166156446851821/.

the evening my cousins met with friends to play their regular Monday evening bridge game, this time at Birna's home not far from the foot of Mount Helgafell.[33] They were novices but were getting practice in the complicated rules for taking tricks.

When two or more members of this family met up, laughter and fun were always on the agenda, and so it was this Monday evening between bids. It was getting late and darkness was descending. When the game was at its most exciting, Birna's house began to vibrate and she thought that something must be wrong with the central heating. Her bridge partners became concerned. The furnace in this house, as in many others in the Westman Islands, could be fractious; the boiler was capable of anything, and it was best to check the fuel supply and the pump system. If the radiators in the whole house started singing, something was wrong. Birna nudged her husband, Theodór, who went to check. Nothing was wrong with the furnace, but the vibrations continued.

Now one of the women phoned the Westman Islands Radio Station, which acted as the civil defense service connected to the fishing fleet, the mainland, and the outside world. "Are they earthquakes?" "No, no," was the reply. More people had seen reason to call that evening and ask about the strange vibrations and droning sounds, but it was safe to go to bed: Nothing was happening. Perhaps the women had picked up some sort of radio transmission. They continued to play cards, but the low-level vibration persisted.

They finally threw down their cards when a new day had begun, around 1:30 a.m., even though four hands were left in the rubber. The tremors were making them uncomfortable, and they also needed to rest before the work day. Lilla, Birna's sister, was going to give a lift to the other bridge players on the way home. When they had left and Birna was getting ready for bed, the window in the bathroom started vibrating. Birna closed it,

---

33 Aðalbjörg Jóhanna Bernódusdóttir, interview, Hafnarfjörður, February 2016.

but then the mirror took over, shivering as though it were terrified. What on earth was happening?

Lilla tells me she was driving a sleek saloon, a light grey 1972 Sunbeam, with four headlights. The eastern part of town was dark; east of the village were only fields and rocks, and beyond them the deep Atlantic Ocean. The women drove past two young men that they knew well. They considered offering them a lift home, but thought it wasn't worth it, as it was such a short distance home for them to go. The young men were in no rush, coming back from an evening stroll. They had obviously not noticed anything odd.

Suddenly, the women saw a glow of fire towards the east, apparently on the slope of Helgafell. Birna's house was silhouetted against the fire, and they were filled with terror. It was as though the house were aflame. Had the furnace, in spite of everything, blown the house up? Lilla was half ashamed of her first reaction, "Thank goodness we got out in time and avoided this trouble," knowing that her sister Birna and family seemed to be directly between them and the blaze. They hurried back towards Birna's house. The beam of the car headlights swept between houses. Would they be able to help if the house were on fire? It was just as well that no one else was on the road right now.

"It's an Eruption"

They got closer to the glow, and just before they reached Birna's house, her friend Sjöfn suddenly exclaimed: "It's an eruption!" There was no need to continue east and Lilla stopped the car. Now they could see that Birna's home and family were safe, for the time being at least, but behind the house was a huge conflagration. The incandescent glare spread and moved northwards. The ground opened suddenly, with a thundering noise, releasing fountains of fire and glowing lava. The women didn't approach close enough to see the fissure itself because houses and hills partially obstructed their view, but they could see one lava-fountain after another spouting up in front of them, six or seven glowing jets. They thought that the eruption was in Helgafell's crater, the same thing that most Westman Islanders initially assumed that night. In the history of Iceland there are few examples of people witnessing the start of an eruption, and this was the first time a volcano had erupted in an inhabited area.

The village was strangely silent in spite of this momentous event happening right on its doorstep. No one was around now except the women, but there were lights in many windows all the same. Many people were attending to their furnaces, checking the weather, or puzzling over the changes in atmospheric pressure and vibrations, or the glare of light farther east on the island. Before long, most of the locals would be astir, in the middle of the night, with a new and urgent task.

They made haste. Lilla was terrified that the island would split in two. She turned abruptly west, wanting to stay in the western part of the village, on the right side of the divide if the worst happened. She wanted to get home and be with her family, whatever happened. When the car approached her house, Sjöfn opened the door and practically jumped out before it came to a halt. Lilla continued to her own home. Her husband Jói was standing in the doorway and asked what was happening. He had been sleeping restlessly and was thinking of checking his fishing nets first thing in the morning, even though the weather prospects were not good. He had been awoken by the vibrations in the house just before Lilla came home. When Lilla told him there was an eruption, Jói jumped into the car to go "take a look," leaving Lilla at home on her own. He drove around the south of Helgafell, by the airport, where he saw the eruption in all its glory. The ground was still ripping open, and it seemed to him that the fissure was heading towards him. When the crack opened it was like a zipper slowly being unzipped along the ground. In his panic he couldn't tell if it was safer to run the shortest way home in the glow from the eruption, or to drive back the same way he had come. He chose the latter option.

Shoulder Stone

The eruption began by *Axlarsteinn,* "Shoulder Stone," a man-high rocky cliff on the northeast shoulder of Helgafell just above the road that circled the mountain (fig. 13). It used to be a popular

Fig. 13. Shoulder Stone (to the left) in the hills of Helgafell where an eruption broke out on 23 January 1973. Eyjafjallajökull in the background. Photo by Sigurgeir Jónasson.

place for kids to practice their sprang technique, in preparation for gathering seabirds' eggs from the cliffs when they got older. Around the mid-twentieth century, before the rapidly growing village approached the foot of Helgafell, the dell below Shoulder Stone was a popular campsite for youngsters, at a convenient distance from home. People spoke of a bare patch around here, popular with teenagers in wintry conditions, where natural heat in the earth prevented the snow from settling. Not far from the cliff was a cave, which also attracted youngsters in search of adventure.

The old tales about Shoulder Stone sometimes have fantastical overtones. According to a 1906 newspaper article, a certain Einar from Eyjafjöll, who lived early in the nineteenth century, is said to have recounted that once, when he was on his way from the mainland, "the sea seized the boat and drove it past Klettaskor (in the Westman Islands) and into the high ground east of Helgafell, and drove it there into Shoulder Stone as far as the second thwart."[34] The rock clearly had a powerful attraction.

I remember the annual New Year bonfires at Shoulder Stone well. In the final weeks of the year, kids in the east part of town started to collect old timber and other stuff that to burn. Sometimes they even stole the wooden formwork for concrete from building sites. They sneaked from house to house taking a little here, a little there, not removing too much from any one site. Then all the firewood was stacked up on New Year's Eve. Oil was thrown over it and the pile was set on fire. Some kids experimented, with varying success, with firecrackers when they were on bonfire duty, dividing them into smaller units to have more fun and get more out of them.

The kids, mostly boys, who built the bonfire at Shoulder Stone were in competition with groups from other parts of the village. During the last few nights of the year the bonfire had to be guarded. Björn Th. Björnsson, in his book about growing up in the Westman Islands between the wars, writes:

> They daren't come, the bastards, I said and struck the stick against the pile of barrels [...] The year before last they managed to light our bonfire the night before New Year, or almost. Even though the boys were on guard — Ási, Nonni from Sjólyst, and Daddi-the-Turd. That was the fight when Daddi-the-Turd got the nail in his head. Right into his brain, or nearly.[35]

Things have often become heated below Shoulder Stone, and some accounts are reminiscent of the blood-curdling deeds of the medieval Icelandic sagas. But the sheets of flame by Shoulder Stone that January night were bigger than any bonfire.

---

34 Björn Jónsson, "Eftir tíu ár: Úr ferð um landskjálftasvæðið frá 1898," *Ísafold* 67 (1906): 266.
35 Björn Th. Björnsson, *Sandgreifarnir* (Reykjavík: Mál og menning, 1989), 7–9.

What Was To Be Done?
Many Westman Islanders thought at first that the volcano Katla, a well-known monster on the mainland, long overdue for an eruption, was stirring. They couldn't believe their own eyes when they looked out and saw the glow of fire, so close, in the east. Some thought that dry grass was burning, or something else had caught fire. Others wondered if a new underwater eruption had started near Bjarnarey, an out-island just east of Heimaey. But the wail of sirens and the fire klaxon that the police switched on suggested otherwise. Now the radio station, which earlier that night had refused to admit there were any unusual tremors, sent out a call for help on the international distress frequency 2182 kHz:

> MAYDAY, MAYDAY, MAYDAY. THIS IS WESTMAN ISLANDS RADIO. ERUPTION IN THE WESTMAN ISLANDS. WE NEED HELP FOR 5000 PEOPLE. WESTMAN ISLANDS RADIO.[36]

Here, all sorts of earthly factors were in the mix, including the volcano and humanity in desperate straits. The islanders hurried down to the harbor, not knowing what would happen next. On the mainland, people sat speechless by their radios.

Skippers on the fishing grounds off the Westman Islands who heard the Mayday call thought they should do something but did not know what. Soon after the eruption began, the Icelandic Coast Guard vessel *Týr* cut one of the net wires of a British trawler, the *Ross Altair* from Hull. From 1972 to 1973, Britain and Iceland were engaged in a territorial dispute known in Iceland as the Second Cod War. The net cutters were the Icelanders' most effective weapon, causing great consternation, taking the British by surprise, and working better than many other weapons. The British trawlermen claimed that the Coast Guard crew had snipped the wire without warning as they sailed at speed toward Heimaey while the British skipper had intended to offer aid because of the eruption. Icelandic wits retorted that it was

---
36 Jón Kr. Óskarsson, interview, October 4, 2016.

highly unusual for a trawler to speed to the rescue with its fishing nets out.[37]

Fortunately, the weather was favorable. The storm had died down, and the wind had dropped. The police went house-to-house, woke the residents, and explained what was happening. Many people checked that their neighbors were up or called relatives and friends who might have slept through it all, not forgetting the elderly and sick. Urgent questions sprang to mind. There were no clear answers or any organized plans. All the same, most people seemed calm and composed — probably dazed or in shock. Some older people refused to leave their homes. Some yielded to persuasion, while others stuck to their guns and were left alone for the time being.

At the police station in Reykjavík, just before three o'clock in the morning on Tuesday, January 23, the Icelandic civil defense committee met to make arrangements for receiving the five thousand Westman Islanders on the mainland. The state broadcasting station RUV went on air just before 4 a.m. and delivered news of the eruption. The mayor of the Westman Islands was interviewed. He said that no one was in immediate danger, but that people were being encouraged to make their way to the harbor.

The few farmers on the Westman Islands would not consider leaving without first taking care of their livestock. A few hundred meters from the eruption was a corral full of horses. They became so agitated they had to be released. One horse bolted into the lava flow and had to be put down. A few others were safely led to the harbor to be transported to the mainland. About fifty cattle from the farm of Kirkjubær were taken to one of the fishing plants to be slaughtered and soon their bodies were transported to the mainland for the meat market. It was strange to watch them being herded down to the harbor. When the farmer at Kirkjubær, Þorbjörn Guðjónsson, was asked if it was hard to lose his cows, he said, "I've got nothing to complain

---

37 "Eru náttúruöflin að kenna okkur að standa saman?" *Tíminn*, January 24, 1973.

Fig. 14. One of the first photographs of the Heimaey eruption. Photo by Kristján H. Kristjánsson.

about; my forebears fled here, escaping from the Laki eruption, with everything they owned in a single chest."[38]

A LONG NIGHT UNDER THE VOLCANO

In the first few hours of the eruption few people thought to photograph what they saw. One exception was Kristján H. Kristjánsson, a student at the secondary school. When the eruption began, Kristján woke from a deep sleep at his home in the pharmacy his parents ran in the village center. Kristján was an amateur photographer, and when he was told about the eruption his first thought was to hurry out with his camera. He was relieved, in spite of the strange and terrifying sight in front of him, as he was supposed to be taking an Icelandic literature exam that morning on the *Saga of Gísli*. He had exam nerves and felt he had not studied properly. Many other students were worried about exams that night. Some were sure they would not avoid the exam even if they were evacuated to the mainland; the teacher would be waiting there with the exam papers. A

---

38 Information relayed by Svavar Steingrímsson, interview, January 2017.

few years after the eruption, Kristján attended classes I taught in my first teaching post, although it wasn't until decades later, however, as I began writing this book, that I learned about his photographs of the eruption (fig. 14).

A relative of mine, Sigurgeir Jónasson, was considered the unofficial public photographer for the Westman Islands. He had recorded human life and human–earth relationships on Heimaey with incredible diligence and resourcefulness for decades, and later photographed the eruption and its victims from various angles. But on the eruption night itself he was fully occupied saving himself and his family, with no time to think of his camera.

They and the other Westman Islanders would soon become refugees, cut off from their habitat. No wonder there was uncertainty about when the eruption had actually started, time had little meaning. It either flew unaccountably fast or seemed to stand still. Modern science speaks of "geological time," an almost infinite time scale, extending millions or billions of years, but now the geological history of Heimaey somersaulted forward in just a few minutes.

In the pitch dark of the early morning Icelandair, together with helicopters and planes from the US military base at Keflavík in southwest Iceland, began operating an airlift between Heimaey and the mainland. The weather made flying possible, which was not always the case in the Westman Islands. Geologists, reporters, and photographers arrived from the mainland, while pregnant women and the old and infirm were carried back.

At the same time, the Westman Islands' rescue service began preparing a plan to station rescue boats on the northern coast of Heimaey, in case the fishing fleet should be trapped in the harbor by the rivers of lava, and people had to be ferried to the mainland or to boats from other fishing ports. But the local skippers, undeterred by the ash and flames at the harbor's mouth, decided to board their boats and sail out that night with their families and friends.

Many people drove eastward on Heimaey first, as close as possible to the eruption, to comprehend the enormity of it all and to convince themselves that they really had to leave. Some thought they should wait a while, in case the volcano should be kind enough to complete its work within a few hours. Perhaps there was no need to say farewell to Heimaey. But soon nearly everyone reached the conclusion that it would be best to sail to Þorlákshöfn on the mainland. It was the closest harbor that could receive several large boats at the same time.

Tempest Tossed
Earlier in the century, when many motorized smacks were longline-fishing at this season of the year, the Westman Islands' boats would line up in the harbor mouth and wait for the signal or "green light" that authorized sailing to the fishing grounds. This was done to avoid line-disputes. Now there was no squabbling about the best area of sea. Instead it was necessary to allocate the passengers, around five thousand people, places on seventy boats, and make arrangements for them at Þorlákshöfn, an hour's drive over the mountains from the city of Reykjavík.

When my uncle Magnús Bjarnason came down to the harbor, he went to the motorboat *Bergur* which had a 170-ton capacity. Magnus's wife was studying in Norway, and her mother Sólveig had been taking care of the home and their two children in her absence. Sólveig's son was one of the skippers, and Magnús was reassured to see him and his family on deck and to have their company: "There was no need to ask to be taken along, instead outstretched hands greeted us."[39] The engineer had started the engine, and it was clear that they would soon depart, because the boat was filling up. Over one hundred and sixty passengers were on board.

Magnús put Sólveig and the children on board, but was conflicted about going with them himself. His parents, grandmother, sister, and her two children were still on the island — and

---

39 Magnús Bjarnason, "Privatissimo: Eldgosið í Heimaey 1973," unpublished manuscript, 2003.

there was his home, all that his family owned. Then he made the decision:

> As I stood there on deck, and looked at the eruption, I sensed that I needed to stay behind. I didn't know how I could be of help, but something told me that I just couldn't leave. [...] I was obsessed by some indefinable sense of responsibility that I also felt on a different level could be against all common sense. But still I decided not to go. It reinforced my decision that the children and my mother-in-law were in safe hands. I told them what I was planning. Later Sólveig told me that she practically froze at my words, but did not want to stop me.[40]

What was the "indefinable sense of responsibility" that Magnús referred to? Probably his decision to remain was a sign of the power that the human habitat—and its intimate connection with the earth—has over us.

Naturally enough, there was no advanced planning for assigning places in the boats. The boats tied up at the quay, several vessels deep. Those who were unused to sea travel tried to get on one of the larger ships, hoping that the journey would be safer and less turbulent. When a signal was given on the radio, the boats sailed one after another out of the harbor mouth, with the volcanic fire on one side and the cliffs on the other.

It was hardly possible to stay on deck because of the ashfall. The eruption had produced a huge quantity of ash from the start, first blowing it out to sea, but when the wind changed it piled up, it soon engulfed dozens of houses. Some passengers still remember the noise and stench of the eruption. The temperature of the sea had risen rapidly, and clouds of steam rose from the water. A glowing lava river cascaded off the edge of the ancient lava field and flowed along the sea floor. This unusual submarine floodlighting was certainly magnificent to look at, at least for those on the deck or the bridge who dared to look over the side of the boat. During the crossing, the passengers on

---
40 Ibid.

the way to Þorlákshöfn looked back to observe the glow from the volcano. There seemed no end to the eruption and nobody knew what would happen to their homes or to the people who had stayed behind.

The vessel *Ísleifur*, with a 216-ton capacity, transported 109 people that night, including the crew's families and many of their neighbors. In the summer season the ship's crew sometimes went on long and rigorous tours fishing for herring in the North Sea. One time, the crew sent their wives greetings over the radio, on the *Seamen's Requests* program, with the Beatles' song "Help!" The next program had a greeting from their wives — a song made popular by Tom Jones, "Help Yourself."[41] Now it was time for the Westman Islanders to give their famous sarcastic humor a rest.

The passengers were of all ages, and most were not used to fishing boats. The inhabitants from the east end of the village and the houses closest to the eruption site felt the worst, well aware that their homes would not be spared. The swell was strong. The convoy of boats sailed slowly on in the dark for the four-hour passage to the mainland. The pilots in the airlift said it was spectacular to observe the convoy from the air, like traffic on a highway at night in a big city. Many men were on the deck of the boats at first, rolling with the waves and watching the eruption, while most women and children went below. They lay packed together, under the whaleback, in the mess room, the wheelhouse, and the fo'c'sle. Seasick passengers found there was nowhere to vomit except the sink, the saucepans, and on the floor.

That day, January 23, 1973, the sun rose at about ten-thirty. Most of the boats reached land at Þorlákshöfn well before then, between seven and eight in the morning, still in inky darkness. Despite the discomfort and anxiety, the crossing itself went off without incident, with a few exceptions. My bridge-playing

---

41 Jón Berg Halldórsson, "Frásögn á 40 ára gosafmæli," *1973 í bátana*, March 2013, http://1973-i-batana.blogspot.is/2013/03/utbjo-essa-blogg-siu-til-i-tvennum.html. .

cousin Lilla set off for the mainland with her family aboard the *Andvari*, which her husband Jói skippered. It so happened that the engine of the *Hrönn*, which he and his partner Hörður had recently bought, had failed. The men were keen to get both boats safely out of the harbor, so the *Andvari* set off with the *Hrönn* in tow. About forty passengers were on the *Andvari* and twenty on the *Hrönn*.

When Jói got out of the harbor, he didn't like the look of the swell. The *Andvari* was a medium-sized wooden boat, with a 100-ton capacity, and the *Hrönn* — a large steel vessel, with a 200-ton capacity — was a bit large for the *Andvari* to manage. Jói contacted the skipper of the nearby *Gjafar*, with a 200-ton capacity, and asked him if he could take *Hrönn* in tow. The skipper declined, as he had a boat full of people. That night, the *Gjafar* transported more passengers to land than any other Heimaey boat, close to four hundred people. Jói then cast off the tow line, left the *Hrönn* behind, with skipper Hörður in charge, and sailed back into the harbor. He said that he must pick up more crew and his parents and would not go to the mainland without them. The *Hrönn* tossed helplessly around in the waves, until the *Andvari* returned.

Some people feared a bad ending for *Hrönn*, and even questioned Jói's decision not to head straight for Þorlákshöfn with the forty people he had on board. Lilla, who was with her husband on the bridge of the *Andvari*, was terrified. When she protested, Jói told her to "get below."[42] No doubt Jói had discussed his plans with Hörður on the shipping wavelength. When he tied up at the quay back at Heimaey the police asked him to wait a while for a few islanders who had refused to leave earlier. He agreed.

Around 4 a.m., about two hours after Jói's operation had begun, he left the harbor again with his father and some of his crew. He took the *Hrönn* in tow once more as planned, but unfortunately the line broke soon afterwards. The boats danced in

---
42 Aðalbjörg Jóhanna Bernódusdóttir, interview, Hafnarfjörður, February 2016.

Fig. 15. Evacuees from the Westman Islands arrive in Þorlákshöfn on the morning of January 23, 1973. Photo by Sveinn Þormóðsson. Courtesy of Brynja Pétursdóttir.

the waves, almost side by side and full of people. The two ships' crews fought to get a new tow line between them, but the towline broke over and over. Sometimes the people on the wooden *Andvari* feared that the prow of the steel *Hrönn* was going to smash into them in the heaving seas. Rubber tires were hung from the gunwales to cushion the impact if the boats were to collide. The crews of the *Andvari* and *Hrönn* battled until nine o'clock in the morning, while the two ships made slow headway. Then additional boats came to the rescue from the mainland, and one of them took the *Hrönn* in tow. The three vessels finally sailed into Þorlákshöfn about two in the afternoon. Many passengers were feeling very unwell and shaken after their long sea voyage (fig. 15).

Although I was not on any of the boats that night, being far away at graduate school in England, I can easily put myself in their shoes. In my years at Laugarvatn, I sometimes had to sail on the Reykjavík ferry when I travelled to or from Heimaey. The sea journey took all night, and when I took the ferry at the last minute all the berths were taken, so I had to make do with lying on the floor, under tables, and between bunks. In all the rolling when the ship sailed through the infamous Reykjanes Race, the churning water between the Reykjanes peninsula and Eldey island, it was hard not to throw up, and vomit flew in all directions. At the end of this ordeal by water, I would step ashore in the early hours of the morning with vomit on my face and the unsteady legs of *mal de débarquement*. It must have been an exhausted and anxious group that stepped onto land at Þorlákshöfn after eleven tempest-tossed hours.

When the boats arrived at Þorlákshöfn after a long and difficult overnight journey, they had to wait in line until they were given a signal on the radio. Only a few boats at a time could dock so their exhausted passengers could be helped ashore. Parents lifted their children over the gunwales. In no time the boats pushed off the quay to free up a berth, making way for the next boat. Sometimes there were ten boats at a time maneuvering into the harbor or proceeding out of it, heading for a different port now that they couldn't go back, or, like the practical Icelanders they were, they took their boats out to sea, as if it were an ordinary workday, to fish. The boats would find other harbors, at least as a temporary base, occasionally visiting Heimaey as the crews checked on their houses and friends. For the time being, and perhaps for good, there was no fish processing on Heimaey. The harbor was no longer secure.

Raining Ash

The few people left behind on Heimaey, perhaps one hundred, were in the thick of it. One of the mainland photographers, Gunnar M. Andrésson, took a memorable photo of the volcanic fissure as it headed for the harbor while a group of people watch in astonishment from the slopes of Helgafell and the Coast Guard ship lies just outside the harbor. The ground is still ripping open (fig. 16).

When Magnús Bjarnason had escorted his family to the boat, he hurried towards his brother-in-law's house. He had promised to look after it, but the intensity of the eruption seemed to be

Fig. 16. The eruptive fissure on the first morning. Photo by Gunnar M. Andrésson.

steadily increasing: "Once I was indoors I realized more clearly than before what a devastating force it was — the whole house was shaking and the noise was deafening. I shut the windows, turned the lights off, and locked the outside door, which had stood ajar when I arrived."[43] He hurried off to his own house. On his way Magnús met people heading in the opposite direction, towards the harbor. Magnús, who is an unusually tall, powerfully built, and authoritative figure, slowed down so as not to attract attention: "I didn't feel it was right for me to be seen running as fast as I could, to get away from the volcanic ash raining down on us. That was no time to show fear." When he reached home, he put his car in the garage, brewed some coffee, and poured himself a cup: "I sat down in the living room and tried to collect my thoughts. Of course nothing sensible came of that." Then he phoned his wife in Norway and told her the news. When the Norwegian broadcasting service announced, soon afterwards, that half of Heimaey island had sunk into the ocean

---

43 Bjarnason, "Privatissimo."

and all the inhabitants had been evacuated, at least she knew that was not precisely true.

A rain of ash, to any Icelander, brings to mind Pastor Jón Steingrímsson's precise account of the catastrophic Laki eruption of 1783. Immediately on the first day of the "Fires," he wrote, "a black haze of sand appeared […]. The cloud […] was so thick that it caused darkness indoors and coated the earth so that tracks could be seen. The powder which fell to earth looked like the burnt ash from hard coal."[44] A few days later "the entire area around here was covered by the fall of cinders […]. They were blue-black and shiny, as long and thick around as a seal's hair […]. They formed a continuous blanket over the ground and where they fell on bare patches of sand and gravel and the winds tossed them about, they were twined together to form long hollow rolls."[45]

Along with the ash, the Laki eruption emitted toxic gases that killed livestock and tainted vegetation, and the fine volcanic dust in the air blocked out the sun for months, leading to a prolonged period of hardship known as the Haze Famine. Three-quarters of Iceland's livestock died, as did one-fifth of the human population. In Pastor Jón's parish, which was in close proximity to the volcano, 225 people, over a third of the inhabitants, died. Farms by the coast came off better than many others, showing "how much the juices of the sea can do to counteract pestilence on land," wrote Jón in his account of the eruption. He continued: "The same is true of the Westman Islands, where the scourge did not kill a single beast. But as things turned out the people of these areas lost much of, and some of them all of, their livestock the following year, just as we did, due both to the pestilence and lack of sufficient hay."[46]

Humans played no part in events leading up to the Laki eruption, even though Pastor Jón, traditionally known as the Fire Priest, saw the volcanic fires as divine retribution for the sins of

---

44 Steingrímsson, *Fires of the Earth: The Laki Eruption 1783–1784*, 25.
45 Ibid., 27.
46 Ibid., 75–76.

fallible men and women in his county. But the huge global impact of that eruption calls to mind the environmental problems of the current age. That first night, as the ash rained down, no one knew the Heimaey eruption would not be accompanied by a global environmental impact equivalent to that of Laki, and the news that instantly travelled around the world, like that of the Norwegian broadcasters, often assumed the worst.

News from Iceland

At Manchester University, where I was studying, the weekend had been uneventful. We students were gradually settling back in after our Christmas break. A group of Icelanders at the university were in the habit of meeting up for lunch now and then to exchange views and share news of home. Sitting down to lunch that day, Tuesday, January 23, someone announced that, according to the BBC news that morning, a volcano was erupting on the island of Heimaey. The island might even split apart and sink into the sea, said the BBC.

I was taken aback. Most of the other Icelanders took the news calmly: Surely even the ever-reliable British Broadcasting Corporation made mistakes? I was the only Westman Islander there, and it seemed to me unlikely that the eruption could really be taking place on Heimaey itself. Mount Helgafell, the only volcano on the island, was extinct, I protested, or at least had been dormant for thousands of years. Children on the island used the crater as a playground, I told them. Surely the BBC must mean Surtsey island, I speculated, recalling the eruption there only ten years earlier.

Although I had my reservations, I was deeply unsettled and the matter warranted further investigation. So, after lunch I made my way to a student reading room nearby, which offered such newspapers as *The Guardian,* the *Times,* and the *Manchester Evening News.* I had often gone there to read the latest news about the Second Cod War between Britain and Iceland, then at its height. Despite its name, the *Manchester Evening News* rolled off the presses in early afternoon. Would it have something to say about an alleged eruption on an archipelago far away in the north Atlantic?

I glanced around in search of the *Evening News* and saw that there was only one copy in the reading room. A young student lolled, reading the paper at his leisure. I took the seat facing him, hoping that it would soon be my turn. Although students here, as elsewhere, were politically conscious and active at that time, there was rarely any competition for access to the papers. I tried to conceal how eagerly I was waiting, to avoid embarrassing him. He had every right to read the paper for as long as he liked. The *Evening News* was a large-format broadsheet, so it is quite possible that, engrossed in his reading, he did not even notice my impatient presence, hidden as I was behind the pages, even though I had unconsciously inched forward to the edge of my seat and was gazing at the front page, aghast.

At the top was a report on the heavyweight boxing match between George Foreman and Joe Frazier. Foreman had won the encounter and was now officially world champion. All I could read was the headline: "Foreman KOs Frazier." I couldn't decipher the small print, but that didn't matter. I'm not a boxing fan. Nor did I pay much attention to the report on the death the previous day of former US President Lyndon B. Johnson. My eyes were inexorably drawn to an item in large print on the middle of the front page, the news I had hoped was an invention, or a misunderstanding, "VOLCANO BLAST SPLITS ISLAND: 5,000 SAVED." It was the paper's lead story. Had Heimaey island truly sunk beneath the waves? That thought was unthinkable.

I have no idea how long it took for the young man to finally finish reading the paper. As he tossed it down, I snatched it up and devoured the report:

> A mini-Dunkirk rescue operation today carried 5,000 people to safety after a volcano, inactive for 7,000 years, erupted on a small Icelandic island, almost splitting it in half. It was 2:30 am when the volcano blew open tearing a 1mile rift in the main Westman Island, 10 miles off the island's coast. [...] Experts thought it may explode and disappear into the sea.

> Terrified inhabitants, dressed only in nightclothes, crowded the streets as the lava first spurted from Helgafell mountain, just two miles south of the village, lighting up the whole island. Mercifully, it flowed down into the sea, missing the village except for one house, which was burnt out. [...] British trawlers [...] offered help but Icelandic Coast Guard said there were enough boats there already. [...] A horse had been seen to fall into the glowing rift when the ground opened beneath it.[47]

The eruption coverage continued on the inside pages, under the headline "River of Flames." There were two photographs: one of the blazing lava in the darkness of the night, the other of a woman and child — the first evacuees arriving on the mainland. There was no mistake, an eruption had started on Heimaey. I was hugely relieved to learn that no lives had been lost to the flowing lava.

Likening the overnight evacuation of the islanders to the famous Dunkirk operation during World War II was entirely apt. When the British Expeditionary Force in northern France found itself trapped by rapidly advancing German forces in the summer of 1940, volunteers had set off across the Channel on vessels of all sizes to rescue thousands of stranded men from the beaches at Dunkirk. "We shall fight on the beaches, we shall fight on the landing grounds, we shall fight in the fields and in the streets, we shall fight in the hills; we shall never surrender," declared Prime Minister Winston Churchill in those dark days of war, when the Dunkirk rescue restored faith in what ordinary people could do. Likewise, the local fishing fleet transporting Heimaey's inhabitants to the mainland in rough seas restored my faith in my countrymen. But although I had learned a lot from the *Evening News*, I still had many questions. The university campus offered no other sources of information about

---

47 "Volcano Blast Splits Island: 5,000 Saved," *Manchester Evening News*, January 23, 1973.

events in Iceland, and I was too restless to sit and focus on my anthropology texts.

As twilight fell, I strolled down Oxford Street toward the railway station and the train home to my residence hall. I lived in the Sale district on the outskirts of Manchester with my fiancée, Guðný, whom I had met at school in Laugarvatn. Guðný was also a graduate student at the university, and we lived in a multinational community of students. On the way to the station, however, I was brought to an abrupt halt opposite an electrical-goods shop. In the window were big color TV screens, turned on to capture the attention of passers-by. Color TV was a recent innovation, dismissed by some as unnecessarily fancy — after all, black-and-white had been good enough until now. But many people believed that color TV would be a revolutionary change, and a bonanza for sellers of electrical equipment. Regular broadcasts in color had begun around 1969, although the first color TV broadcast in the UK had taken place in 1967, from the Wimbledon tennis championships.[48] As I passed the shop window that Tuesday evening, the film footage being broadcast was of the eruption in Iceland. I was transfixed. The colorful spectacle made an extraordinary impression, repeated across dozens of color TVs. Molten lava and ash were flung high into the air from the crater, and a river of red-hot glowing lava flowed down the fissure, from the crater toward the sea.

That may have been the first time that a volcanic eruption was televised in color, practically live, all around the world. In the moment, it was hard for me to register its historical importance or even to define what I was feeling. I stood there for a long time, mesmerized by the TV, trying to imagine what was happening back home on Heimaey, and what these events would mean for the community, particularly the members of my own family. My parents and siblings were, thankfully, in no danger, as they had moved to the mainland four years before. But the house I had

---

48 *Wikipedia,* s.v. "Timeline of the introduction of color television in countries," https://en.wikipedia.org/wiki/Timeline_of_the_introduction_of_color_television_in_countries.

grown up in, Bólstaður, my first habitat, was still there. Or was it? I had to call Iceland.

The train trundled out of the city center, passing the Old Trafford football ground on the way to Sale. The residence hall had a public telephone. It was much in demand, and on this occasion it was hard to get through to Iceland. All the international lines were busy. Late in the evening I finally reached my parents. I told my dad what had been reported in England, and asked him whether it was true that Heimaey might sink, or explode? He reassured me with a laugh that the news reports were somewhat exaggerated. Heimaey island was not about to disappear. There had been no fatalities, and all our people were safe. He told me that the evacuated islanders would all be provided with shelter on the mainland, but it remained to be seen whether they would ever be able to go back. It looked as if the flowing lava might fill up the harbor, the heart of this busy fishing port.

The international operator interrupted to ask for more coins if I wanted to continue. Sometimes this phone's coinbox filled up, and then we international students would talk for hours on a single coin that had gotten stuck in the slot. But tonight, I inserted a river of coins, so that we would not be cut off.

When we finally hung up, I sat down and tried to make sense of this conversation with home and the awful news that had turned out to be mostly true. Asleep for thousands of years, Mount Helgafell had woken up with a bang, right on the doorstep of Bólstaður, my first habitat. The Westman Islanders' connection with the Earth was in question and under review. My friends and neighbors might have to find new habitats on the mainland, perhaps for the rest of their lives. Looking back on that night now, my feelings were like those of many people today who are reluctant to acknowledge that we have entered into an unprecedented period of human influence on the Earth — the Age of Humans, or Anthropocene — and that it is necessary to take radical actions to reverse disastrous environmental changes or else we will lose our homes. While to those on Heimaey that night in 1973 it was blindingly obvious that their relationship with the Earth had changed, to me, at a little distance, it simply seemed surreal.

THE BATTLE FOR HEIMAEY

LAVA

In 1864, a little more than a century before the Heimaey eruption commenced, distinguished US environmentalist George Perkins Marsh had warned against harmful human impact on the Earth's ecosystems. It was necessary, he said, to resist, to reinstate the equilibrium between humanity and nature, to protect forests, and to plant new ones. Otherwise nothing would be left but bare rocks, and all the life that had flourished on them would vanish. At the same time Marsh emphasized the limitations of human action in the face of nature — including volcanoes: "No physicist," he claimed, "has supposed that man can avert the eruption of a volcano or diminish the quantity of melted rock which it pours out of the bowels of the earth."[1] It was commonly assumed that a glowing stream of molten lava would go its own way. Until 1973, that is.

Fires and Freezing
On the morning of January 23, as many of the boats bringing the evacuees from the Westman Islands were mooring in Þor-

---

1 George Perkins Marsh, *Man and Nature,* ed. David Lowenthal (Cambridge: The Belknap Press of Harvard University Press, 1965), 459.

lákshöfn harbor, the Westman Islands Council gathered for an emergency meeting on the top floor of the bank building in the middle of the village. Plans had to be made for damage control, and a response to this unprecedented situation. Everyday political divisions were set aside. From time to time, as they discussed the situation, the councilors stood up to peer apprehensively out of a small south-facing window which offered a clear view of the fiery volcano.

At the same time, a group of experts had been called to the University of Iceland's Science Institute, in Reykjavík, to discuss "practical measures to prevent damage to people and infrastructure" on the Westman Islands, especially the harbor. Three main ideas were discussed: raise dikes to divert the lava flow; cool the edge of the lava; or use explosives to blast open the crater edge in a more favorable direction. The minutes of the meeting include that, "Reference was made to the moral support to be derived from experts with measuring devices," and "The meeting was transformed into a flurry of preparation, as time and daylight were at a premium."[2] Quite unusual minutes.

Following the meeting in Reykjavík, three of the experts — one of them a Westman Islander himself — speedily made their way to Heimaey by helicopter. After familiarizing themselves with what was happening, the three returned to Reykjavík later that same day. Another meeting was held at the Science Institute the next morning, January 24. Among the resolutions reached was that they "should be in contact with locals on the Westman Islands and try, in consultation with them, to check or restrain the lava flow."[3] Later that day eleven experts went out to the Westman Islands, bringing their morale-boosting measuring devices. Some of them collected samples and tried to form an idea of what kind of eruption this was and what might be expected to happen next. Others considered where and how protective

---

[2] Minutes of the Board of the Westman Islands, January 23, 1973, Westman Islands Archives.

[3] "Eldgos í Heimaey í Vestmannaeyjum," Minutes of The Science Institute, University of Iceland, January 23, 1973.

measures could be applied. Would Heimaey split up, explode, or sink into the sea? Would the eruption last for weeks, months, or years, as in the case of Surtsey?

On January 25, more experts flew to Heimaey, including the renowned Icelandic geologist Sigurður Þórarinsson, who had long had an interest in Mount Helgafell, having decried the damage done to the mountain by gravel quarrying in 1950 and wondered, as late as 1972, what would happen if it erupted. A young geologist who accompanied them, Ari Trausti Guðmundsson, later wrote a short article describing the experts' reactions, especially their bewilderment.[4]

The experts were provided with accommodation by the harbor, in a workers' hostel, another one of my old haunts, belonging to one of the fish-freezing plants where fish were normally gutted, processed, and frozen for export. I had worked at the freezing plant for a few summers, the last being in 1969, to work off debts I had accumulated during my stay at the Laugarvatn school. The winter had been difficult, and by spring my debts were heavier than usual. When I phoned home to the Westman Islands looking for work, the foreman, a friend of my father, remarked sarcastically: "So you're about to graduate! Are people like that any use in a freezing plant?" It was far from clear at the time that I would pursue an academic career, but perhaps I was already a dud in the context of fish and guts.

The foreman's suspicions were partially born out on my very first day. My job was to load the fresh fish onto a conveyor belt that delivered it to the floor above for filleting, packing, and freezing. I was staying with relatives close to the foot of Helgafell. Exhausted after the first day of backbreaking toil, I overslept the next morning, and had to walk, shamefaced, down past my boyhood home at Bólstaður to the freezing plant. Fortunately, I managed to keep my job and settle my debts. I knew the foreman had dry humor and, perhaps, he was simply using the opportunity to comment on social class, the people who

---

4   Ari Trausti Guðmundsson, "Annar og þriðji gosdagur í Eyjum," *Jökull* 33, no. 1 (1983): 162.

left their hometown to acquire degrees, positions, and money. Would they ever return?

Now the freezing plants, the key workplaces of Heimaey, were out of function. An army of rescue workers, mostly men, from both Heimaey and the mainland, struggled to save the storage from the freezers, loading boxes of high-quality fish onto vessels destined for the mainland. Also, some of the most expensive and valuable machinery of the plants had to be removed and taken away, in case the eruption would destroy the fishing plants. The workers had to be provided with food and places to stay, and solutions were often invented on the spot.

Shortly after Sigurður Þórarinsson and his colleagues settled into their rooms at the freezing plant, there was a clattering of ashfall and lumps of lava on the roof. One after the other, the doors on the scientists' floor were flung open. Sigurður hurried out into the street, wearing a hard hat. His intention, like that of the other scientists, was to get "as close to the eruption as their sheepskin-lined coats would allow," wrote Ari Trausti. Sigurður "did not pause. Rushed downstairs and out, with his coat half-on." After him hurried another geologist, waving Sigurður's boots and calling out to him. He caught up with Sigurður, in his stockinged feet, out on the road. Sigurður shoved his feet into the boots and, armed with his long experience of Icelandic volcanoes, hurried off to meet this latest crater that had taken people by surprise. The eruption had not, it was now clear, begun in the crater of Mount Helgafell after all. Instead, a new crater had formed and was erecting around itself a new mountain that would be named, "Fire Mountain."

At Kirkjubær farm, some reporters accosted Sigurður and another well-known geologist, Arne Noe-Nygaard from Copenhagen, as they watched the new mountain being born. The wind direction was favorable, but lumps of lava whizzed down to crash onto the ground between the men as they talked. Sigurður was used to reporters' questions and spoke with caution, unwilling to say much about future developments but suggesting that the eruption might last two to three months. Arne astonished the reporters by saying: "'*Vi måler tiden efterpå* — we measure the time afterwards' and the reporters wrote it down and nodded."[5]

The Kitchen Experiment

It was clear from the start that the harbor, the beating heart of the community, was at risk from the lava flowing from the new crater, Eldfell. Of the three ideas advanced by the experts from the University of Iceland's Science Institute — to divert the lava flow with dikes, blast open the crater edge in a more favorable direction, or cool the edge of the lava — there was time to try only one, as the lava would soon reach the harbor. Tensions ran high. On a geological time-scale, things were happening extraordinarily fast, and it was vital to make the right decisions before the shape of the island was irrevocably changed. It was time to think about the larger picture and the future. While efforts soon began to bulldoze up ramparts to protect the east side of the village, the proposal to blow an opening in the edge of the new crater was postponed for the time being. To save the harbor, they would try to cool the lava's advancing edge.

It was Þorbjörn Sigurgeirsson who came up with the innovative idea of pumping seawater onto the lava, in an attempt to divert it from the harbor. He had first thought of this idea a decade earlier on Surtsey island, where he had made preparations for trying to cool the lava and influence its path. He had noticed that the lava tended to snake long distances along the shoreline in both directions when it met the cold sea, instead of flowing straight into the ocean depths. Could we, he asked, affect the shape of our new island neighbor? Curve it into a harbor? The experiment didn't materialize, as the lava flow stopped.

In the Westman Islands another story is often told of Þorbjörn's proposal. Þorbjörn, as the story goes, got the idea after he ate a meal of fish served in the traditional way, with melted suet. He was struck by the sight of the suet spilling off his plate onto the table. I imagine the table had a plastic top with a metallic frame, a modernist fashion at the time. The molten mass

---

5 Guðmundsson, "Annar og þriðji gosdagur í Eyjum," 162.

initially flowed directly towards the edge of the table, but as it cooled and congealed it started to flow out to the sides.[6] The molten suet had changed its course. Þorbjörn seems to have leapt to the conclusion that if the lava front could be similarly cooled, it too would change direction. With all the rooms at the freezing plant taken, he was staying in the Westman Islands fire station and the eruption response team there reacted favorably to his suggestion of an experiment. They agreed to try pumping cold water onto the lava, initially using fire engines, and then fireboats. Westman Islands Civil Defense took action, and on February 8, in the eruption's third week, the first three pumps were deployed.

Þorbjörn was a man who went his own way. It was strictly forbidden to venture onto the advancing lava flow alone, being that there were many dangers, not least those from emissions of noxious gases and flying lumps of glowing lava. Yet Þorbjörn would be out in the early morning, observing the flow of the lava and making notes on its direction, taking readings, making calculations, and mapping out the changing landscape in his mind. It was vital to listen to the groaning of the lava and the thunderous rumblings of the volcano — to hear what the mountain had to say — and down at the harbor every other sound was drowned out by the din of the powerful water-pumps. After his morning stroll Þorbjörn spoke to the teams working in the lava field, gave them instructions for the day, pointed out dangers to be avoided, and told them where to direct the water. No doubt there was a lot of consultation, but Þorbjörn's guidance was crucial.

Who was this man who walked through the burning lava field every day, usually on his own, with woolen mittens on his hands and a hard hat on his head, determined to save the harbor, whatever the objections of both experts and ordinary people? Þorbjörn was a farmer's son, the eldest of five brothers, born in 1917 in northern Iceland. After early schooling in a rural

---

6 Sigrún Inga Sigurgeirsdóttir, interview, January 20, 2017; Ragnar Baldvinsson, interview, January 20, 2017.

school, he went to Copenhagen to study physics at the Institute of Theoretical Physics, founded by Nobel-prizewinner Niels Bohr, now named the Niels Bohr Institute. During Þorbjörn's time as a student, World War II broke out and Germany occupied Denmark, but he managed to complete his MSc degree and then make a daring escape from the Nazis via neutral Sweden. In 1945 Þorbjörn went to Princeton University in the US.[7] On his return to Iceland he embarked on research into radioactivity and was an active participant in Iceland's Nuclear Science Commission, established in 1956. In 1954, Þorbjörn was among those who planned the foundation of CERN, the European Organization for Nuclear Research, located near Geneva, Switzerland. CERN is home of the Large Hadron Collider and other particle accelerators used in research on various unanswered questions about the nature of the universe. In later years, Þorbjörn returned to Princeton to pursue research on cosmic rays.

During the Surtsey eruption, while he pondered cooling the hot lava, Þorbjörn had practiced swimming and scuba diving in the cold sea surrounding the island. Later, when he undertook to chart magnetic fields over Iceland, he trained as a pilot in order to be able to fly all over the country to make his observations. His pilot's license proved useful during the Westman Islands eruption, as he could fly back and forth between the islands and Reykjavík at his own convenience. He was universally regarded as stoical and level-headed. On a flight out to the Westman Islands with Valdimar K. Jónsson, Þorbjörn, in the pilot's seat, twisted and turned the light plane from side to side, "zigging and zagging; sometimes he turned in the direction of the south pole, and sometimes the north pole," as Valdimar put it.[8] On the way out to the islands, as he stood up and stretched out to grasp a bag he had brought with him, he inadvertently knocked the elevator control with his rear end. The plane went into a sudden dive, but Þorbjörn calmly resumed his seat and

---

7   Steindór J. Erlingsson, "Veirur, kjarnorka og eðlisvísindi á Íslandi," *Morgunblaðið*, October 8, 2016, 30.
8   Valdimar K. Jónsson, interview, January 20, 2016.

brought the plane back onto a level course. Valdimar felt compelled to admit that Þorbjörn had been "a little absent-minded" on that occasion. But that was not necessarily deemed a flaw, more a sign of his capacity to be deeply absorbed in the task at hand, and not to be distracted by trivia.

Hlöðver Johnsen, another of his close collaborators during the eruption, also tells an amusing anecdote about Þorbjörn and the men risking their lives on the lava:

> [O]ne time, when some of the men were having difficulty connecting water hoses atop the half-molten lava, in scorching heat and clouds of steam, a man was standing at a distance, watching. One of them called out to him: "Come here, you bastard, and help us out." And the man didn't hesitate, he did all he could to help, and did well. They managed it, as usual, and the men set off back to their digs at the fire station, where they told the others about the weirdo who had been wandering about in the lava field. He'd lent them a hand, admittedly, but he certainly wouldn't be back, as he'd set off in the opposite direction, out into the lava field, and vanished into the murk. They were asked to give a more detailed description of the mystery man, and it transpired that it had been The Man himself, Þorbjörn Sigurgeirsson. And of course he turned up again, safe and sound.[9]

The geologists and other experts who were observing events on the Westman Islands were often asked their views on the probable course of the eruption, and whether such cooling efforts had any chance of success. Þorbjörn had expressed his opinion, and convinced others to try what he suggested, but not everyone was persuaded. One dissenting voice in particular stood out.

---

9 Hlöðver Johnsen, *Bergið klifið: Minningar veiðimanns* (Reykjavík: Almenna bókafélagið, 1986).

The Aquarium
The French geologist Haroun Tazieff, known for his writings as well as for his dramatic photographs and films of eruptions, visited Heimaey island as the pumps began their work and a report of his journey appeared in the French daily *Le Figaro* on February 21. There, Tazieff maintained that the village on Heimaey was "virtually doomed" should the eruption continue. The Icelandic ambassador in Paris noticed the report and mailed a copy home to Iceland that same day.[10] The following day, the Associated Press sent out a report much the same as the *Figaro* article. On RUV radio news in Iceland, Tazieff was reported as expecting the village to be destroyed. Another eruption was foreseeable in the village itself, he said.

Tazieff was described in the radio news report as "one of the most renowned volcanologists in the world" who had "spent time on Heimaey island doing research for UNESCO." He had descended into a deep volcanic crater in the Congo, crawled through caves in the bowels of the earth, and walked alongside flowing lava in many places around the world, according to an interview in daily Icelandic newspaper, *Morgunblaðið*, with "the famous volcano man Tazieff."[11] What was the correct response to this authoritative voice? Should the people striving to save the village and the island from destruction simply give up, one month into the eruption? At the University's Science Institute, Tazieff's challenge was taken seriously. The same day that his views were broadcast, the Institute called a meeting to address the issue.

Þorbjörn, who had organized the pump brigade and who could be unceremoniously blunt at times, at the meeting got straight to the point: "What are we supposed to think of this H. Tazieff?" he asked. "As a scientist, a photographer, or what? […] If we don't respond we'll be seen as accepting his views."[12]

---

10 Minutes of the Science Institute, University of Iceland, February 23, 1973.
11 "Með rannsóknum má segja fyrir um eldgos," *Morgunblaðið*, August 21, 1965, 15, 27.
12 Minutes of the Science Institute.

According to the Associated Press report, Tazieff had stayed on Heimaey at the local aquarium, along with other visiting experts. "We slept on the floor there, surrounded by twelve fish tanks," he said. "During the night, as the volcano raged and the thundering din resounded around the doomed village, we observed big fish swimming towards us, their teeth glinting. I have never experienced another such night."

Established in 1964, the aquarium was an exciting place for children and teenagers, especially at feeding time. The strange worlds in the fish tanks were microcosms of the North Atlantic that surrounded Heimaey and fishermen would sometimes donate specimens of rare species they caught alive at sea. The aquarium was run by Friðrik Jesson, a gym teacher at the elementary school, and his wife Magnea Sjöberg. Friðrik, who demanded discipline in both the fish tank and the gym, seemed to have developed a relationship with the wild catfish, as if he had domesticated them. When the eruption began, he and his wife refused to abandon their sea creatures, moving into the aquarium and providing lodging for a few scientists as well, rather than leaving the island.

Tazieff had audaciously ventured up onto volcanoes. His bravado in the vicinity of erupting craters and glowing lava was well known from one of his documentary films, *Le rendezvous du diable* (1959), released in English as *The Devil's Blast*. But his reputation for a cool head was undermined by a story told in Iceland that during his night among the fish Tazieff had woken up in terror, gazing straight into the horribly fanged maw of a gigantic wolffish (*Anarhichas lupus*). After that he was adamant about wanting to get off the island and about the doomed fate of Heimaey. Perhaps the wolffish wasn't the best of roommates. Writer Stefán Jónsson once remarked of it: "No other fish has such a deep-seated will of its own — and under the hooded, rounded brows are blue eyes, hard as nails and glittering with something that is either divine or demonic."[13]

---

13 Stefán Jónsson, *Mínir menn: Vertíðarsaga* (Reykjavík: Ægisútgáfan, 1962), 200.

Was the wolffish afraid as well? Did the fish sense the tremors and the thundering din, like the horse that was startled on the first day of the eruption? Nobody seems to have considered that possibility. At that time, feelings were regarded as an exclusively human domain. Other animals — or "animals" in the parlance of the time, as if we humans were not animals, too — and all other living beings were seen as insensible and incapable of feeling pain. Ethical principles applied only to humans.

It was an interesting chance that placed some of the visiting scientists in amongst the fish. Aquaria, like the decorative but informative botanical gardens created in many cities, represented in tangible form the dominant attitude in science that assumes a dichotomy of man versus nature. The aquarium was separate from the human world, while subject to human influence, with humans alone able to understand what went on within it. They "read" the book of nature, able to understand the living conditions of the fish, the relationships between the different organisms, the food chain, and so on. I have maintained elsewhere that many of those who address the future of the oceans have a tendency to regard them as giant aquaria, and therefore imagine that we stand apart from them.[14]

To some extent, the battle with Eldfell and the lava flowing from the new crater was similar to managing a fish tank. Both are microcosms of humanity's conflict with a subjugated Earth that serves human interests. The Science Institute had even proposed to drop explosives on an erupting volcano, an idea that typified the twentieth century's relationship, or lack thereof, with Earth. Human beings placed themselves at the imaginary *Punctum Archimedes,* looking down on the earth from afar, keeping it mentally at arm's length, while considering its content and revising it at will. Archimedes would have been thrilled. Or would he? The Ancient Greek sage is probably best known for discovering the principle that bears his name:

---

14 Gísli Pálsson, "Nature and Society in the Age of Postmodernity," in *Reimagining Political Ecology,* eds. Aletta Biersack and James Greenberg (Durham: Duke University Press, 2006), 70–93.

Fig. 17. Þorbjörn Sigurgeirsson in the lava field on Heimaey. Photo by Sigurgeir Jónasson.

the law of buoyancy, which states that an object immersed in liquid is buoyed up by a force equal to the weight of the liquid it displaces. Would he have swung himself up into the tank with the wolffish, and enjoyed the spectacle as the displaced seawater gushed out onto the floor?

Fiery Lava

Þorbjörn's diaries from the time of the eruption recently came to light.[15] They comprise four small notebooks in which he made scribbled notes of readings taken as he walked about the burning lava field, and observations recorded after he returned to his lodging. He assessed the situation, determining where the greatest danger lay and what had been achieved (fig. 17). His handwriting varies according to the circumstances, sometimes

---

15 Þorbjörn Sigurgeirsson, Diaries from the Westman Islands, 1973.

tired out after a long day, or night, walking in the lava. His notes are not always in chronological order, the reason for which is unclear, but it is disconcerting for the reader. Perhaps he simply grabbed whichever notebook was at hand and scribbled his notes wherever he could, focused above all on writing down the important points, the ones which might prove useful in the following days. Why should he care about anyone who might try to decipher his notes when the eruption was over?

The disorder of his notebooks probably accords with the chaos that reigned out in the lava field during the eruption, including all the factors that Þorbjörn had to keep in mind in order to achieve his goal; the constantly changing conditions, which must be addressed; and the absolute imperative of not giving up. For that very reason his diaries are, in their way, vital documents, alongside the detailed formal reports that were written about the salvage and rescue operations on Heimaey. Þorbjörn does not, admittedly, provide anything in the nature of a personal narrative; he doesn't mention his feelings, disappointments, or victories, nor report on his interactions with other people out in the lava field. His focus is all on the essentials: The work of cooling the lava by a combination of means, as he experienced it in the hard toil out in the lava field, surrounded by pumps and the men who were operating them. On occasion he was roused in the middle of the night, if the lava suddenly gushed forward. On March 10, for instance, he notes: "Called out at 4 a.m. Lava flowing into the sea right by the harbor wall."

As the work of cooling the lava continued, Þorbjörn took temperature readings and samples of gases, and recorded photographic evidence using film and still photographs, carefully noting the time and location. Interspersed with these details are references to flights over Surtsey island, or to the mainland. His days were crammed with activity. In view of the huge task confronting him, and how much was at stake, one can only admire his cool head and patience.

It was not easy to find one's way in the lava field, the "Newfound Land" or *Terra Incognita,* as explorers and cartographers called unknown territory in the Middle Ages. Familiar landmarks such as "Shoulder Stone" had been swept away in the eruption, and the clouds of smoke and steam over the lava were often so thick that Þorbjörn and his colleagues lost their bearings. The shifting landmarks in the lava field were sometimes given names by the men working there. Some names were derived from someone on the island.

Humorous tales are sometimes told of seafarers who tried to navigate using clouds as their "landmarks." Like clouds, the landmarks in the lava were mutable and ephemeral. One of these was Flakkarinn, "The Wanderer." This huge rock had split away from the rim of the Eldfell crater during a massive explosion in the middle of the night in late February. It then started its progress down the lava field, making a getaway, like the stones that Þórbergur Þórðarson pictured in his book *The Stones Speak*. In the Middle Ages people spoke of the *homo viator,* a pilgrim travelling in a quest for salvation; here was a whole mountain on the move — with no apparent goal. Some of the men working in the lava field tried hitching of the ride on the Wanderer. The wandering "mountain" juddered beneath them as it careered onwards, they said, as if propelled by a malfunctioning engine. This denoted the extraordinary relationship these men had with the Earth.

The first victory in the battle with the lava was a joint achievement by bulldozers, firefighters, and fireboats, won at the harbor in late February. A stream of lava heading straight for the harbor was halted at a manmade barrier. Those who observed the pilot boats spraying seawater onto the edge of the lava field were convinced that the harbor had been successfully defended by this method — at least for the time being. The scientists felt that they now knew what had to be done. As confidence increased, some fish processing was resumed. Some of the Heimaey boats, as a result, would return, occasionally landing their catch, in this case mainly capelin for "melting" or grounding as fish meal.

Interestingly enough, a fortification erected in the sixteenth century, to defend the assets of the King of Denmark against English merchants and foreign raiders, played a useful role in the battle for Heimaey. Skansinn, "The Fort," was a high stone wall built in 1586 for King Frederik II and rebuilt after the "Turkish Raid" of 1627, when Barbary corsairs captured hundreds of Westman Islanders to be sold into slavery in north Africa. That Skansinn proved itself a sturdy obstacle to the lava flow of 1973 calls to mind the roads made by inhabitants of Fogo in the Cape Verde archipelago that unexpectedly made history in 2014, when the volcano Pico do Fogo began to erupt. There, though, the impact was different, as the roads invited the lava straight into the villagers' homes.[16] As in the Westman Islands, ever since the days of colonial rule, many generations had unknowingly played their part in the disaster, be it for good or ill — just as may be said of people all over world today.

Drilling into Magma

Geothermal sources of energy play an increasing role in Iceland, partly because the damming of wild rivers is contested by environmental groups. An ambitious Deep Drilling Project was recently launched to explore deeper sources of energy with exceptionally high temperatures at the Krafla volcano in northern Iceland. In the spring of 2009, drilling progressed until 2066 meters in depth, when the machinery got stuck.[17] It turned out the drill had, unexpectedly, reached into the mixture of molten and semi-molten rock between the Earth's surface and the mantle around the planet's core. The drill, an extension of humans much like the white cane of a blind person, had ventured into

---

16 Ármann Höskuldsson, email, April 2016; AFP, "Volcanic Eruption in Cape Verde Destroys Two Villages," *Daily Mail*, December 16, 2014, https://www.dailymail.co.uk/wires/afp/article-2876017/Volcanic-eruption-Cape-Verde-destroys-villages.html; Christopher Marc Lilyblad, "Between Hope and Despair: The Community of Cha das Caldeiras after the Fogo Volcano Eruption," *Europa Archives*, January 7, 2014.

17 W.A. Elder, "Drilling into Magma and the Implications of the Icelandic Deep Drill Drilling Project (IDDP) for High-Temperature Geothermal Systems Worldwide," *Geothermics* 49 (2014): 111–18; Kathryn Yusoff, "Anthropogenesis: Origins and Endings in the Anthropocene," *Theory, Culture & Society* (2015): 1–26; Nigel Clark, Alexandra Gormally, and Hugh Tuffen, "Speculative Volcanology: Time, Becoming, and Violence in Encounters with Magma," *Environmental Humanities* 10, no. 1 (2018): 274–94.

a magma reservoir, a rare occurrence despite thousands of geothermal drilling projects worldwide.

Keeping in mind the threats posed by major magma extrusions (i.e., volcanoes) throughout history, some of those involved no doubt wondered if drilling into magma would be catastrophic. Some may have pondered what such a capture of fire by humans, no less remarkable than the playing with fire at the dawn of humanity, would involve. What would be the consequences of such an intrusion, a conflation of the familiar rhythms of human life and the deep time of the Earth and the solar system? Surely, this was a far more spectacular scientific advance than the "domestication" of a lava flow during an eruption — and with totally unpredictable consequences. Would the stunning opportunity to touch magma and study it before it cooled and lost its magmatic qualities disrupt the flow of time? Hadn't this encounter with magma violated the long-standing barrier between the dead geologic interior of the planet and its living, cultured surface?

"THE HOUSES HAD NO TIME TO BURN"

While the battle for Heimaey progressed, I remained in Manchester, attending lectures in the imposing house which had been home to Friedrich Engels in the nineteenth century at the height of the Industrial Revolution. Now occupied by the University of Manchester's Department of Anthropology, where I was a student, this house must have been where the comrades Marx and Engels hammered out their *Communist Manifesto*, whose ideas would reverberate around the world, shaking up human societies with the power of an erupting volcano. While the Industrial Revolution was central to their theories, they could have had no idea that one of its consequences would be an insatiable demand for energy, or that this demand would sow the seeds of our current environmental crisis. Certain elements of their ideology may hold lessons for us, in particular their analyses of inequality, the laws of capital, and the global financial system. But in their day coal and oil were simply resources, elements of the economy, while the focus was on growth, and human control of nature. They foresaw the end of capitalism in a revolution of the proletariat, but that would have made no difference to human progress down the primrose path to the everlasting bonfire. Perhaps the Industrial Revolution and the steam engine blew smoke into the eyes of Marx and Engels, and the Marxists who followed their lead.

I had initially wanted to write my thesis about the society of the Westman Islands and its proximity with the sea. The department was not sure what to make of my idea, as anthropological studies then tended to focus on societies of nomadic herders in East Africa, for instance. Now that the Westman Islands community was in crisis, and I had no wish to take the crisis as my subject, I would have to shelve the idea. I don't suppose I would have known where to start, as an individual or as an anthropologist. Did anthropology have any contribution to make in such circumstances? Did I have any contribution to make? Wouldn't I be too focused on myself and my own relatives, given the circumstances?

Far away in England, I made do with the news of the eruption that I could glean from packages of newspapers sent by my parents. Sometimes there was a letter with the papers, and occasionally I phoned home for an update. My father kept up with developments through his job: He worked at a petrol station in a new suburb of Reykjavík, where he met a lot of Westman Islanders. Dad was a sociable, helpful man, who made friends easily. Many of the evacuated islanders were living in Reykjavík for the duration of the eruption, and they often dropped in at the petrol station to exchange news. During Dad's shifts the station was a hub of activity. The family joked that it was part of the social service. Mum was in frequent contact with relatives who had remained behind, who recounted their adventures and told her about the fate of the homes that fell prey to the falling ash or the advancing lava, one by one.

The last mistress of the house at Bólstaður, Íris Sigurðardóttir, had never been at ease alone in the house, although she had no objection to being on her own in other places. It was as if there were some mysterious presence in the house, not found in other houses.[18] Now Íris was in Reykjavík. She would never return to Bólstaður, which had been her family home for over a decade. Her husband Hafsteinn Ágústsson soon went back to the island to take part in the salvage operations. He seized the opportunity to retrieve the family's furniture, clothing, and crockery, and transported their household goods to the mainland aboard the boat which had evacuated the extended family that fateful January night. The old worker's cottage of Bólstaður was left standing empty and deserted.

In the Path of the Lava

In the middle of March, lava engulfed a large section of the east village. The teams manning the hoses that cooled the lava were repeatedly forced to withdraw before the capricious advancing flow. The following days marked a turning point in the story of the battle with the lava, which was inexorably advancing in two parts of the east village. The part regarded as doomed was known as Death Valley. According to one press report, "[t]he lava is moving so fast that the buildings don't even have time to burn."[19]

On March 22, Pastor Þorsteinn Lúter Jónsson summoned the remnants of his Lutheran congregation on Heimaey to mass in Landakirkja. The islanders called it the Fire Mass (fig. 18), referencing the famous Fire Mass held in 1783 by Pastor Jón Steingrímsson, whose detailed descriptions of the catastrophic Laki eruption were well known. Pastor Jón had urged his parishioners to repent their sins if they wished to be delivered from destruction. Tradition tells us that the lava in 1783 halted when it reached the church, sparing the building and the faithful gathered, praying, inside it. Wrote Pastor Jón:

> Both myself and all the others in the church were completely unafraid there inside its walls. No one showed any signs

---

18 Hafsteinn Ágústsson, interview, January 23, 2016.
19 "60 hús undir hraun í nótt," *Vísir*, March 23, 1973.

Fig. 18. The "Fire Mass" in Landakirkja, March 22, 1973. Photo by Sigurgeir Jónasson.

of fleeing or leaving during the service, which I had made slightly longer than usual. Now no length of time spent talking to God could be too long. [...] From this day onwards the fire did no major damage to my parish in this way.[20]

At Pastor Þorsteinn's Fire Mass in 1973, "It was a congregation of exhausted men, unshaven and dressed in woolen sweaters and overalls, who attended church that night [...]. In the chancel some of the men stood holding lit candles. Pastor Þorsteinn gave an impassioned sermon."[21] The congregation sang the Icelandic version of Gerhardt's hymn *Entrust Your Way,* expressing willingness to confide one's fate to the hands of God in times of travail. Among those who attended the Fire Mass that night was Sigurgeir Örn Sigurgeirsson, the only person to die in the eruption.

---

20 Jón Steingrímsson, *Fires of the Earth: The Laki Eruption 1783–1784,* trans. Keneva Kunz (Reykjavík: University of Iceland Press, 1988), 49.
21 Ibid.

Landakirkja was a sturdily built historic building dating from the eighteenth century. Its massive stone walls rested on bedrock that, until now, had never been disturbed. The church was a vital element of island life and played an important role in my early memories. I had been christened here, and, in due course, confirmed. Like other confirmands, I had attended Sunday masses as part of my instruction and taken Communion. The mass in Landakirkja at the height of the eruption was psychologically empowering, but neither the mass nor the prayers of the congregation could halt the advance of the lava. "That was a horrific night on the Westman Islands," wrote a reporter:

> The lava was flowing so fast you could see it move, in part of the village; it smashed houses in an instant and then engulfed them. Window panes were constantly shattering, roofs and walls were pulverized; the deafening din was like the houses wailing. Nothing could be done.[22]

Black humor offered many who were on the front line a way to cope with their anxiety. As the lava rushed inexorably onwards, and one building after another burst into flames, a ball of flaming lava crashed through a skylight in the western part of the village. As the fire took hold, the householder phoned the fire station to request assistance, as he was unable to put the fire out. The fireman quipped: "Have you got a booking?"

Most Westman Islanders who were monitoring the progress of the eruption, whether on the ground or from afar, attached particular significance to the electric power station. I was aware that the efforts to safeguard this essential building might well be doomed to failure, and I kept up with news of it as long as possible (fig. 19). It was an impressive concrete building in the modernist style with a hipped roof, which had brought a cosmopolitan touch to the little fishing community. Its powerful generators supplied electricity to the entire community all year, around the clock, like the sun that reliably rose and set

---

22 "64 hús hurfu á 8 klst," *Morgunblaðið*, March 24, 1973.

Fig. 19. Retreat from the electrical power station on Tuesday, March 26. Photo by Sigurgeir Jónasson.

every day. Behind it rose the Heimaklettur cliffs, with their own hipped roof.

To Westman Islanders the power station stood for progress and human potential in the age of technology, calling to mind other, bigger power stations and ongoing technological advances — even flights to the moon. But in the end the men fighting to save this beacon of the future had to admit defeat. Some of those who watched as the building succumbed to the lava shed tears. Every light on Heimaey went out. Darkness reigned, as if the island had been transported back to the ancient times. The modern world had symbolically crashed and burned, vanquished by the flow of lava.

Bólstaður Goes Up in Flames
A person's habitat — the hearth, the home, the manor, the castle — has both economic and emotional significance. It is the world and the environment in which people function in all societies. Even those who are constantly or seasonally on the

Fig. 20. The advancing lava a week before Bólstaður (shown by arrow) was destroyed. Photographer unknown.

move, for whatever reason, have a camp or a hearth. Perhaps it would be more correct to say that the environment, the people, and the community are one. Nowadays that unity is constantly being sundered and the concomitant trauma leaves no-one untouched.

On Heimaey in late March, the pressure was so great that few people on the island took the time to stop and observe individual buildings being consumed by fire and lava, but when some unusually important building was in danger a crowd might gather. On the night of April 1, the fishing boats that had been slowly returning sailed out of the harbor, as it was impossible to tell whether the harbor mouth or the harbor itself might be closed off. On April 2, the lava destroyed my Bólstaður and the nearby buildings (fig. 21). The event was reported in the newspaper in Reykjavík the following day.[23]

---

23 "1000 sek. lítrar af sjó — á 1100 stiga heitt hraun," *Morgunblaðið*, April 3, 1973, 32.

Fig. 21. The eastern part of the village of Heimaey, April 2, 1973. Photo by Eiríkur Þ. Einarsson.

My mother heard the news that Bólstaður had been consumed from her nephew, Siggi, who was operating a crane as part of the lava-cooling operations. Siggi owned the only crane on the island during the eruption, and he and other men were working night and day, transporting the pipes that carried the cold water out onto the lava, as well as fetching valuable machinery out of danger.

On occasion the thirty-ton crane maintained a delicate balance as it transported heavy machinery dangling from its sixty-foot boom. But Siggi knew what he was doing. One day he took a short break to show a workmate the house where his grandmother had lived. Siggi's father, Óskar, had grown up in Bólstaður, and for years he had himself been a frequent visitor to our grandmother, Auðbjörg. A few days earlier, a bulldozer had crafted a temporary road for the cooling team onto the new massive lava behind the house, as if the house were safe. Now Siggi heard that Bólstaður was in imminent danger from the lava. As he and his friend approached, they saw a huge rock come flying down from the lava flow, right through the house. The old house "disintegrated and was destroyed in a moment," Siggi reported. My mother did not necessarily say much, but when she did it was always to the point. When she heard the news of Bólstaður, "it gave her a disagreeable feeling," she told me later: "It made me feel strange in my body."

As I explore footage from the days of the eruption, stored in the film archive of Icelandic State TV, I notice a few seconds of coverage of the Bólstaður neighborhood. The camera slowly follows the lava front around Bólstaður. I notice that a bulldozer has carved a road onto the lava piled up behind the house. This must have been to provide access for the cooling team. I was not aware of this. It seems to indicate that the experts thought Bólstaður was reasonably safe. A few hours later, the house and the road disappeared.

Of Bólstaður, I recall the dark and dampness in the basement and attic, and the light and warmth on the ground floor. I recall listening to stories from Grandma Auðbjörg, and visits from my grandfather Gísli, who in the last years of his life came to the Westman Islands each year from the East Fjords for the fishing season. I recall the family eagerly listening to the radio in the tiny best parlor, card games in the dining room, playing ball in the garden, visiting the neighboring homes, sledging down the road, and so much more. At the basement entrance there was much to catch a little boy's eye. Dad would pluck the puffins caught from the cliffs, sharpen skates, paint car hubcaps, make various things, humming a random melody as he worked. Sometimes he would dig out a primus stove and a saw and sear some sheep heads in the flame before sawing them open to reveal the brain, tongue, and so on — traditional delicacies that I really didn't like.

Our habitat tends to play a dominant part in our consciousness. It is no coincidence that concepts such as *economics* and *ecology* derive from the Greek *oikos,* meaning house. Likewise, the Latin *domus,* meaning building or home, is the root of many words, such as *domesticate,* literally to "bring into the home."

It is no exaggeration to say that Bólstaður, and the other buildings destroyed by lava or ash, had a "sudden death" and Westman Islanders have found that an appropriate way to put it. One local man raised a flag in front of his home as the final moment approached, and when the house had breathed its last breath, he lowered the flag to half-mast in its honor. The police objected that his action was in contravention of Icelandic flag law, but the men nearby clustered around to defend the flagpole. And then the house was gone.

THE FIREWALKERS

Would it prove possible to domesticate the fast-flowing lava, to lead it, not into the house, but away from our habitat? Would Þorbjörn Sigurgeirsson and his pump brigade be forced to admit defeat, as George Perkins Marsh might have predicted? Four years earlier humans had taken a "Giant Step" on the moon, and it seemed as if we could achieve anything we wanted. Or had the human drive to conquer nature, dominant since the Industrial Revolution, finally met its match?

The efforts of the Westman Islands fire brigade to cool the advancing lava were working. But by the time the eruption had been going on for two months it was clear that the fire pumps could not cope with the strain. Following a series of explosions in the crater, a new stream of molten lava spewed out to flow in two directions: towards the harbor to the north, and towards the houses in the eastern quarter of the village. There, the buildings were overcome one after the other, going up in flames or collapsing under the weight of ash and molten rock. The scale of the task was far beyond what ordinary firefighting could cope with.

Professor of Engineering Valdimar K. Jónsson, whose field was heat and heat transfer, was called upon to help. The chair of Iceland's Natural Disasters Compensation Fund asked him to compile a list of pumping equipment which would be suitable for the large-scale lava-cooling efforts on Heimaey. He had returned to Iceland a few months before the eruption, after many years of working and studying in the UK and the US. The plan was that Valdimar would go to the United States to select the appropriate pumping equipment and piping.

In 2014, two years before Valdimar died, I sat down with him to discuss the eruption. We were good friends, although we saw ourselves as belonging to different generations, as well as to different fields of scholarship. We had met through our work at the University of Iceland, representing our respective disciplines on committees, and sometimes taking opposing views. The university has long been divided along traditional lines, with natural sciences on one side and humanities and social sciences on the other. Suðurgata, "South Street", the road dividing the university campus, stands for that rupture — a sort of North Atlantic Ridge between the two "tectonic plates" of thought, floating on fiery magma. Suðurgata is something of an accidental black spot, both literally and metaphorically. It is a real danger to life and limb, as well as an obstacle to free dialogue. Yet both Valdimar and I knew what it was like to move from a small community, one a little rough and unfinished, to the neat and tidy environment of the university campus with its elitist traditions. I think he identified with John Lennon as a "Working Class Hero." I know I did.

Realpolitik in the Cold War

Valdimar had kept up with the progress of Þorbjörn and his pumping team, but their efforts made him smile a little to himself: "That's not good thermodynamics," he thought. Many Westman Islanders also had their doubts about the soundness of the lava-cooling theory. The Homeowners' Association of the Westman Islands, for example, felt that priority should be given to helping people resettle elsewhere.[24] Nevertheless, Valdimar agreed to lend a hand. He rapidly compiled his shopping list and made ready to go to the US. As he was waiting to board his flight at Keflavík Airport, he was paged on the public address system, informed that time was now of the essence, the eruption was intensifying. The pumps and other equipment on his shopping list had already been located and would be sent immediately by air. Valdimar hurried back to Reykjavík, a little puzzled about who had providentially stepped in to help. One of the Americans who had helped find and gather the new pumping system

---

24 "Þurfum bætur jafnt fyrir heil sem ónýt hús," *Vísir*, April 2, 1973.

was physicist Charles B. Moore of the New Mexico Institute of Mining and Technology. Moore had visited Iceland during the Surtsey eruption in 1963 to study the lightning in the pillar of volcanic ash and smoke. His photos of the spectacular bolts of lightning within the clouds of volcanic smoke were widely published.

Immediately after the eruption began, the US government offered Iceland a range of emergency equipment and technology. In the ongoing "Cod War" between Iceland and the UK, Iceland had two means of attack — one using the infamous trawl-wire cutters, and the other involving more diplomatic methods as a fellow-member of NATO — and the US had proved to be a useful ally. But Iceland's relationship with the United States had been complicated by a statement from the new left-wing Icelandic government, when it took office in 1971, that the treaty regarding the US naval air base at Keflavík, an hour outside of Iceland's capital, should be reviewed. The base, established just after World War II when the US and the UK occupied Iceland, had always been controversial. By the 1970s many Icelanders felt that the US military presence, far from protecting the island from a possible Soviet incursion, in fact made it a potential target. The future of Iceland–US cooperation was uncertain. The government thus found itself in a predicament with regard to the emergency assistance offered by US authorities. They accepted the offer of a rescue helicopter but hesitated to go further.

The Icelanders were "fully capable of dealing with this challenge without requiring outside support," a minister from the radical People's Alliance Party, who was the former editor of a left-wing newspaper, declared in late January.[25] He lashed out at those who "concentrated day after day on maligning the Icelandic authorities, Civil Defense, and the hundreds of people who have worked day and night to resolve the problems — at the

---

25 "Þjóðin í heild verður að glíma við örðugleikana," Þjóðviljinn, January 26, 1973, 9.

same time singing the praises of any assistance provided by the military at the Keflavík air base."[26]

Þorbjörn Sigurgeirsson, who had come up with the idea of cooling the lava, vehemently opposed to the American base at Keflavík himself, no doubt faced his own conflicts on the subject of accepting US technical aid. But Westman Islanders of all political stripes simply thought the government was shilly-shallying. A left-wing leader among the islanders was asked to telephone their government minister to urge him to expedite the acquisition of the pumping gear. The Cold War took on its own strange forms on this little North Atlantic island.

No doubt personnel at the US Embassy in Reykjavík had been closely following these debates. Once the Icelandic government decided to accept the Americans' offers of help, Ambassador Frederick Irving was ready to act. His wife, Dorothy J. Irving, has described the impact of the water pump issue on family life at the ambassador's residence: "A young scientist at the university," she said, had requested that Sveinn Eiríksson, the Westman Islands Fire Chief, meet with the ambassador, as so much was at stake. The Americans, Sveinn believed, probably had suitable pumping equipment at their disposal. "I'll do what I can," replied the ambassador. Sveinn gave the ambassador the shopping list that Valdimar had compiled — and so began what the ambassador's family would call "the spring of pumps and pipes":

> For three weeks every meal, even breakfast, was interrupted by, "It's a call from Washington, or San Diego, or Norfolk." It became an expected part of our mealtime. So expected that when one Sunday dinner was interrupted by a call from our Washington daughter, we spent five minutes exclaiming to her how wonderful it was to have a call from the States that wasn't about pipes and pumps, hose lengths, or delivery days. Finally, she forcefully interrupted our enthusiastic greetings.

---

26 "Það eru afrek þjóðarinnar sjálfrar, sem skera úr um alla framtíð hennar," *Þjóðviljinn*, February 2, 1973, 16.

"Whoa, Mom, Dad, wait a minute. I'm calling to tell you I'm engaged."[27]

Sometimes major family events had to take precedence over the interests of NATO, the Westman Islands harbor, and the Icelandic nation.

Through the mediation of the US Embassy, arrangements were made to send forty-three powerful pumps and the necessary metal water pipes to the Westman Islands as rapidly as possible. They arrived at the end of March, transported by four military heavy-transport aircraft, including three Lockheed Starlifter C-141s and one huge Lockheed C-5 Galaxy, said to be the largest plane in the world at the time. The vast transport capacity was needed for the many tons of equipment.

The American water pumps were installed by the Heimaey harbor and were connected so as to maximize efficiency and provide a continuous water supply. They were set up in four separate units, to ensure stability and reliability. Some were suction pumps, bright yellow in color, while others were high-pressure pumps, painted green. Valdimar K. Jónsson was assigned to manage the installation of the pumps, meet the thermodynamic requirements of the task (i.e., estimate how much water was needed to cool a given quantity of lava), and ensure that the pumps functioned properly, delivering the required water to the right areas of the advancing lava flow, in accordance with Þorbjörn Sigurgeirsson's instructions, as the lava moved. Various other operations also required coordination, such as running repairs to the pumping mechanisms, connecting the pumps to the water supply via pipes, and bulldozing up earth barricades to facilitate water-cooling the edges of the lava and prevent landslides (fig. 22).

Plus, food and accommodations had to be provided for all the people involved in the operation, numbering up to seventy-five at a time. Some were housed in the aquarium next door to the

---

27 Dorothy J. Irving, *This Too Is Diplomacy: Stories of a Partnership* (Bloomington: AuthorHouse, 2007), 132.

Fig. 22. Pumps and pipes on the harborside. Photo by Sigurgeir Jónasson.

fire station. Others found rooms at the nearby HB Hotel, or in a fishermen's hostel by the harbor, or at the power station — until it was engulfed in lava. Some sheltered in abandoned houses. For months these were the habitats, places, and ground that the teams striving to save the town and harbor bonded with.

Fire versus Water
The arrival of the new pumping gear marked the commencement of a new period in the Battle of Heimaey, as it was sometimes called, as well as a whole new chapter in the ongoing story of humankind's battle with volcanoes. The American pumps were activated, one after another, at the beginning of April. They could provide a thousand liters of water per second, up to a height of 100 meters above sea level. In calm weather, the stench and smoke of the diesel and gasoline engines hung over the quay. The din was intolerable at times. Some of the pumps pumped seawater out of the harbor, while others propelled it onwards, far out into the lava field. Designed to pump fuel in short

spurts, the machines were strained to their utmost by pumping seawater continuously for weeks at a time. Naturally, components failed under the stress and had to be regularly replaced. The machinery was in the care of a team of mechanics and technicians, some from the Westman Islands and others brought in from Reykjavík, who strove to keep the pumps running, in the hope that the cooling project would be a success and that the eruption might soon come to an end. The plan was to pump water around the clock for weeks, or even months if necessary.

The question was, would it work? Would pumping cold seawater onto hot lava, at temperatures up to many hundreds of degrees, slow or stop its advance, which was sometimes as fast as walking speed? If so, it would be a magnificent feat of engineering ingenuity. Running the pumps was one thing, but it was quite another to ensure that the water flowed unhindered through the heavy, rigid metal pipes across a bed of scorching lava that was constantly shifting. The aluminum and steel pipes moved around and had a tendency to break or leak as the lava heaved beneath them. Earlier during the eruption, the islanders had discovered that they could use plastic pipes, which had been brought to Heimaey originally for other purposes. Provided that cold seawater flowed through them continuously, the plastic pipes did not melt in the heat. Sometimes small holes were drilled in the pipes, allowing a little water to trickle out and thus cool the plastic and the lava directly underneath it. The plastic pipes adapted to the unstable lava much better than the metal ones and, in the end, plastic pipes comprised three-quarters of the pumping network. Here, as elsewhere in this unprecedented project, resourcefulness was key, as the participants had to work closely together in order to achieve the best results.[28]

Roads were bulldozed up in the lava field, leveling the rough, fresh lava and making it more accessible. Yet in this weird and wandering landscape, a road might move by dozens of feet from one day to the next. Sometimes the bulldozers towed jangling water-pipes behind them into areas too hazardous to enter on

---

28 Valdimar K. Jónsson, interview, Reykjavík, January 2014.

foot. Then my cousin Siggi's crane would swing them the final yards, as close as possible to the red-hot lava, only about five hundred feet from the crater's mouth. A total of over seven miles of pipe were laid. In a little hut close to the crater, two men were on watch duty. It was their job to observe sudden spurts in the lava flow and tell the lava-fighters below where the lava seemed to be heading.

The lava-cooling project brought many newly invented jobs, and a need for new terminology. The *bunustokksmenn,* meaning flowpipe men, were responsible for laying the pipes from the pumps on the quay up onto the lava, while the *sprautarar,* sprayers, directed the jets of water onto the advancing lava as well as glowing patches. The word *bunustokkur,* flowpipe, had been used previously for the system of pipes that distributed natural hot water from geothermal supplies to heat the cold houses of Reykjavík; now that relationship was reversed, as the pipes transported cold water onto the scorching-hot lava.

Both the flowpipe men and the sprayers, who worked out on the lava field, were known as the Suicide Squad or Death Squad. They were engaged in a life-or-death struggle. As one eyewitness reported, "In the worst spasms the teams and their water pumps were thrown into confusion, as hoses and tools were engulfed by the lava." The ghoulish name was not inappropriate, but the members of the teams I have spoken to disliked it — and who can blame them? Perhaps it is more apt to call these brave men who risked their lives atop the glowing, flowing lava "firewalkers."

Being on the move in the lava could entail mortal danger. As the cold water gushed onto the lava, huge clouds of steam rose up, blocking the view, so it could be hard to keep one's bearings. In many cases, the men could only find their way by following the kinks and curves of the water pipes, up to the edge of the crater, or back down towards the harbor. Protective goggles were a necessity, to safeguard their eyes against injury from tiny flying particles of lava or ash.

The firewalkers often had to pick their way delicately forward over a thin crust of solidified lava atop a still-molten mass, as if they were on the thin ice of a just-frozen lake. If they slipped and fell, they could suffer burns to their hands and wrists, and therefore as a preventive measure they made sure to keep them well wrapped up. They could not remain in one place for long, as the lava would burn through their boots. Each man had several pairs; as one pair gave way to the heat and the jagged edges of the lava, they would have fresh footwear ready to put on. Many wore over-sized boots, with two or three pairs of socks, and some carried a flask of water to pour into their boots and socks to cool their feet.[29] Nonetheless, a number of men needed medical attention for burns to their feet. Young men with nerves of steel, who as boys had leapt from stone to slippery stone down by the seashore, prided themselves on scampering nimbly across the glowing lava — until the soles of their shoes melted.

A major risk for the firewalkers came from flying lava bombs flung high into the air, which could crash down to Earth far from the crater. Such bombs are lumps of hot, glowing lava, ejected by the volcano and molded into spheres as they fly through the air. On occasion lava bombs rained down between the firewalkers and the safe territory below, trapping them in the hot lava field. It was even more dangerous to try to escape than to remain where they were. The men had hard hats for protection, but these were hot and sweaty, and they often removed them and wore ordinary headgear instead. Many of the firewalkers had narrow escapes from the lava bombs, but it was their astonishing good fortune that this hazardous job led to no deaths or major injuries.

It was a crude masculine life. Only one local girl, it seems, joined them on the lava. Sixteen-year-old Sigríður Högnadóttir started work in early March on the old Skansinn fortifications, where she was put in charge of pumps and helped the men move hoses and machinery around.[30] But she did not stay there long,

---

29 John McPhee, "Cooling the Lava," in *The Control of Nature* (New York: Farrar Straus Giroux, 1989), 95–179; Sigurður Þ. Jónsson, interview, January 20, 2017.
30 Gunnhildur Hrólfsdóttir, *Þær þráðinn spunnu* (Reykjavík: Frum, 2015), 382.

as the firewalkers are said to have been so concerned about her wellbeing that she was transferred to safer work, in the kitchen.

The ash that rained down on the village, accompanied by toxic gas, was disturbingly reminiscent of a war zone. This was a period of retreat and disappointments, as the lava continued to advance. The people working on Heimaey became thin-skinned, hypersensitive to the criticism they encountered when they visited the mainland. Personnel of the government's Natural Disaster Compensation Fund were sometimes met with abuse when evacuated Westman Islanders spotted them on the streets of Reykjavík. Homeowners from the island seemed to feel that the salvage teams should be watering their plants for them as they hurried from house to house boarding up windows and draining water systems. When Westman Islanders attended a meeting on the mainland to discuss compensation for their losses, it was suggested that they send good wishes to the salvage teams on Heimaey, but the proposal was resoundingly defeated. Some of the rescue workers recall avoiding places where they would meet fellow islanders:

> We had felt it was right to combat the advancing lava and resist; but with the wholesale destruction of the past few days many of us were, at heart, beginning to have doubts. And the idea was even starting to get to us, that maybe it was right, what people were accusing us of — that we were wasting public money [...]. A certain feeling of guilt was coming over us, slowly but surely.[31]

But still, was it working? Þorbjörn Sigurgeirsson was well aware that his experiments with lava cooling were controversial. Doubts were frequently expressed, and the newspapers published caricatures of scientists armed with tiny water-pistols aimed at the glowing hot lava. The lava-cooling project required massive organization, finance, and manpower. So, it is not

---

31 Magnús Bjarnason, "Privatissimo: Eldgosið í Heimaey 1973," unpublished manuscript, 2003.

surprising that this remarkable experiment was the subject of public debate. As a rule, this debate varied from light-hearted raillery to serious discussions of the issues, but on occasion the reaction veered close to outright bullying, as Þorbjörn himself remarked to a colleague.[32] He was a surveyor and pioneering thinker, renowned for his ambitious research. In addition, he was a political radical, a hard-left socialist in the highly polarized political climate of the Cold War. He became an object of envy and hostility. The operation in the Westman Islands naturally kept him very busy, so he did not have much time to write about the process, and little survived other than his detailed description of the cooling operations and a scientific analysis of the thermodynamics of lava and the progress of the eruption.

The biggest victory in the battle for Heimaey was won when the American pumps succeeded in cooling an extensive area of lava around the big rock named the Wanderer, finally putting a stop to its roaming. Valdimar K. Jónsson likened the cooling process to driving nails down into the lava: Each stream of water cooled the lava around it, so that it solidified more quickly, slowed down, and formed a solid protective layer.[33] Ironically, the twenty-year-old pumps which played such a crucial role had been deemed obsolete when they were gathered from US military armories. In Iceland, they proved that they were not defunct, at least any more than was Mount Helgafell.

Absolution

It is tempting to see the lava-cooling project on Heimaey as a harmless and unique event in humanity's struggle with nature. The human being, standing alone, armed with science and powerful machinery, repels a force of nature which had previously been deemed unconquerable. According to the zeitgeist, human capabilities, tools, and machinery could resolve all problems. Volcanic activity was just another challenge and, sooner or later,

---

32 Ágúst Guðmundsson, interview, July 5, 2016.
33 Valdimar K. Jónsson, interview, Reykjavík, January 2014.

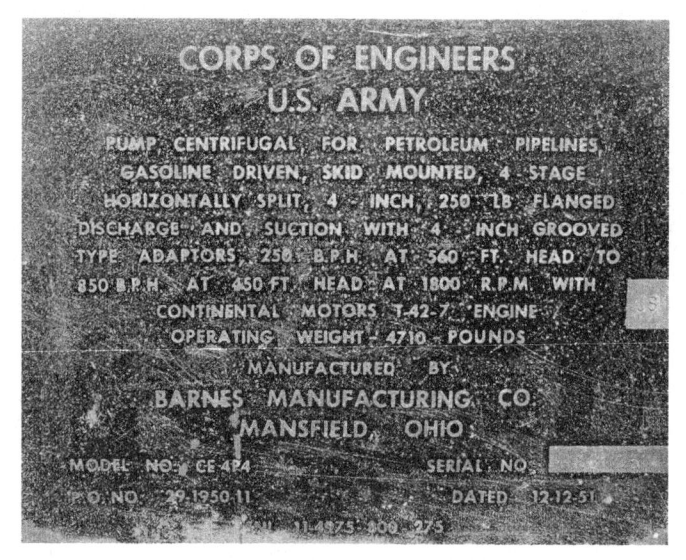

Fig. 23. Manufacturer's specification of pumping gear. Photo by the author).

people were sure to defeat that too, like other enemies of progress.

But the lava-cooling experiment was contingent on other factors. In a sense it was a consequence of global events. The big pumps that made the crucial difference were the offspring of the Cold War, built in 1953, with an original function of accompanying us military forces in order to carry out refueling in the field (fig. 23). Part of the us military arsenal, in Iceland they were known as invasion pumps. Some of them may have played a part in toppling lawful governments and installing dictators.

Many University of Iceland students went to the Westman Islands, together with their tutors, to take part in the battle for Heimaey. At that time, when student life was imbued with radical ideas of changing the world, of Flower Power and student revolt, it is hardly surprising that left-wing students were unimpressed by the pumps contributed by the Americans.

I understood where they were coming from. I'd been one of the long-haired rebels and had published radical papers. I'd been a founder of the "O Party" that ran for parliament in 1971 as a protest against the status quo. I'd organized demonstrations against the Vietnam War and the racist rebel state of Rhodesia, which is now Zimbabwe. On the very day that the eruption commenced on Heimaey, US President Richard Nixon announced the imminent end of the Vietnam War, which had been going on for nearly two decades with a peace agreement that would be signed within days. Now Icelandic students would have to turn their attentions elsewhere. But as a Westman Islander, it was hard for me to turn against the invasion pumps simply for being American. Perhaps the pumps, in the battle of the lava, would earn absolution for their past misdeeds, for their equivocal and dubious past. In the end, in spite of everything, I would have to give the pumps my blessing.

"No Lives Were Lost"

As early as February, people battling the eruption had noticed bubbles in the domestic water supply on the island, as if the water were boiling. Volcanic gases were seeping through the earth to collect in hollows and basements, sometimes via the drains. The few people, mainly salvage teams, who remained on the island were warned not to go about alone and not to lie down to sleep without an open window to admit fresh air.

Many people experienced serious breathing difficulties and nausea. Some islanders, mostly men, whose homes had been engulfed in ash burrowed their way in to try to salvage some of their possessions. The silence down there was overwhelming, they reported. All the noise and commotion outside was muffled by the thick layer of ash. Window glass, if it had not exploded in the heat, had melted and curved inwards. When someone had to descend into a basement, if he was sensible, he took a lighted candle down with him — like a canary in a coal mine. If the candle flame went out at floor level, there was probably a layer of toxic gas there. Sometimes the candle flame seemed to float in the air.

Samples of the gases were sent to Reykjavík to be analyzed by a professor of chemistry, who immediately flew out to Heimaey in a state of agitation. He had concluded from his tests that the composition of the gas was highly unusual, and that it posed a grave danger to the lives of those on the island. It contained not only the toxic compound sulphur dioxide (SO_2), but there was also a large quantity of carbon dioxide (CO_2), which scientists speculated later "may [...] have been released from sedimentary layers with large shell content" when they came in contact with the red-hot lava.[34]

Strict precautions would have to be observed. Guidelines for avoiding the dangers of the toxic gases were read aloud at a gathering on February 14, which was attended by almost everyone on the island. Freedom to move around the center of the village was subject to stringent controls. For a time, the village was practically a no-go area.

In late March the gas pollution reached its peak. The gas was not confined to basements, but also collected in other low-lying areas. Sometimes people walking through the village found themselves passing through a cloud of invisible toxins, only known by the fact that their hearts raced and they had difficulty breathing. Some said it was like walking into a glass wall. All they could do was make for higher ground and take some deep breaths. Cats and wild birds fell victim to the deadly gases, and in low-lying places car engines sometimes choked and refused to restart. People were advised to keep away from the high-risk spots, but that was not always practical. Work had to continue on, cooling the lava and building up protective barriers. On occasion people who were overcome by the fumes had to be given oxygen or transported hastily to Reykjavík for treatment. On the other hand, a physician on the island felt that people were being careless about the dangers of the toxic gases and reported that some people even thought the gas pollution was just a myth.

---

34 Ármann Höskuldsson et al., "Eldstöðvar í sjó," in *Náttúruvá á Íslandi: Eldgos og jarðskjálftar,* ed. Júlíus Sólnes (Reykjavík: Viðlagatrygging Íslands/Háskólaútgáfan, 2013), 424.

Sigurgeir Örn Sigurgeirsson, known as Össi, was not one of the firewalkers, but rather a fisherman. He did not fall prey to the flowing lava or the volcanic bombs, but to the odorless and invisible deadly gas. He was thirty years old. Originally from Reykjavík, Össi had lived on the Westman Islands for some years and married a local girl, though by this time the couple had split up. Össi was one of the crew on a fishing vessel known to have gone ashore on Heimaey on March 22. When the boat was ready to sail out again, he failed to reappear, and some days later the newspapers reported that he was missing. Abandoned houses and basements were searched. There were few indications of where he had gone or what he had done. Perhaps he had gone over to the mainland without telling anyone he was leaving, but it seemed more probable that he remained on the island.

Össi's parents and six siblings on the mainland anxiously awaited news of him. He had told them many times how much he liked life in the Westman Islands and urged them to visit and experience it for themselves. His father called the authorities every day for news about the search for his son. On April 4, firefighters using breathing apparatus that enabled them to search gas-filled premises found a body in the local pharmacy. Össi had clearly lain there for days. The newspaper reported:

> The first death has taken place as a result of the volcanic eruption in the Westman Islands. Sigurgeir Örn Sigurgeirsson, a missing crew member from the *Sæunn VE*, was found dead in the local pharmacy. His death is believed to have been caused by toxic gas. The pharmacy was searched yesterday, as the local doctor reported having noticed someone in the pharmacy the last time he was there. After a thorough search of the premises, Sigurgeir's body was discovered in one of the rooms.[35]

Sometime after moving to the Westman Islands, Össi had suffered severe burns in an accident at sea. He never fully recov-

---

35 "Kæruleysi gagnvart gaseitrun," *Vísir*, March 26, 1973.

ered, and he became dependent on pain medication. When he came ashore after his last fishing trip, according to the later evidence of a friend, he went to the abandoned pharmacy to search for painkillers. Volcanic ash was piled high up the walls of the building, and Össi clambered in through a window on the upper floor. He must have noticed the dead silence inside the building, described by many islanders. Once inside he was able to open a trapdoor down to the ground floor where the drugs were stored. Before entering he had tied a string to the window where he came in, so that he would be able to find his way back out. But he never returned. As he descended into the airless ground floor, where toxic gases had displaced all the oxygen, Össi must have instantly lost consciousness.

I don't recall meeting Össi and I only recently learned about his case. Like many others I have sometimes proclaimed the official line, "No lives were lost." Very little has been said or written about this sole victim of the eruption. Press reports of the only disappearance during the eruption are few and brief. Even after the circumstances of his death were known, there was little coverage of the matter, beyond a report that a man had succumbed to toxic gas in the pharmacy. Perhaps the silence was partly because he had been in the village without permission. For safety reasons, fishermen were not free to wander at will. In addition, he had broken into the pharmacy intending to steal drugs. But during the eruption, the usual rules did not necessarily apply, as fuel tanks, for instance, were broken open with impunity. When food supplies on the island were running low, two village councilors doing salvage work broke into a grocery store to get something to eat. Vehicles, too, were seized as necessary, as owners left them behind on the quay with the keys in the ignition as they were evacuated to the mainland, and rescue workers made use of them as needed. The eruption transformed the Westman Islands into a sort of socialist collective, where everyone was equal and there was little respect for private property. The normal rules of commerce were in abeyance, and money was largely irrelevant.

Some people may have felt that the death of the young fisherman had nothing to do with the eruption. Yet Össi was living under the same conditions as the other islanders, in the shadow of the volcano. The *Sæunn VE,* on which he was a crew member, had evacuated thirty islanders to the mainland on the first night of the eruption, and Össi may well have been aboard on that journey. He had been a fisherman on Westman Islands boats before and during the eruption. He had lived there, married, and made friends. The accident at sea had led to his addiction to painkillers, but it was the volcanic gas that killed him. The cause of his death was the eruption.

Össi slipped, as we say metaphorically in Iceland, "between the ship and the dock." Used literally, the term refers to the kind of accident which may take place when a seaman is returning to his vessel late at night. Misjudging his step on the gangway, he may literally slip down between the ship and the dock, to be swallowed up by the sea. Had Össi died doing salvage work or fighting the advancing lava, no doubt his memory would be honored. Instead, he slipped from view.

But he was not quite forgotten. His death was a major shock to the authorities in charge of operations on Heimaey. The Civil Defense committee on the island was gravely concerned about his disappearance. When the initial search efforts had yielded no results, they asked the rescue teams to search again in all the likely places in the village, including the pharmacy. But it is far from surprising that the islanders buried such unpleasant news in the depths of their unconscious. Such a tragic event was best committed to oblivion, under the layers of ash and lava. As time passed people could say, with no conscious dishonesty, that no lives were lost in the eruption.

One of Össi's shipmates wrote a brief but heartfelt obituary, not simply bidding farewell to an outsider who had been passing through:

> My dear friend, I bid you a fond farewell. But the memory of a good companion and friend will live on, though death has divided us for now. [...] You brought brightness wherever

> you went. [...] Your honesty was remarkable. [...] We were together in the Westman Islands for many years, and there we experienced the natural catastrophe, and saw our beautiful thriving community overwhelmed by a volcanic eruption and lava. I would never have thought, when we were at the Fire Mass in Landakirkja, that the end was so close. [...] We, your shipmates aboard the motor boat *Sæunn* VE 60, thank you for the time we have spent together this winter, and we will miss a good and trusty shipmate.[36]

The day of the Fire Mass, March 22, when the islanders came together in the church to pray, was the day Össi came ashore. After the Fire Mass he was never seen again. Perhaps he headed straight for the pharmacy in search of something to ease the pain of his own burns, and the new pain of seeing his island in flames, with no indication of how long the disaster might go on.

"Outsiders"

After the mass evacuation to the mainland on the night of January 23, many Westman Islanders returned to retrieve what they could of their possessions and their homes, to clear ash off the roofs to reduce the risk of collapse, and to participate in the salvage effort. They were joined by many others, including students I had known at university in Reykjavík. But by mid-April new rules came into effect. Anyone who went to the island — whether as part of the salvage efforts or for other reasons — was subject to strict controls. Civil Defense in Reykjavík issued permits for staying on the island, while local officials were in charge of enforcing the rules and monitoring people's movements. Locals, like everyone else, were issued a serial number and a badge, to distinguish them from those who had no business on the island. The word "outsider" acquired a new meaning. My father had been an outsider, growing up in another part of the country. Yet he had been a Westman Islander, part of the community, until

---

36 Steinar Ágústsson, "Sigurgeir Sigurgeirsson — Kveðja," *Morgunblaðið*, May 8, 1973, 53.

he moved away. The label had always been flexible, as Islanders came and went. Now, however, you either had a permit, or you didn't. It no longer made any difference whether you were a Westman Islander born and bred.

Passenger transport was easily monitored, but the same was not true of seamen, who sometimes went ashore without the necessary permit. Under pressure from Civil Defense in Reykjavík, the district commissioner in the Westman Islands issued a notice requiring every person who went ashore on Heimaey to report to the police. In addition, the harbor would henceforth only be open during the day. Civil Defense authorities on the island were tired of fishermen coming ashore at all hours of the day and night, whenever it suited them. Some pointed out the irony of the fact that the rules were designed, at least in part, to ensure the safety of the seamen when they were on the island. But by April the eruption seemed to be winding down. The dangers appeared much reduced, and in addition seamen were better placed than most people to get off the island in an emergency, as was demonstrated on eruption night, when the fishing fleet evacuated all the islanders at almost no notice.

The district commissioner's press release was sent out to all media. At about the same time, reports were published of looting on the island, particularly from storage facilities at the dockside. The seamen concluded that they were being accused of theft. After playing a vital role in the rescue efforts at the start of the eruption, they were now being portrayed as criminals in print and broadcast media.

The same day that the commissioner's announcement was made public, Páll Zóphóníasson, who bore much of the responsibility for security and salvage on Heimaey, learned that seamen had agreed amongst themselves to all sail back to harbor. The police instantly responded, halting a crowd of angry men headed for the district commissioner's office. Páll made his way between the buildings until he heard the uproar of ten or fifteen police officers, including the police chief facing down nearly 100 shouting seamen. Páll did not like the look of the situation.

Among the fishermen were some well-known strong men, eager to pick a fight.

Páll was a young technical engineer who had been living in Denmark for ten years, and had foreseen staying there, but changed his plans when he was offered the job of municipal engineer on the Westman Islands, just a month before the eruption of Heimaey.[37] It was a life-changing decision. Now he cautiously advanced towards the mass of angry men and tried to make himself heard. But the noise and commotion made that impossible. Accusations flew on both sides, and it looked as if a brawl might break out. Páll, fearful of what might happen, managed to reach the police chief and ask him for a private word. They withdrew from the fray to confer. They agreed that the police would back off for the moment, while Páll tried to negotiate with the seamen. After a heated discussion, the seamen agreed to Páll's suggestion that they nominate three men to go and meet with the district commissioner. They would all turn around and go back to their vessels, and in a little while the three representatives would meet Páll on the quay, and they would go together to the district commissioner. They did so, and the dispute was successfully resolved. A statement was issued that the seamen now had freedom of movement.

It is impossible to say what might have happened, had Páll Zóphóníasson not intervened. The dispute had looked likely to escalate into something from a Western movie, or an Icelandic saga of good versus evil, rebels versus authority. It was all part of the Battle of Heimaey. On one level the dispute was a matter of citizenship, though the revolt of this small and homogeneous group was hardly comparable with the nationalistic confrontations that had long plagued Europe and torn apart old-established nation states. Even so, if the eruption had continued on longer, more outbreaks of this nature might easily have taken place.

---

[37] This account is based on Páll Zóphóníasson, "Þegar sjómenn gengu á land," speech, Westman Islands, April 4, 1993.

Some Westman Islanders were financially secure, while others lived in poverty. Many of the islanders had strong bonds with the homes they had built, or where they had grown up. Others did not. Some wanted a chance to put down new roots and start over. Others did not. Children were particularly vulnerable. While the eruption was in full force, 910 children and teenagers from the Westman Islands were invited to Norway for two weeks, under the auspices of the Norwegian Red Cross and the Icelandic Association in Norway. No doubt, this relaxed some of the pressure on their parents and their hosts on the Icelandic mainland, but under the circumstances it may also have created additional anxiety.

New relationships with the earth gave rise to new pressures. Many bonds were sundered by this seething volcano, when families and friends were scattered. Some islanders salvaged their goods, but never returned to the island and had to settle for a distant relationship and virtual membership of their island community. Some marriages could not withstand the strain. Some new relationships were formed in that melting-pot of activity. Some young people found their life-partner on the very first night of the eruption, and although there was no talk of engagement, let alone marriage, at that point, the sea journey to the mainland sealed the bond.

In time some of the islanders became unwelcome outsiders. The permits and badges were disconcertingly reminiscent of the rise of nationalism in Europe, only decades before. And the islanders had much in common with the environmental refugees of the twenty-first century: stripped of their rights, denied citizenship, and forced to break their bond with their place on Earth. I think of herders in Africa forced out by drought, hunters of the far north forced out by the melting of the ice, each suddenly having to adapt to a different way of life. Some have nowhere to go, no footing on the earth. Others find new hope for the future.

VICTORY

Late on the evening of Easter Sunday, April 22, the watchmen at the edge of the Eldfell crater gave warning that a new tentacle of lava was unfurling directly east, across pastures and farmland. People rushed to the east of the island to watch in awe as the powerful lava flow plunged off the cliffs into the sea. Some of the lava flowed westwards, towards the harbor and the town, where it stopped, met by water pipes and solidifying lava. The cooling operation had worked, and the harbor had been saved. The Battle for Heimaey had been won.

At that moment the sceptics who had dismissed the pumping effort as "nonsense," as just "pissing on the lava," fell silent. Þorbjörn pointed out that just that single spurt of lava would have been enough to lay waste the heart of the town and fill the harbor. People came together to celebrate after long weeks of strenuous effort. No speeches were made, no banquets were held, but everyone involved felt a welcome sense of relief, even though the eruption had not yet died down. That moment was in truth the victory. Rather than the "end of the eruption," it was that day that was the crucial day of the eruption. Afterwards, the cooling effort was gradually scaled down.

One of the consequences of the lava-cooling operation was—to quote American writer John McPhee, who visited the Westman Islands in the 1980s and published a *New Yorker* article about the battle with the lava in 1989—a specific kind of rock: "Among the natural patterns of lava flows, it was utterly anomalous. In a very real sense it was man-made."[38] The idea of the new geologic Age of Humans had not been codified when McPhee wrote that succinct description, but his use of "man-made" lava is a telling example of human impact on the face and infrastructure of the Earth.

New and historical connections with Earth were being forged here. On Surtsey, the approach had been different. Ac-

---

38 John McPhee, "Cooling the Lava," *The New Yorker*, February 22, 1988, 142–43.

cess to that island, after it suddenly appeared out of the sea in 1963, was prohibited to all but scientific researchers. A decision was made to exclude humans from this natural laboratory in order to observe its evolution. In contrast, on Heimaey island every effort was made to tame the emerging landscape in the interests of the human population of the island, to shape the lava and ash to humanity's needs. Many years later related disputes would arise, where the traditional boundaries between human society and the landscape took on new forms. Opinions differed widely, for example, with respect to harnessing geothermal energy or building hydroelectric power plants in Iceland's uninhabited wildernesses, as well as the desirability of restricting visitor numbers at popular natural attractions and historic sites.

The End

Eventually Eldfell calmed down and stopped erupting without any human intervention. The final day was June 26, 1973, though Westman Islander Hlöðver Johnsen, who had been assisting the geoscientists, didn't declare it as being over until three days later. In his memoirs, he wrote that it had been "mainly wishful thinking": June 29 was his wife's birthday, and the end of the eruption made a "nice birthday present."[39] He added that, although he did not feel he had the "standing" to declare the volcano officially dead, he did it anyway. Then he got hold of a rope, with the intention of entering the crater to ascertain that truly nothing was happening there anymore. Hlöðver was renowned for his sprang technique, his skill in climbing down cliffs on ropes to collect seabirds' eggs in the Westman Islands tradition. When Þorbjörn, the volcano's unofficial spokesman, returned to the Westman Islands on July 2, Hlöðver was waiting for him: "I told him everything was ready—I'd taken the rope up to the crater, and we should just go straight on down." At that moment the end of the eruption was officially set in stone. The two men took gas masks, a walkie-talkie, and asbestos socks. Wrote Hlöðver:

---

39 Hlöðver Johnsen, *Bergið klifið* (Reykjavík: Almenna bókafélagið, 1986), 222.

> I slid rapidly down the rim of the crater; it was damned hot at the top and there was quite a lot of steam rising, but as I went lower there was less heat, no discernible gas, and I felt better and better with every step down I took. The rope didn't reach quite to the bottom — I had underestimated the depth — so I ran down the last bit and gave a cheery wave to Þorbjörn, who wasted no time clambering down the rope. Then more people followed. We sat down there in the bottom of the crater — which wasn't even warm. We had a chat [...], and photos were taken, and Þorbjörn suggested that we ought to put some tents up and camp out there overnight.[40]

Photographs taken on the occasion by my old schoolmate Guðmundur Sigfússon, not suprisingly, show apprehension in the faces of some of those who took part in this highly unusual expedition. Guðmundur recounted the event in a press interview the following day:

> We went down at about ten last night. The idea [...] was to take readings of temperature and gas at the bottom of the crater, but that proved unnecessary [...] Down at the bottom the air quality was good [...] We had taken asbestos garments with us, in case [...] we needed them, but we left them behind, because there was no need, far from it. We estimated the depth of the crater at about 30–40 meters from the rim. The bottom itself is about 3–4 meters in diameter.[41]

"It was a wonderful feeling," added Guðmundur. The following day, July 3, Westman Islands Civil Defense issued a statement that the eruption was over.

Joy was unconfined in the Westman Islands. The relief was overwhelming, and people gathered down at the harbor to celebrate this keenly anticipated day. Fireworks were fired in the direction of the volcano, and sparklers were lit. The time

---
40 Ibid., 222–23.
41 "Eigum við ekki bara að tjalda hérna," *Vísir*, July 3, 1973.

had come, people were thinking, to start moving the islanders back home and reconstructing the village, time to adapt to the changed environment. On July 7 the last of the pumps were turned off. Six million cubic meters of seawater had been pumped onto the lava, about as much water as cascades every three hours or so over Dettifoss, one of Iceland's most magnificent and voluminous waterfalls.

According to an American geological report, this was "the greatest effort ever attempted to control lava flows during the course of an eruption."[42] It is possible that some parts of the town that were engulfed in lava might have been saved had the primary emphasis not been on protecting the harbor. Could the cooling of the lava have saved my childhood home, Bólstaður? Towards the end of the eruption some geologists maintained that if powerful pumps such as those provided by the Americans had been deployed earlier, dozens of homes might have been saved. There were many ifs and buts, and the outcome was not perfect, but the crucial point was that the harbor was not destroyed by the eruption. In fact, it was improved, providing better shelter for ships and seafarers.

Humans have long worked with rock and stone of various kinds — sometimes on a gigantic scale, as in tunneling and mining. But this was a historical first, humans toiling as the rock was forming in the midst of an eruption.[43] Humans had altered mountains before by building cairns on them, cleaving them asunder, or leveling them. But now it had been proved possible to stop a mountain in its tracks, to halt the famous Wanderer, which had sped down the lava flow towards the harbor, as if intending to sail away.

The Twin Island: Hawai'i

The story of the successful lava-cooling operation on Heimaey spread like wildfire around the globe. Journalists and scholars

---

42 McPhee, "Cooling the Lava," 144.
43 Gísli Pálsson and Heather Anne Swanson, "Down to Earth: Geosocialities and Geopolitics," *Environmental Humanities* 8, no. 2 (2016): 149–71.

visited the Westman Islands in order to ascertain for themselves what had happened and to tell the stories. Individuals who had directed the operations were invited to share their experience to assist in places where similar challenges were faced. Some of the leaders of the Heimaey project went abroad to talk about the lava-cooling exercise. Geologist Þorleifur Einarsson was invited to New Zealand and Valdimar K. Jónsson took part in a seminar at Penn State University in the US, where he had worked for several years before the eruption. Little is known of these events. At Penn State, Valdimar apparently spoke about *A Volcano in Town*.

The subject was naturally interesting to the Americans, as Hawai'i is one of the most active volcanic regions on Earth, and eruptions there often endanger human habitation. "Iceland and Hawaii in a sense are twins. They are geophysical hotspots, the two most productive in the world," wrote John McPhee.[44] In that sense, the two islands, on opposite sides of the globe, are bound together by a special connection, as are the people who live there. Today the "twins" seem to have even more in common than before. The tourist industry, which plays an important role for both, is predicated upon the attractions of fresh lava fields and active volcanoes, along with the appeal of exotic tales of ancient warriors. People flood to these hotspots in the millions, like a flow of glowing lava, in a quest for adventure — to escape something at home, or something inside themselves. On the largest island of the Hawai'ian archipelago is a young volcano, Kilauea, meaning "spewing," which has been erupting almost continuously since 1983, to the delight of tourists and geologists. Kilauea was the very volcano that farmer Einar of Skammadalshóll had been reading about in between scrutinizing his soot-seismograms in the weeks before the Heimaey eruption.

---

44 McPhee, "Cooling the Lava," 159. On tourism in Hawai'i, see Wells Tower, "The Hawaii Cure: A First Trip to the Island, in a Desperate Bid to Escape the News," *New York Times Magazine,* March 21, 2017, https://www.nytimes.com/2017/03/21/magazine/hawaii-travels-escape.html.

Could the Hawai'ian islanders learn from the experience of the Westman Islands? After the Heimaey eruption, US military engineers considered storing water in a reservoir, which could halt future lava flows in Hawai'i. The islanders did not favor the idea, feeling that it would be better to do as the Westman Islanders had done and cool the advancing edge of the lava flow with seawater. In 1986 firemen in Hawai'i tried to save a building by spraying the lava with water from nearby fire hydrants, but the lava flow was too powerful.

Although it was not clear they would do any good, the US authorities were interested in large-scale engineering solutions, while the islanders themselves tended to apply other approaches. In Hawai'i it was an ancient custom to present a *lei* or floral garland to dangerous lava fields, or bring offerings of food, tobacco, or gin to placate them and Pele, the volcano goddess. Such rituals are not unlike the Fire Masses held in Iceland. Were the engineers' pumping operations no more than magical rituals too?

The authorities in Hawai'i had also tried other military actions in their battle against advancing lava, sometimes in face of opposition from the local people. In 1935 bombs were dropped on the Mauna Loa volcano, but no conclusions could be drawn about their effectiveness, as the eruption came to an end shortly afterwards. In 1942 bombs were once again used against an erupting volcano when the lava flow headed for the historic town of Hilo, where the first Polynesian settlers on Hawai'i had landed between 300 and 800. The bombs split the lava flow into two, but the streams reunited farther down the mountainside. While Hilo was saved, this experiment, like many others, yielded limited benefits, and posed major questions. The situation was uncertain, and on occasion it seemed clear that one district of the town would have to be sacrificed in order to save another.

During the Cold War the superpowers used bombs to display their might. In 1958 the US Air Force launched Project A119, with the objective of exploring the impact of detonating nuclear bombs on the moon.[45] The bombs the US had in mind were of similar magnitude to the Hiroshima bomb. Nothing came of the plan, but the project remained top secret for 45 years. The Soviet Union was hatching similar plans.

The idea of bombing the crater rim on Heimaey was one of the first three responses of the team of experts called together by the University of Iceland's Science Institute on January 23. It was given consideration, then postponed, and after more debate finally rejected.[46] Municipal engineer Páll Zóphóníasson declared on February 7 that using explosives to divert the lava flow would be absurd and that the islanders would never approve such a bombing, which could in any case have unforeseeable consequences and might destroy buildings which remained undamaged from the eruption.[47]

The story goes that a crucial voice in this debate was that of Stirling Colgate, an American who visited Heimaey and worked with Þorbjörn for some days. Colgate was a complicated man. The heir of the toothpaste corporation of that name, Colgate campaigned untiringly around the world against the growing power of the sugar corporations and the consequent impact on dental health. He was also a professional physicist, and worked for many years at the Los Alamos laboratory, which housed the Manhattan Project and yielded the atom bomb. Now he was on a tiny island in the north Atlantic, watching over a volcano through a February night, closely observing the glowing lava and estimating the possible impact of bombing the crater rim. In the early morning, having finished his calculations, he met

---

45 Richard Sandomir, "Leonard Reiffel, Who Studied Lunar Nuclear Bomb, Dies at 89," *The New York Times*, April 26, 2017, https://www.nytimes.com/2017/04/26/us/obituary-leonard-reiffel-nuclear-bomb-moon.html.
46 Stirling A. Colgate and Þorbjörn Sigurgeirsson, "Dynamic Mixing of Water and Lava," *Nature* 244 (1973): 552–55. See also "Report of Dr. Stirling Colgate and Prof. Charles B. Moore to the Science Institute, University of Iceland, in cooperation with Prof. Þorbjörn Sigurgeirsson," February 26, 1973.
47 "'Leyfum ekki sprengingar,'" *Vísir*, February 7, 1973.

with the rest of the team and made his recommendation: "For God's sake, don't bomb it!"

There appeared to be a risk that a manmade explosion in Helgafell could lead to a chain-reaction, and thus spark a far more powerful explosive event, arising from the interaction of molten lava, water, and steam — something like the massive explosive eruption of Mount Krakatoa in Indonesia in 1883, one of the biggest eruptions in historic times. On the second day of the Krakatoa eruption water flowed into the crater, causing a gigantic explosion. About 36,000 lives were lost, and the mountain and the surrounding land subsided into the sea, setting off tsunamis which wreaked havoc on the neighboring islands of Java and Sumatra.

The physicists' calculations indicated that Heimaey might explode as Krakatoa had done, setting off a chain reaction in the same way. Less heroic measures would have to suffice here, though it was not clear in advance what the consequences might be. It was probably advisable to steer clear of Cold War posturing.

After the eruption was over, Westman Islanders recalled that in 1958 General Electric had submitted a proposal to Iceland's State Electric Power Works for construction of a small nuclear power station on Heimaey island.[48] Looking back, we were glad nothing came of that idea.

Dramatis Personae

Volcanoes possess enormous power, which many people have found out for themselves. As a rule, a volcano will have its own way, whatever humans or other creatures try to do. The volcano on Heimaey, which sent a vast mass of magma from the depths pouring out over streets and fields, into the sea and over houses, is obviously the main character in the drama that took place in the winter and spring of 1973. But many other actors had joined it on the stage, and even upstaged it. The role of the pumping

---

48 Björn Kristinsson, "Kjarnorkuver fyrir Vestmannaeyjar: Lýsing á tilboði General Electric," unpublished manuscript, 1959.

equipment and the pipes that crisscrossed the glowing lava fields was key. The ungainly, noisy, polluting pumps at the harborside had already performed years of service when they went on their long journey to the far north.

Þorbjörn Sigurgeirsson and Valdimar K. Jónsson, who were first among equals, were not in the habit of flaunting their achievements on Heimaey. As Þorbjörn looked back, he praised others, not himself.[49] When the pumps had been in action for some days a journalist asked Valdimar, sometimes called the "general" in the lava fields, how a professor who normally spent his time lecturing at the university found himself laying pipes. "You have to be in touch with reality," he replied, "and this has certainly been a huge experience."

A vast number of other people were involved in the effort, teams of men (and one woman) out in the lava field, caterers, mechanics, crane operators, excavator drivers, technical staff, engineers and geoscientists, all striving to make a difference. The plastic pipes, which were such an essential element of the lava-cooling operation, were produced in the workshops of Reykjalundur outside Reykjavík, a rehabilitation center founded in 1938 to battle tuberculosis, where production continued at full capacity to meet the demand. And in Reykjavík metalworkers were kept busy producing replacement spindles of robust steel for the pumps. Not to mention Páll Zóphóníasson and the other officials on Heimaey, as well as those at Civil Defense. And of course, the North Atlantic Ocean that provided the seawater for pumping. The contribution of those whose task it was to save buildings was no less important. A large team of volunteers and skilled tradesmen prevented buildings from collapsing by reinforcing rafters, clearing volcanic ash off roofs, and boarding up windows. Here, as in the lava field, initiative and innovation were key. The whole team, including the volcano, the machinery, the organizations and individuals, the ocean, and many more factors that made their contributions, wrote a new and

---

49 Þorbjörn Sigurgeirsson, "Hraunkæling," public talk, Nordic House, Reykjavík, November 4, 1973.

extraordinary chapter in the long history of volcanoes and the natural calamities that have arisen from them.

In the Heimaey eruption, time may have been the most important factor. Had the eruption gone on much longer, the outcome would have been different. All the efforts made to safeguard the town and the harbor would have been for nothing. And the same applies to our current global rescue efforts. If we do not come to terms with the problem, particularly climate change, the days of Earth as we know it are probably numbered.

Descriptions of the lava-cooling effort are often framed — as I have done — in military terms, as a "battle" or "operation," and the metaphor is an apt one. It reflects the widespread uneasiness in the twentieth century regarding global environmental issues, issues which remain in the spotlight today, more than ever before.[50] Since Heimaey erupted, the global climate has displayed more extreme fluctuations, with towns and cities threatened by flood and storms, and glaciers melting and adding their water to the sea. Humanity, it seemed in the 1970s, could achieve anything, yet the scientific and technological solutions that were available, which were supposed to save mankind from annihilation created new problems and were met with growing criticism. Although nobody knew it then, these are the problems of the Age of Humans.

French volcanologist Haroun Tazieff, who had declared the Westman Islands doomed after a brief visit in February, appears to have left the island without saying goodbye, somewhat to the surprise of the local people. Tazieff returned to Iceland in 1980, during an eruption of Mount Hekla. He made his way up the slopes of the volcano, hoping to make contact with geologist Sigurður Þórarinsson, with whom he had travelled to the Westman Islands in 1973. Tazieff had probably been told that Sigurður would be found, as usual, closest to the eruption site.

---

50 Joseph Masco, "Bad Weather: On Planetary Crisis," *Social Studies of Science* 40, no. 1 (2010): 7–70, at 14; Magdalena E. Stawkowski, "I Am a Radioactive Mutant: Emergent Biological Subjectivities at Kazakhstan's Semipalatinsk Nuclear Test Site," *American Ethnologist* 43, no. 1 (2016): 144–57.

After walking some way up the slope, Tazieff spotted a tent. No one else would think of camping in such a place. In the entrance to the tent, a man with a red cap on his head sat cross-legged with a guitar. Tazieff asked him where the famous geologist might be found and was astounded to learn that it was Sigurður himself in the red cap playing the guitar.[51]

Tazieff has sometimes been described as a reckless adventurer. But, while he may have taken risks in his expeditions, he was not always misguided. Three years after his verdict on the Westman Islands, he took the opposite view in a dispute over another volcano. During an eruption of the Soufrière volcano on Guadeloupe in the Caribbean, a scientist proposed that all seventy-two thousand people who lived in the vicinity should be evacuated. Tazieff disagreed, volubly, and in that case he was right.[52] The authorities ordered the population to evacuate, and they all loaded up their cars and sped along the narrow road out of the mountains towards the nearest city. But the eruption caused little damage, most of which was due to the traffic chaos caused by the evacuation.

Four years after the Heimaey eruption Tazieff published a brief but interesting piece in *Nature* on the subject of eruption predictions. Tazieff points out that geoscientists have often been gravely mistaken, and so it is vital to learn from experience. In the last six years, he writes, the experts' predictions have been wrong at least four times and once was the Heimaey eruption. One might expect Tazieff to expand on that subject, but in fact, he mentions it only briefly and superficially, with no reference to his own mistaken prediction. He writes:

> The third case happened in 1973 during the last days of the Heimaey eruption. Persuaded by a somewhat inexperienced foreign volcanologist, Icelandic authorities agreed to use fire-

---

51 Ari Trausti Guðmundsson, interview, April 2016.
52 "Haroun Tazieff, 83, a Volcanist and Iconoclast on Environment," *The New York Times*, February 8, 1998, https://www.nytimes.com/1998/02/08/world/haroun-tazieff-83-a-volcanist-and-iconoclast-on-environment.html.

boats to sprinkle water on a tongue of the thick lava flows which over several weeks had progressed at a distressing speed towards the harbor entrance. No arguments could prevent the exercise: not even the evidence that the Atlantic [O]cean itself, with all its water, had not been able to stop the main part of the flows which had crawled over the sea-floor for two months.[53]

It is not entirely clear who Tazieff means when he references "a somewhat inexperienced foreign volcanologist." Þorbjörn Sigurgeirsson seems a likely candidate, although he was neither foreign nor inexperienced. And Tazieff appears to know nothing of the big pumps brought in later from the US. Tazieff concludes:

The main lesson […] is perhaps to confirm the absolute necessity for a good volcanological interpretation of all the available […] data before expressing any forecast. Volcanologists, just as medical doctors, should be responsible, skilled, experienced, different specialists closely co-operating with each other. And they should keep as cool as a cucumber.[54]

In 1984 Tazieff was appointed by the French government as Secretary of State for the Prevention of Natural and Technological Disasters. Until the end of his life in 1998 he remained a vocal advocate of environmental issues. In this, as in other matters, he was controversial. The errors and inconsistencies in his accounts of the Heimaey eruption have not attracted particular attention, but in 1991 he caused a sensation when he declared that carbon dioxide in the atmosphere posed no threat, including that ideas about the greenhouse effect were nonsense, that the thinning of the ozone layer was not due to human influence,

---

53 Haroun Tazieff, "La Soufrière, Volcanology and Forecasting," *Nature* 269 (1977): 96–97, at 96.
54 Ibid., 97.

that global warming was an outright invention, and that reports about the dangers of warming were fake news.[55]

Now, more than a quarter of a century later, many people, including powerful politicians and national leaders, despite the overwhelming scientific consensus that Earth is changing in ways that will make our lives more difficult, still dismiss climate change.[56] "Welcome to the trampoline!" the jokers say, as Iceland's glaciers melt and the land lifts, the pressure on Earth's crust is eased, and the magma beneath is released. And increased volcanism is only one of the many challenges we will face in this new Age of Humans.

ACCEPTANCE

The destructive impact of the Heimaey eruption was not confined to the human inhabitants of the island. The entire ecosystem suffered massive damage. As the hot lava flowed into the harbor it boiled the fish alive. Grass withered in gardens and hayfields. Migratory birds which return to the Westman Islands every year to breed were bewildered in the spring of 1973 upon their arrival. They too had lost their footing on the earth. Yet the bird population did better than one might expect. Puffins, which spend the winter out on the ocean waves and return each spring to nest in the same burrows year after year, dug their way down through the thick ash layer to reach their burrows — just as the humans did to reach their homes upon their return. Puffins, whose breeding grounds had been near the lighthouse, now buried beneath a layer of lava rock, fluttered around their old breeding grounds, finding shelter in hollows in the lava. They could not dig down through the lava to their burrows, but they knew where they were supposed to be. In more recent times, as Iceland's puffin population has been decimated by climate

---

55 Bill McGuire, "Obituary: Haroun Tazieff," *The Independent,* February 7, 1998, https://www.independent.co.uk/news/obituaries/obituary-haroun-tazieff-1143330.html.
56 Gísli Pálsson, *The Human Age: How We Created the Anthropocene Epoch and Caused the Climate Crisis* (London: Welbeck, 2020).

change, the little bird has become an iconic symbol of Iceland and a popular souvenir for tourists.

In July 1973, the time had come for the Westman Islanders to decide whether to return to their "Home Island," Heimaey. While the geoscientists were pretty certain that the eruption had come to an end, it was not inconceivable that it might start up again. The toxic gases remained a source of concern for many, especially parents of young children. Some of the evacuees had made a new life for themselves on the mainland, finding new opportunities and adapting to their changed circumstances. They shrank from the prospect of returning to Heimaey, where huge challenges of reconstruction awaited. When the opportunity to return finally arose, many were undecided. They needed encouragement, to be convinced to relocate again. Some islanders briefly visited Heimaey and looked around, only to be sorely disappointed by what they saw.

Clearing and excavating the town after the eruption seemed an insurmountable task, and the new mountain, Eldfell, loomed menacingly over the town it had ravaged. But in time Westman Islanders did start to make their way home. The mayor predicted, only slightly incorrectly, that within a year seven out of every ten islanders would be back. Their roots and history as well as their bonds with the community, the old homestead, and the island's natural life were deep. Like the puffins who returned year after year to breed in their same burrows on the Westman Islands, the Westman Islanders needed to find their old nesting places.

Svanhildur Gísladóttir and her husband were among those who were long conflicted about whether to go back. They had renovated their first home just before the eruption. On their first night there, they had only been asleep for an hour and a half with their one-year-old baby when there came a knock on the door and they were told they must leave at once. Svanhildur was seven months pregnant at the time. After the end of the eruption the family had to make a decision about their future. Svanhildur was keen to arrange their three-month-old daughter's christening, and got in touch with Pastor Karl Sigurbjörnsson, who would in later years be Bishop of Iceland. Karl had served his island flock from Reykjavík, but now he was back on Heimaey. He proposed that the little girl be baptized at the first service in Landakirkja church since the eruption. Svanhildur was hesitant. Wasn't everything still "all black" in the town? The pastor admitted that it was but told her that the weather was beautiful there at the moment. The family flew out to Heimaey and the baby was christened in the church crammed with people.

Svanhildur has a vivid memory of walking into the church with the baby in her christening dress and seeing piles of shoes in the lobby. Most of the congregation was disheveled and exhausted, having labored hard to save what could be salvaged from the lava and ash. Now they had taken a break, wading through drifts of black ash to the church, and they had removed their shoes to avoid dirtying the church floor. When the young couple walked down the aisle with their little girl, tears of joy and relief were shed. There was no turning back. In October, once accommodations had become available, Svanhildur and her growing family returned to Heimaey.

Ash and Lava

The Heimaey that met the returning refugees was different in many ways from the "beautiful isle" that so many poets had lauded. But it was time to make peace with the forces of nature. Gradually, the town came back to life. Every new family that arrived was warmly welcomed. Old relationships were renewed. Life went on. But many faces who had been part of the community were now missing, especially those of elderly people who had felt unable to face moving back, as well as those who had lived in the newer districts closest to the volcano, whose homes had vanished under the lava. About four out of ten islanders never returned home.

The first challenge for those who returned was to clean things up, as the town was buried under a thick layer of ash. The light, fine-grained black dust got into everything, but with mechanical diggers, lorries, and shovels the cleaning progressed well. Between one and two hundred people worked on clearing the ash, starting at the west of town where the ash layer was thinnest, and gradually working eastward toward the districts where houses were completely buried. People came from far and wide to help, including students from Reykjavík, people with family ties to the Westman Islands, and others from all over Iceland who wanted to do their part; military personnel from the US air base at Keflavík; and Europeans and Americans in search of adventure combined with doing a good deed. Misunderstandings sometimes arose, and even cultural clashes. The staff canteen did not offer a large menu, and the diverse group of workers had various culinary customs. Locals, for instance, were taken aback when Americans took *skyr*, a milk curd usually eaten as a dessert with cream and sugar, and used it as a sauce on their meat. And then the sightseers arrived. As one of the islanders remarked: "In the drifting ash we were like Bedouin in the desert; when the tourists arrived we were like penguins in a zoo."[57]

The town emerged from its ashy shroud in record time, as the clearance teams worked on shifts around the clock. As a rule, they cleared one street at a time, and soon had established an effective routine. The mechanical digger drove over the thick ash layer into each individual plot, then scraped the ash out towards the street. There were four men with each digger, and they dug the ash out by hand where the mechanical digger couldn't reach it. Pipes had been welded onto the lip of each digger's bucket, so it scraped the surface without tearing up the grass underneath. Then the ash was loaded on lorries and trucked away.

The ash proved useful on construction projects, especially in the old lava field to the west, where a new district was built. In retrospect many islanders regretted this, wishing that the old lava field had been preserved. A large quantity of the ash was also used at the airport, to lengthen the runway. If Helgafell avenged itself on the islanders for daring to quarry scoria from its slopes, at least it provided compensation in the form of near-endless quantities of grading materials.

---

57 Guðmundur Karlsson, interview, Reykjavík, August 9, 2016.

The new lava field was harder to accept. The lava had engulfed part of the town and flowed out into the sea, enlarging the island eastwards. This was unexplored territory, and it seemed to pose more of a threat. It could not simply be removed, like the loose ash. Islanders gradually ventured up onto the jagged new lava, which was still hot to the touch. Families drove out into the new territory to see for themselves. New landmarks had been formed, in addition to those the firewalkers had named during the eruption. The fine old lighthouse had been swept away, but before long a replacement was built nearby.

Visitors to Heimaey often talked about the impressive spectacle of the eruption, but islanders did not share their delight, focused as they were on the destruction the volcano had inflicted. But, despite that, did the new lava field have a beauty of its own? Some were able to make their peace with it within the year, while others took years to accept it, and still others never did. Sigrún Inga Sigurgeirsdóttir, former chair of the Westman Islands town council, recalls going on a walk with her husband near the edge of the new lava field in 1983. Suddenly she stopped in her tracks and said, "Now I'm home." Her husband gazed at her in perplexity, asking, "What are you talking about?" It had taken her ten years to accept the new face of Heimaey and that evening, she felt that she had "suddenly put down roots, halfway down the mountainside."[58]

In 1978 the thermal energy of the new lava field was harnessed to provide heating for the town. Water was sprayed onto the thick layer of porous ash on top of the new lava, and as it trickled down towards the still-hot layer of lava beneath, it was converted to steam which rose back towards the surface. The steam was extracted and piped to a heat exchanger, where it heated the water in the town's central heating system. The thick layer of ash atop the lava provided good insulation, slowing down the natural cooling process, and the heating system operated for ten years. Using the warmth of fresh lava for heating was unprecedented. The project was a remarkable experiment,

---

58 Sigrún Inga Sigurgeirsdóttir, interview, January 20, 2017.

carried out on the initiative of Hlöðver Johnsen, the man who had declared the eruption "over" on his wife's birthday.[59]

Although everything seemed to be going well, and the eruption's products were being put to good use, many Westman Islanders remained nervous for a long time afterwards. My bridge-playing cousin Lilla, who had witnessed the very beginning of the eruption and had spent many hours being tossed about at sea trying to reach the mainland, did move back to Heimaey but needed some persuading first.[60] For many years afterwards, she was always on edge in late January. "Would it happen again?" she asked herself, though she rarely spoke the words aloud. As the anniversary of the eruption approached, she became more and more restless, and it was not until after 1:43 am on January 23 that she could breathe more easily—at least until the next year. On one occasion when a fire alarm went off, she rushed from the house, along with many others. Her neighbors had thrown a few possessions into a shopping bag, as they had on that fateful night, and run out into the street, prepared to leave for the mainland again if necessary.

When a pile of old tires caught fire on Heimaey, and a column of black smoke rose into the air, many islanders were convinced that the volcano was erupting again. Some still regularly keep up with reports of seismic activity just like weather forecasts. During the two great earthquakes, each a 6.3 on the Richter scale, in South Iceland in 2008, "when the earth undulated like a stormy sea," as one Westman Islander put it, people were shaken, in two different senses. Another eruption of Mount Helgafell seemed to be imminent.

Home Is Where the Heart Is
Geological events are deeply unsettling and personal for those who experience them. They disrupt people's lives, turning them

---

59 Hlöðver Johnsen, *Bergið klifið* (Reykjavík: Almenna bókafélagið, 1986), 216; Sveinbjörn Björnsson, "Nýting hraunhita í Vestmannaeyjum," radio talk, December 8, 1976.
60 Aðalbjörg Jóhanna Bernódusdóttir, interview, Hafnarfjörður, February 2016.

into outsiders, compelling people who have grown up trusting each other, their community, and their environment to leave their homes and move to new and sometimes exotic places, to establish new relationships with the environment and the people already there. In the Heimaey eruption, the bond of the cheerful, hard-working, and resourceful Westman Islanders with their habitat was severed. That relationship was no less important than the bond between fellow islanders. Many homes vanished beneath the lava, while others sustained major damage, some even becoming unrecognizable. A lot of the islanders acquired a new home on the mainland, putting down new roots. This was not easy. Some islanders have said that the eruption ruined their lives. And that is no exaggeration. Although the term was not yet in general use, many were traumatized. Some always heard the rumbling of the volcano as they tried to sleep — in some cases for months, if not years, after the eruption ended. They knew the noise was not real, but that was no help.

My uncle Magnús Bjarnason, who had put his children and mother-in-law on a boat, then turned back to help fight the lava, driven by an "indefinable sense of responsibility," had not cried since he was a little boy. Yet as he watched the splendid electric power station being crushed to dust by the advancing lava, he felt that all was lost. Darkness fell over the town as the electricity failed, and Magnús made his way home past the churchyard:

> As I stood there in front of the lychgate, with its inscription *I live and ye shall live,* something gave way inside me. I leaned against the drystone wall and started to cry [...] I was all alone there in the dark, and I let my feelings out. I turned to God and prayed the most heartfelt prayer I have ever prayed. I prayed for it to be over. I asked questions, as if I stood face to face with Him: Why? And again, why?[61]

Magnús's detailed account of his experience is known to many Westman Islanders. I recently visited him and his wife in a home

---

61 Bjarnason, "Privatissimo."

for the elderly on the islands. We talked about the early bond between our families and the shattering impact of the eruption. Then he added with a mischievous smile that, following his honest personal account of the eruption, his friends had begun to call him "The Man Who Wept."

Occasionally during the clean-up effort, vehicles and diggers that were being driven atop the thick layer of ash would suddenly tumble down several meters into concealed buildings that had tolerated the strain until then. *Has the earth split open?* wondered the shaken drivers as they scrambled back up to the surface of the earth. During the eruption, many of the people involved could make no sense of what they had seen or experienced, as reality gave way to the surreal. Advancing lava might flow uphill, as if the law of gravity were no longer in force. In such circumstances, something had to give. The lychgate, with its message of solace and hope, *I live and ye shall live,* came to be an icon for the life-and-death struggle in progress on Heimaey. It is no coincidence that the lychgate was one of the most-photographed subjects on Heimaey in the spring of 1973.

Trauma counseling and psychotherapy were not yet widely recognized or readily available, and those who had lived through the eruption felt that they must resolve their problems themselves, as best they could. The Red Cross offered counseling from social workers during the eruption, but few people took up the offer. The unwritten rules of no complaining while keeping calm and carrying on were still in force. Perhaps that process of self-suppression was a kind of self-defense, comparable to the cooling of the lava during the eruption. In the Westman Islands that had generally been seen as an effective way to cope with grief, for instance when men were lost at sea, or fell from the cliffs when gathering seabirds' eggs. The islanders had grown up with death always just around the corner, and now the only option was to get on with things and let time heal the pain.

But the two parish clergymen, Karl Sigurbjörnsson and Þorsteinn Lúter Jónsson, realized that their parishioners had a deep need to meet, talk, and pray together. They needed to get their bearings, with the help of God and other men. During the eruption the pastors were given space in a warehouse on the mainland in Reykjavík, along with the evacuated Westman Islands town council and the Natural Disasters Compensation Fund. A café in the warehouse provided a place for Westman Islanders to meet for company and mutual support, and a TV showed live footage from the islands. A tense hush fell as the islanders watched their homes go up in flames, helpless to prevent it. One man could not stop weeping when his home was consumed by the burning lava. A doctor had to be summoned to take care of him.

Iceland's national radio devoted a special program to the Heimaey eruption. Broadcast every evening, it was hosted by two brothers who were Westman Islanders, plus the writer Stefán Jónsson, who had described the wolffish in the aquarium as "divine or demonic." Each show ended with a prayer and the sound of the church bells from Heimaey. The radio show was important to the Westman Islands diaspora and brought them together into an "imagined community" like those that led to the creation of nation states in past centuries. Then it was new print media which crafted these imagined communities and connected people long-distance, people who would never meet in the flesh.[62] Without such media, it is hardly possible to imagine the evolution of strong and united societies.

The morning after the eruption started, psychologist Einar Gylfi Jónsson was sitting down to take an examination at the University of Iceland when he heard the news. Like many Westman Islanders, he initially thought it must be a misunderstanding. Perhaps it was the crater on Surtsey island that was waking up? Then he heard on the radio that all five thousand Westman Islanders had been evacuated to the mainland. His immediate response was to sketch a map of the island, with the fissure and the new crater. He was reassured to see that the town seemed to be in no immediate danger. His parents had reached Reykjavík and had found a place near him to stay. They got in touch later

---

62 Benedict R. Anderson, *Imagined Communities: Reflections on the Origin and Spread of Nationalism* (London: Verso, 2010).

that day. The following days and weeks were a welter of activity, disrupting Einar Gylfi's university studies. He felt he must help out, so he volunteered to go out to Heimaey to assist in saving the islanders' worldly goods from their abandoned homes. When he later received a check in payment for his work on the island, he was affronted: He had gone there as a volunteer.

Einar Gylfi's knowledge of conditions during the eruption and afterwards, together with his clinical experience, led many people to consult him about their psychological issues after the eruption.[63] They did not talk much about the events of the eruption night, and some had only a hazy recollection of fleeing to the mainland. But most had feelings of guilt. They had the idea that they could have reacted differently, could have behaved in another way, that somehow, they were to blame for the eruption. They were not generally eager to delve too deeply into their emotions. If they opened that Pandora's Box, who knew what might fly out? It was a psychological "compromise," according to Einar Gylfi. It did its job, and it worked, up to a point. Ultimately the time came when their defenses crumbled, and people found that they needed to talk through their experiences properly. That shock often only occurred long after the eruption, and out of the blue — like the eruption itself.

Before and After
Today the Westman Islanders' chronology is based on January 23, 1973. "For us, it was always Before the Eruption and After the Eruption, not BC and AD," remarks my old schoolmate Jóhanna Helena Weihe.[64] During the Eruption, the interlude between Before and After, was a strange and troublesome time. It was a rootless, timeless period in which most of the islanders were far from home, out of touch with their roots, yet constantly thinking of home, and consumed with anxiety. No doubt many of those who were far away felt they had failed their island in some way, even regretting not being there to share in their neighbors'

---
63 Einar Gylfi Jónsson, interview, Reykjavík, December 2016.
64 Jóhanna Helena Weihe, interview, June 2016.

ordeals. Perhaps this feeling of guilt is why many Westman Islanders feel compelled to recall the eruption.

Most of the evacuees who arrived by sea at Þorlákshöfn harbor on the night of the eruption were transported straight to Reykjavík by bus. There, a range of new challenges awaited. More than five thousand "new" townspeople had to be registered, and basic necessities had to be provided. Many of the refugees were able to stay with friends and relatives, while others were housed by strangers who had opened their homes. Within hours all the islanders had a place to stay. Some received assistance from the Natural Disasters Compensation Fund. Many found work, and all twelve hundred children were guaranteed a place at school.

Still, the islanders missed the social safety net they were used to. Often pure chance determined where people found themselves, whether it be in the Reykjavík area or farther away, living in other people's homes, in a poky basement, or in a comfortable new house. The community of the Westman Islanders stretched all around the country, anticipating the virtual reality of more recent times. The community was real, yet nowhere and everywhere, nebulous, mutable. In addition to other challenges, some families had to settle for being separated for weeks or even months. Many of the men went back to Heimaey to save their own possessions and those of others, to try to safeguard the assets of the town and its businesses, to cool the lava, and finally to sweep the fallen ash from homes and buildings. If some buildings collapsed under the strain, doubtless the same was true of some families.

At the beginning of the eruption the Westman Islanders were bombarded with help from other Icelanders. But as time went on there was something of a backlash. The islanders encountered resentment, even hostility, in schools and workplaces, and out on the streets of the city. "You've done well out of the eruption," scoffed some resentful voices. "You've got compensation for your homes, and then some, haven't you?" Such reactions resemble those that environmental refugees have encountered recently in the US and Europe. They may be welcomed with impressive ceremonies at borders and in airports, with speeches and toasts, yet as time passes their hosts may have second thoughts.

"What Boat Were You On?"

The future is uncertain, but the past is fixed and immutable, though new generations may view it differently. In the Westman Islands, as in other places that have experienced natural disasters, people have a strong need to remember past events, to erect monuments, and to write down the story, even though it will never be told in final form.[65] One year after the eruption came to an end, hundreds of people gathered in the new lava field that lay over my first habitat, Bólstaður, where a brass band played. Over the years, the annual End of the Eruption event has grown into a major community festival, with a range of arts performances, educational seminars, and talk of the eruption and related subjects. In this way the islanders nurture their memories and rejoice that the story ended well.

The Eldheimar, "Home of Fire," Volcano Museum plays a vital role in these community acts of remembrance. For many Westman Islanders, the opening of the museum in 2014 provided a welcome opportunity to face the pain that the eruption entailed. Some found they had tears in their eyes as they examined for the first time the wealth of objects on display from the eruption, as the recorded din of the volcano thundered from loudspeakers. Thousands of people now visit the museum every year. As in Pompeii in Italy, which was engulfed by a thick layer of volcanic ash from Mount Vesuvius in 79 BCE, visitors to Eldheimar can

---

65 James Hamilton, *Volcano: Nature and Culture* (London: Reaktion Books, 2012); Karen Holmberg, "Beyond the Catastrophe: The Volcanic Landscape of Barú, Western Panama," in *Living Under the Shadow: Cultural Impacts of Volcanic Eruptions,* eds. John Grattan and Robin Torrence (Walnut Creek: Left Coast Press, 2015), 274–97; Lisa Hill, "Life after the Volcano: The Embodiment of Small Island Memories and Efforts to Keep Montserratian Culture Alive in Preston, UK" *Area* 26, no. 2 (2014): 146–53; Felix Riede, "Volcanic Activity and Human Society," *Quaternary International* 294 (2016): 1–5; Sri Warsini et al., "Living through a Volcanic Eruption: Understanding the Experience of Survivors as a Phenomenological Existential Phenomenon," *Mental Health Nursing* 25 (2016): 206–13.

look inside a home that was abandoned in haste in the middle of the night on January 23, 1973 that has been excavated from the ash. Displays include visual material about the eruption and a wealth of information about the events. It is possible to see which buildings, when and in what order, were destroyed by the eruption — a subject of fascination to both Westman Islanders and other visitors.

Another monument to the eruption is a virtual one, existing only on the Internet. Ingibergur Óskarsson, now an electrician on the mainland, was a nine-year-old boy when he fled with his family to Þorlákshöfn aboard the *Leo*. Long afterwards he started to compile information about the fleet of fishing vessels that had transported the islanders to safety that night, including the names of the crew and passengers on each boat, and the stories they told. He sent questionnaires out to Westman Islanders and appealed on social media for information on their experiences.

Forty years after the eruption, with the anniversary receiving extensive media coverage, Ingibergur's information-gathering took off. Many islanders sent him detailed information about themselves and their families, as well as photos and accounts relating to the evacuation, and Ingibergur put all this information online.[66] The vast majority of the evacuees are now documented on the right boat, and the website has become a valuable source regarding the fateful events on Heimaey and the journey to the mainland on the night the eruption began. At social events in the Westman Islands, one often hears the question: "What boat were you on?" Now the answers are accessible online. More and more stories are being told and increasing numbers of people want to hear them.

Helgafell Returns

Jóhanna Hermannsdóttir, the owner of the historic painting *Helgafell's Revenge* which seemed to anticipate the Heimaey eruption, has always maintained a strong connection with the

---

66 Ingibergur Óskarsson, "1973 - Allir í bátana," https://en.1973-alliribatana.com/ingibergur.

Westman Islands, despite decades living in the US, a connection, she has often argued that "runs through" the iconic painting. I learned about Jóhanna and her painting during one of my visits to Heimaey and arranged to call her in the US. She knew my mother from her early years and remembered my house and my grandmother well, known for their close bond, occasionally strolling together in the village, well dressed and hand in hand. This was news to me; I was deeply touched and could easily imagine the scene.

I was aware of the fact that the Westman Islanders wished *Helgafell's Revenge* would someday return "home." During one of our discussions, I asked Jóhanna if she might donate her painting to the islands. The question wasn't prepared, and I was surprised that I raised it out of the blue. But Jóhanna responded without hesitation. She would be happy to give it away, to be shown and taken care of by the Art Museum of the Westman Islands. Afterwards, I thought to myself, why would I engage in such negotiations, stepping in front of the camera, so to speak, changing the course of these events that I was only recording and describing? Should the narrator place himself right into the scene? In the autumn of 2017, Jóhanna formally donated the painting to the Westman Islands.

Several Westman Islanders, on Heimaey, on the Icelandic mainland, and abroad, including Ambassador Stefán Haukur Jóhannesson, facilitated the painting's return. Stefán used an opportunity between sessions at the United Nations Assembly in New York to visit Jóhanna in New Jersey, along with his wife and a couple of friends, to fetch the painting and to present Jóhanna with Icelandic gifts. For all who were present, the event was particularly moving. *Helgafell's Revenge* was officially received at a large public gathering on Heimaey in January 2018 (fig. 24). Jóhanna's son, Helgi Hannesson, who lives in Iceland, was present to receive thanks and flowers from the community.

In the summer of 2014, I was passing close to Manchester University, so I seized the opportunity to revisit the place where I had first learned of the eruption on Heimaey island more than forty years before and to reimagine how I had reacted to the

Fig. 24. Guðni A. Hermansen, *Helgafell's Revenge* (1971). Photo by Sigurgeir Jónasson.

news. The obvious first step was to call in at the library and trace that article in the *Evening News*. The sight of the Central Library, in a graceful circular building by St. Peter's Square in central Manchester, brought back fond memories of my three years as a student in the city. The librarians were quick to retrieve the news report in question, which was stored on microfilm. They offered me a digital copy. It was a strange experience to re-read the newspaper after all these years, and the feeling of dread seemed to well up — although this time I knew how the story ended.

The press report was largely as I had remembered, although my memory had played some tricks on me. In retrospect, I am not at all sure that I walked past the electrical goods store in Manchester on the very day that the eruption began. Surely film of the eruption could not have reached British TV on the same day. And I am not certain that the store window with its bank of new color TVs was on the left-hand side of the street. Nor that it was dark when I saw the colorful images. And so on. But in my mind, that was how it happened, all in one day.

REFOUND LAND

Westman Islanders after the eruption perceive their islands as "refound land." In the words of poet Gyrðir Elíasson, "[i]t is the land which was found / and lost / and found again."[67] The islanders had to get to know a changed island, to resettle there and relearn it.

Shortly after the end of the eruption, in August 1973, I visited Heimaey with my wife, Guðný, and another couple. I hadn't been home for four years, and now the place was unrecognizable. Much of the island was still carpeted in a thick layer of ash. We stepped out cautiously onto the new lava, on which all eyes had been focused earlier in the year. In the middle of our walk it started to rain, and instantly we were surrounded by clouds of steam rising from the hot lava and blocking our view. We thought back to the lava-cooling operation and the people who had been working here a few months before. We didn't want to risk getting lost so, we turned back towards the town.

The few people we saw in town were restoring order, clearing the ash and excavating buildings. We peeked into some wrecked buildings, some still hot indoors, with the smell of the ash strange and pungent. Then we got to Bólstaður. Scattered here and there at the edge of the lava field were tattered fragments of the house that had been leveled by the lava at the beginning of April. Unexpectedly, I had a feeling of emptiness. My childhood was gone, buried under rock and lava to become part of geological history. Under the thick layer of lava that now concealed the former site of Bólstaður, dozens of people had lived, rested and slept after long days at work, made love, played, told stories and said prayers, and made lives for themselves. Before we left for Reykjavík, we went up onto the Heimaklettur cliffs and looked out over the new lava, the columns of steam that rose from it,

---

67 Gyrðir Elíasson, *Tvífundnaland* (Reykjavík: Mál og menning, 2003), 62.

Fig. 25. On Heimaklettur soon after the end of the eruption, 1973, l–r: Guðný S. Guðbjörnsdóttir, Gísli Pálsson, Jóhannes Þorsteinsson, and Valgerður Einarsdóttir.

and the streets that had narrowly escaped destruction (fig. 25). The sun had come out, and we sat down on the grass and the volcanic ash.

I knew before I made my visit that Bólstaður had fallen prey to the eruption, so the event itself was not a huge shock, and I had never before missed the old place. The traces of the house that could be glimpsed, between lumps of rock, made its former location clear. But although the map coordinates were obviously the same as before, this was no longer the same place. Some neighboring houses had been spared, although the distinction between one garden and another, jealously guarded by the neighbors from incursions by unruly children, had been erased. The house that stood west of Bólstaður, called Jaðar, stood untouched, and still does today. Its name, which means "Edge" or "Boundary," proved more apt than anyone could have foreseen.

The house my parents had built on Nýjabæjarbraut, "New Town Street," where they had lived until they left for Reykjavík four years before the eruption, did not vanish suddenly like Bólstaður, but died a slow death. A spacious, modern brick house, it stood farther up in the town than Bólstaður, much closer to the volcano, and it was gradually engulfed by ash. By the end of the eruption most of the houses in the "New Town" district were buried under the ash and people could walk on their roofs — it looked like a barren black wasteland. My parents' house on Nýjabæjarbraut has not been excavated, and its fate does not touch me in the same way as the disappearance of Bólstaður, even though I had taken part in its construction, put up formwork, built walls, pulled nails from timber, and painted the house, inside and out. Perhaps my second home on Heimaey is best described as a seasonal dwelling, as I only lived there in summer months as my studies took me away from home. My parents naturally lamented the demise of the home they had built for themselves with such effort, but not in the same way that they mourned Bólstaður. The enchanted rock Friður in front of their house was buried under the ash, although its shape can still be traced. Nature herself had violated her own sanctuary, disrupting the lives and homes of the elves or Hidden People whom my grandmother, and no doubt many others, had observed from afar.

Brothers

In recent years, I have often walked on Eldfell on Heimaey, strolled along the stretches of new lava, onto Mount Wanderer (which finally settled down), into the depth of the crater, and along its smooth edges. The new lava with its changing contours and shifting colors continues to amaze me. I wonder what the striking blue colors will be named: true blue, glaucous blue, royal blue, steel blue? Perhaps all of the above. On a good day, the view to Eldfell's siblings, the volcanoes beneath Eyjafjallajökull and Surtsey, is spectacular.

On a recent visit to Heimaey in 2017, I travelled with my brother Karl, usually called Dalli, who is twelve years younger than me. We both knew that this would be his last visit, although we did not speak openly about it. Half a year earlier, he had been diagnosed with brain cancer, glioblastoma, an incurable disease. He was slowly losing speech, memory, and emotions, as if a huge cloud of volcanic ash was busily burying his life and history, but he was still able to travel and was eager to join me. He had bought a new car, perhaps challenging his predicted fate, and meant to enjoy his last months in this world. We drove slowly along the southern coast of Iceland and took the ferry to Heimaey from a new port. Instead of the four-hour crossing of 1973, it now took only about half an hour to travel from the mainland to the island.

I was reminded of my very first trip abroad, in 1971, when I had traveled to Copenhagen with my other brother, Sigurður Þór. Four years my junior, Sigurður Þór was diagnosed with a brain tumor when he was a student. I went with him to Denmark for an operation. I kept him company, spoke with his surgeon in my flawed Danish, and relayed the bad news home, walking to the Central Station to make the call. It was impossible to remove the tumors, but radiation therapy might work. If Sigurður Þór survived the year, he would beat the disease, but he did not.

Copenhagen was strange and cold to me and I had little money. A damp, bitter winter wind chilled me to the bone, but I had friends in the city who were good to us both. The highlight of my stay was a concert with Crosby, Stills, Nash, and Young. They presented *Déjà Vu,* one of the best albums of the century. The auditorium was packed, filled with the distinct smell of marijuana.

Sigurður Þór was a lively boy who got up to various shenanigans. Unlike most of his peers he wrote poetry, both rhyming and free verse, about love, hope, space travel, the Vietnam War, Uncle Sam, and the world's shame; they were published posthumously. In an untitled poem, probably his last, he wrote:

> Now rings out a new song,
> a bright new song of freedom
> of love,
> hope,
> life.

I'm going to
find Guðfinna
in the New Year.[68]

Sigurður Þór had foreseen his own death, personified with the feminine name of *Guðfinna*, "Godfinder," and come to terms with mortality. His illness and death were "the worst thing that happened to us," as my mother said when she recalled her life in her final years; "but I've had a very good life," she added. His death truly was a cataclysm.

Now another cataclysm awaited my family. I again felt a deep sense of impending doom and heard in my mind the strains of Crosby, Stills, Nash, and Young's *Déjà Vu*. Dalli seemed to enjoy the trip, though he said little. Sometimes he began a sentence or two, but invariably he gave up mid-course, missing the point or out of words. We visited relatives on Heimaey, stopped by the graves of our grandparents, and explored the new lava. Half a year later he was gone. The cancer had spread throughout his frontal brain, like a subterranean magma flow preparing for a violent eruption.

Dalli had always been a quiet person, thoughtful and considerate, always available for our sisters Auðbjörg and Lilja and myself. During his last years, he had erected a log house, virtually single-handedly, on a relatively recent lava flow under Mount Hekla. His last ambition was beekeeping, something unheard of under Icelandic volcanoes. Dalli was down-to-earth in the fullest sense.

Professionally, he was an electronics engineer and programmer. One of his early jobs was to work with geologists to establish a system of sensors to monitor Icelandic volcanoes. During his last years, he managed the machines that track and regulate air travel across the North Atlantic. He had witnessed the Eyjafjallajökull eruption of 2010 both from the ground and from high above, so to speak, with the bird's eye view of electronic

---

68 Sigurður Þór Pálsson, *Skriðið úr skrápnum* (Reykjavík: Bókbindarinn, 1972), 47.

monitoring of ash clouds and the sudden interruption of air travel.

The impending loss of my brother affected me more than I had ever imagined. We had always been exceptionally close. Early on, I had been his mentor and role model and later, the relationship tended to be reversed. Two months before he died, I experienced unprecedented nausea. As I got up in the morning, I would lose my balance, forcing myself to sit up straight for a few seconds or to crawl out of the bedroom until I figured out which way was up and which way was down, as the world seemed to swirl endlessly around me. This occurred every morning for weeks. My doctor told me it was a relatively harmless condition called "Benign Paroxysmal Positional Vertigo" (BPPV). She asked me to throw myself down on a bench several times, alternating from left to right, and I left her office an hour later reasonably balanced but a little seasick. Sudden vertigo occurs, she explained, as the otolith organs, the mineral stones in our inner ears, are rearranged, scrambling our sense of space. Why had the stones spoken?

The reason was most likely emotional trauma, triggered by the tragic fate of my brother Dalli. It mattered too that my other brother, Sigurður Þór, had died in 1971 from the same condition, glioblastoma. I tracked down his medical records from the state hospital, about eighty pages of horrid reading. Somehow, my study of his records reminded me of reading the seismographs preceding the Heimaey eruption and the diaries of the firewalkers on the lava. I soon learned that the disease was not genetic, and that losing two brothers to the same rare condition was a striking coincidence. My sisters and I still requested brain scans and were relieved to know that we had no tumors.

Volcano Collection in the Garage
The scientists who went to the Westman Islands on the first day of the eruption, after their emergency meeting at the Science Institute in Reykjavík, along with their colleagues who followed, accumulated large quantities of equipment and tools as the eruption progressed. Many of these items are now stored as

monitors, thermometers, rock samples, cameras, reels of film, and more in a garage in an elegant old district of Reykjavík. The collection is dusty and uncatalogued, and few of the items are labelled. Much of the equipment has long been obsolete, yet people are reluctant to get rid of it. It tells the story of a unique eruption and efforts by Iceland's leading geoscientists to explore and understand the nature of the eruption, how it progressed, and its impact on the community.

This remarkable collection is not open to the public. When geophysicist Leó Kristjánsson invited me into this world in 2016, I remarked that these objects should be on display in the Eldheimar museum on Heimaey. Leó just smiled. He handed me a big plastic bag crammed with spools of film. I was instantly excited. These films had probably never been viewed, at least not so far as Leó knew. There were thirty spools of varying sizes, most still in their metal or cardboard cases. Most were color films, hastily labelled. There was sometimes a note of the date and time when the filming began, but little information on their content. Several cameras, Leó told me, had been installed far above the eruption site on places like the Heimaklettur cliffs, which commanded a good view of the new crater and the lava flow. The person in charge of the camera had carried it up the mountain, set it up to cover a certain view, started it, and then walked back down into town, to return several days later to retrieve the film. This bag of films thus consisted of time-lapse sequences. When the first camera was installed, on the tenth day of the eruption, no one knew how long the eruption would go on, or what the consequences would be. Some of the geoscientists on Heimaey had never operated a movie camera before. Still, the photo sequences ought to make it possible to observe the progress of the eruption, and to answer the question of what it was like to have a volcano in one's living room.

I borrowed the bag of films and studied them in the company of geologist Ari Trausti Guðmundsson, who had worked on the island as a young man and written about the experts' bewilderment. Sadly, many of the films are blank. Sometimes the camera toppled over, or the lens was obscured by ash, rain, or snow, or

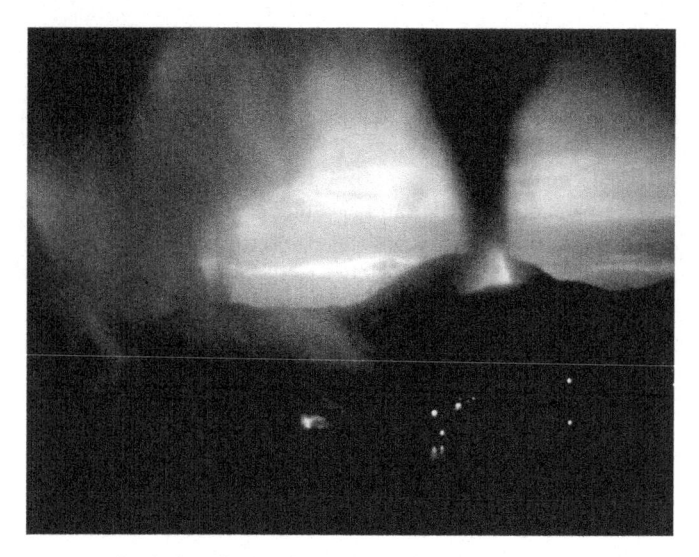

Fig. 26. A "time-lapse" photo taken during the Heimaey eruption. Courtesy of the Science Institute, University of Iceland.

the battery ran down unexpectedly. We picked five spools and had them scanned, so that we could work with them in digital form. In total, the footage came to about twenty minutes, representing several days of the eruption.

The viewpoint is of course different from what people saw down in the lava field and the town. And the film is silent, far from the roaring of explosions in the crater, the groaning of the advancing lava, and the drumming of the ash raining down that existed. It is extraordinary to watch twenty-four hours pass in two or three minutes on the computer screen. The column of lava and ash is flung up in an instant, and the red-hot lava surges down towards the sea (fig. 26). In the winter darkness, car lights are seen speeding around town, as people check on their houses, cool the lava, get something to eat, and get to bed. Clouds build up in the sky and are gone. And then a new day begins.

Leó told me that he had three lava-bombs from the Heimaey eruption. No doubt he often glanced up in the heat of battle, to dodge out of the way of one of the flying red-hot bombs expelled

Fig. 27. Bomb, "LK 27.3. HOT," six kilos. Photo by Kristín Bogadóttir.

from the depths. He seized these three bombs either boiling hot or glowing red, freshly "cooked." I told him that if the bombs were homeless, I would be quite prepared to take one of them in. Leó probably found my offer incomprehensible, and who could blame him? I'm not even sure why I felt this desire to have one of those lumps of rock. Perhaps what appealed to me is that they had been in human hands from the moment they were born. That is not something a rock can generally expect. Leó soon saw that I was serious. "You can have all of them," he said, and I gratefully accepted.

At the garage, Leó placed the lava-bombs in my care and I promised to look after them well. They are remarkable souvenirs, if that is the right word, taken from the molten mass beneath the earth in a historic eruption (fig. 27). They still carry a faint smell of volcano, one I recognize from my visit in 1973. I am sure the odor would call up mixed feelings for the firewalkers who spent months in a life-or-death battle.

The smallest of the three bombs, and the most irregular in form, fell on June 17, Iceland's National Day. Around it is tied a bright yellow ribbon on which is written: BOMB FROM CRATER — GLOWING — ABOUT HALF. The other half was left behind on the lava field. Another, a little larger and remarkably heavy, is neatly spherical. It is labelled: 27–28 MARCH — SECOND. Perhaps Leó had to get out of its path as it fell and caught it at that very moment. The third, the largest by far, weighs six kilos. Streamlined by its flight from the crater, it has the oval form of a rugby ball. The surface is strangely smooth, as if shaped by human hands. On a dark-green tape Leó has written LK 27.3. HOT. It must have been bizarre to dodge such flying missiles. The largest bombs flew through the air dropping in clusters shortly after the Fire Mass in the church. Perhaps, rather than seeing it as adopting these bombs, I should see them as heirlooms that serve to confirm my relationship with Eldfell and the Westman Islands.

The Key

In the early twentieth century, fish-houses were a striking feature of Heimaey. They were gone by my time, but I remember seeing photos of them. They heralded the new, modern era of fishing from motorized vessels. With abundant fishing grounds nearby, the Westman Islands' fisheries boomed. The fish-houses were sheds tightly clustered together on wooden docks above the sea. Wheelbarrows loaded with fish and other goods were pushed through narrow gaps between the buildings. When the boats came in laden with fish, there was a flurry of activity around the sheds.

The cottage at Bólstaður included ownership of such a fish-house, listed in the 1916 valuation of the property. That was where my grandfather Sigurður and his crew gutted and cleaned the catch after a day at sea and it was probably also used to store oars, fishing gear, and so on. Grandpa's fish-house was a vital part of Bólstaður, and when it was not in use, it was kept locked. Now the key to that lock is all that survives from Ból-

Fig. 28. The key from Bólstaður. Photo by the Author.

staður — apparently by pure chance. The story of the key is also the story of the eruption.[69]

My cousin Siggi, the only crane operator on Heimaey at the time of the eruption, had watched as a huge lava-bomb landed on Bólstaður and the old house disintegrated. Siggi is something of a legend in his own time. His colorful *curriculum vitae* includes carpentry, diving, aviation, various business enterprises, the fisheries, and musical composition. Long-haired and bearded, Siggi is cheerful and fun and has a good memory and plenty of stories to tell. In about 1990 a friend of his, Sigurgeir Sigurðsson, brought him a brown paper bag. Inside it was a rather large old copper key (fig. 28). Sigurgeir's conscience had been troubling him, as he had taken the key without permission. He asked Siggi to keep their conversation confidential.

Sigurgeir had worked for many years on Heimaey for the state telephone company, and on occasion he had to go to the Steinasmiðja machine shop. He would pass through a jumble of machinery and equipment coated in soot on his way to the offices on the upper floor, as was natural in a busy machine shop at that boom time in the fisheries. From one of the rafters hung a key. He noticed it but paid no particular attention.

---
69 Sigurður Óskarsson, interview, August 2014.

One night during the eruption in 1973, Sigurgeir was working in the street near the machine shop. The building was clearly doomed. Sigurgeir went inside. He suddenly remembered the key he had noticed long ago. The lava was creeping ever closer to the building, and under such circumstances most people would have given little thought to trifles such as an old key, who knows for what lock? Most people would have grabbed something more valuable from the machine shop, but Sigurgeir went straight in, took the key down, and shoved in his pocket, giving it no more thought.

A long time later, when the eruption was over, he cleaned up the key to examine it. When he had removed the dirt and soot, he saw that it was a skillfully wrought copper key with the word BOLSTAD engraved on one side. This must be the key to a fishing-house, he thought. Since Bólstaður had belonged to Siggi's grandfather, the key should go back to Siggi.

Siggi was fascinated by the story but protested that he could not agree to keep it confidential, as there would be little point in having the key without the story. So Sigurgeir agreed that the story could be shared, and Siggi rang my mother. Hearing the description of the key, she remembered it, adding that Sigurgeir's father and Grandpa Sigurður were "terribly good friends." They used to meet up every weekend and Sigurgeir's father even worked for Grandpa Sigurður, cleaning the catch in the fish-house.

Sigurgeir must have had some kind of premonition when he sought the old key out at the height of the eruption, saving it at the eleventh hour from the lava — for it was that very night that the machine shop disappeared. The key had been taken there for repair long before, and forgotten, as Grandpa Sigurður had given up his fishing boat by then.

Today the key has pride of place on the wall of Siggi's summer cabin, not far from where our grandparents grew up in the lowlands of south Iceland. Perhaps the key to Bólstaður, which unlocked for Siggi and me the little world of our forebears in the cottage on Heimaey island, can also symbolize the door that we all stepped through as we entered the modern age. Through that door, we step into an Earth that we hardly recognize, yet have shaped by our own actions.

EPILOGUE

I had been asking around for some time among Westman Islanders if anyone had photographs of the last moments of Bólstaður. I felt an obligation to seek them out. Bólstaður was where my mother "birthed me in the bed," and was the scene of many of my childhood memories. My requests had rummaged up a number of shots of the neighborhood around the time Bólstaður went up in flames. But all were taken from a distance. The picture quality was not good and Bólstaður was not in the foreground. Steam and ash obscured my view of the scene.

When I had almost abandoned hope, an image of Bólstaður in flames appeared on social media. The photographer was my boyhood friend Eiríkur. He had made a brief trip back to Heimaey with his father to check on the family's home and had taken his camera along. He had walked around our childhood haunts, taking photos of what he saw. From the balcony of a shop near the harbor, he looked over the town. He noticed that the lava had advanced across what had been the square at the junction of Heimagata and Vestmannabraut, and was nearing my house, Bólstaður. He lifted his camera and clicked the shutter. Realizing that things were happening fast, he hurried out and walked towards Bólstaður. He stood in front of my house, watching the flames take hold (fig. 3, p. 22).

Just minutes after Eiríkur took his photo, Bólstaður was gone, burned then buried under lava. The only person present at the moment of Bólstaður's passing was Eiríkur, with his camera. I think it likely that Eiríkur's photo of the last moments of Bólstaður influenced me to start writing this book. I was so deeply affected by that image. The words were eruptions within me, and to paraphrase novelist Jón Kalman; they were "magma" that had to come out.[1]

In all probability the modern Age of Humans will give rise to a whole new literary genre, with accounts of people's circumstances and struggles in the Refound Land that we have created — when people are uprooted, only to face the indifference of authorities, the self-interest of corporations, and recurring environmental disasters.

One of the most important tasks in writing is always to keep in mind the times and spirit of the age. This can be challenging, owing to the vested interests of the powerful. In the latter half of the twentieth century, tobacco producers clamored to tell people that there was no danger from smoking, which has proved to be untrue. Now powerful people around the world are trying to sweep under the carpet facts about global heating, silencing those who monitor the situation, as if the scientific community does not exist or is misguided. American biologist Donna Haraway points out that it is imperative to demand that all who write should "situate" themselves, explain their backgrounds and what they stand for; they cannot expect to be listened to without doing so.[2] Otherwise there is insufficient trust. The poet Jorge Luis Borges expressed a similar idea in his well-known autobiographical essay *Borges and I*, describing his own duality of simultaneously being both the author Borges and "the

---

[1] Jón Kalman, *Eitthvað á stærð við alheiminn* (Reykjavík: Bjartur, 2015); See also Oddný Eir Ævarsdóttir, *Land of Love and Ruins*, trans. Philip Roughton (New York: Restless Books, 2016).

[2] Donna Haraway, "Situated Knowledges: The Science Question in Feminism and the Privilege of Partial Perspective," *Feminist Studies* 14, no. 3 (1988): 575–99, at 589.

one things happen to," adding, "I do not know which of us has written this page."[3]

Who has written this book?

Even if authors are entirely willing to disclose their own context and interests, they are always subject to limits. Sometimes it is said that theories in the humanities are not objective, as they directly influence their subject matter. Theories about economics and politics, for example, shape the society that they are intended to illuminate. It is different for theories about the natural world. The Earth goes its own way, irrespective of any theory advanced. But is that always true? The concept of the Anthropocene, the notion of the geologic Age of Humans, drawn from geology, has already become a geological force, a tool to direct attention to environmental problems of the present, and to resist them. In the light of increased knowledge of humanity's influence on the planet, it is time that people discussing the Earth provide full disclosure.

I have maintained that those in charge of the narrative should identify themselves, so to speak. And their identity, their habitat, is the Earth itself. Terms like *earthquake, fault,* and *plate boundaries* are in common use, and it can be helpful to apply them when discussing the forces at play in the human world. I sometimes use geological turns of phrase to describe the society that has bred me. The closeness of the Earth is to some degree relative, circumstantial, but humanity's connection to the Earth, on the other hand, is chiseled in the material world and in us — petrified, fossilized, solidified — including in our bones, otoliths, and gallstones.

Now and Then

Intimacy with the Earth has taken on a new meaning. Humankind is in the strange position of both reading and recording its future in the layers of rock. It is not completely clear what this will mean. How does time pass and how can we know about

---

[3] Jorge Luis Borges, *Labyrinths: Selected Stories and Other Writings* (New York: New Directions, 1962), 246–47.

it? Icelanders, like many others, struggled with time long before Albert Einstein and his colleagues began to talk about relativity and the curvature of space and time. In Iceland, as elsewhere, our best friend for millennia, the moon, divided time into convenient units of days, months, and seasons.[4] For a long time, though, the uncertainty of time gnawed away at Nature, both in Iceland and elsewhere in Western civilization. Europeans assumed that the history of humankind was theirs alone and even resisted the idea that nature had its own history. The human theatre changed constantly, but the Earth itself stood outside time as a giant stone collection, a memento.

Although the Earth had its own history and its own monuments, the story of the Earth was separate from the human world and obeyed its own laws.[5] Faculty divisions of Western academia and university planning departments kept watch over such dualism, as though it were etched in stone. Human history and the history of the Earth ticked in time with different clocks. In recent decades many advocates for the humanities have questioned this dichotomy. It has been pointed out that it is based on relatively new Western ideas about the separation of culture and nature which hamper an understanding of many of the things that typify the present time. Now geoscientists have unwittingly turned over a new leaf, removing divisions between the Earth and Humanity, virtually at a stroke. Human chronology and the history of the Earth seem to have coalesced at last.

Indian historian Dipesh Chakrabarty, who works at the University of Chicago, has drawn attention to the inequality that accompanies climate change; some Earth-dwellers suffer more than others from global warming, and that must be addressed from the viewpoint of human rights. However, Chakrabarty argues, this is problematic: "We have run up against our own limits as it were […] if we, collectively, have also become a geo-

---

4   Bernd Brunner, *Moon: A Brief History* (New Haven: Yale University Press, 2011).
5   Bronislaw Szerszynski, "The Anthropocene Monument: On Relating Geological and Human Time," *European Journal of Social Theory* 20, no. 1 (2017): 111–31.

physical force, then we also have a collective mode of existence that is justice-blind."[6] Perhaps we should be grateful that Mount Helgafell tempered justice with mercy and that the volcano itself served as "a barrier and buffer" to the new fault, sparing most of the village. It could have been so much worse.

Many things lie forgotten, covered by time's ash layers. The ash from volcanoes sometimes hides memories of past events so completely that nothing can be known about them. A good example is the ancient Roman port of Pompeii. It was not until 1784 that Pompeii was excavated, leading to the realization that it held a precious testimony of human society and the physical remains of two thousand citizens who had died in the eruption. These tableaux from long ago have proved invaluable historical sources about civic planning, architecture, social structure, and people's homes, left just as they were when Mount Vesuvius erupted, and the people breathed their last breath.

In May 2005, I walked among the ruins of Pompeii, marveling at the beautiful streets and ornamentation, and the achievements of the people who had excavated the city. In the nearby city of Herculaneum, also engulfed by Vesuvius, around three hundred papyrus scrolls were preserved. Discovered in 1752, they were immediately recognized as important examples of literature from "before the eruption," as Westman Islanders would say, perhaps shedding new light on ancient times. This discovery of a large library of scrolls was celebrated. Perhaps it is comparable to finding a whole shelf of "new" manuscripts by Snorri Sturluson, Emily Dickinson, or William Shakespeare. But the manuscripts from Pompeii were petrified. The text was literally written in stone, like the commandments entrusted to Moses, but they could not be read. The keepers of the scrolls in the past three centuries have generally resisted the temptation to break the stone apart, trusting that at some time new methods would unlock the content. Only very few stones from the Hercula-

---

6 Dipesh Chakrabarty, "Postcolonial Studies and the Challenge of Climate Change," *New Literary History* 43, no. 1 (2012): 1–18, at 14.

neum library have been destroyed. They were sawed open or bathed in acid by avid and curious would-be readers, to no avail.

Now a way seems to have been found to get into the stone without causing damage.[7] Using x-ray technology, it has proved possible to "unroll" the petrified scrolls, "open" them, and read parts of them digitally. Although much work remains to be done, specialists believe that most of the manuscripts are written in Greek on philosophical themes. Some of them are copies of works by philosopher and poet Philodemus, who lived two centuries before Vesuvius erupted and was known for his ethical theories. Perhaps the voice of Philodemus, preserved in stone for such a long time, holds good advice for a world in trouble.

More often than not, volcanic ash has destroyed all evidence of context and place, as if time has been erased. But ash itself can be a timeline. Repeated volcanic eruptions, depositing ash in stages across an area, can divide history into periods, comparable with the labels of the Viking Age, Renaissance, and Enlightenment that annalists and historians tend to refer to. The science of tephrochronology, literally meaning "ash dating," developed by geologist Sigurður Þórarinsson in the 1940s based on the then-available knowledge of volcanic eruptions, is now widely used by archaeologists.[8] If an eruption is mentioned in historical sources, the ash layer (tephra) associated with it can be used to date human artifacts and remains.[9] In the absence of historical records, chemical analysis of the ash and comparison to the ash layers found in the Greenland ice cores can be used to date the eruption, and thus the archaeological finds.

The fossilized remains of "Lucy," *Australopithecus afarensis,* one of the earliest known representatives of humankind, were

---

7 Richard Van Noorden, "X-Rays Reveal Words in Vesuvius-baked Scrolls," *Nature,* January 20, 2015.
8 Sigurður Þórarinsson, "Tefrokronologiska studier på Island," Doctoral dissertation, University of Stockholm, 1944; Sigurður Þórarinsson, *Heklueldar* (Reykjavík: Sögufélagið, 1968), 5.
9 Karen Holmberg, "The Cultural Nature of Tephra: 'Problematic' Ecofacts and Artifacts and the Barú Volcano, Panama," *Quaternary International* (March 2015): 1–19.

found in Ethiopia in the 1970s under a layer of volcanic ash where they had lain for over three million years. The anthropologists who excavated her bones are said to have been listening to the Beatles song *Lucy in the Sky with Diamonds,* which explains the name she was given.[10] The remains, hundreds of fossilized bone fragments that have been labeled AL 288-1 on the shelves of the Ethiopian museum that keeps her, proved to be of a woman. It has been suggested that she died by falling out of a tree. Although the ash hides what lies beneath it, volcanoes frequently work like irrepressible annalists. A comparison of the tephra on which Lucy rested and the ash which later fell on top of her made it possible to estimate when she lived. In Laetoli in Tanzania, footprints of primitive humans of the same species as Lucy were recently found. They had walked through volcanic ash millions of years ago, and their footprints held and preserved important information about their gait, physical build, and more.[11] Thanks to volcanoes, time sometimes becomes elastic.

Although many recent technological innovations have caused great consternation, they are not all bad. Some innovations provide a clearer view of a world that might have been thought to be a closed book forever, and thus enhance our understanding of the problems and opportunities that humanity faces. Ice cores from Greenland and the Antarctic ice cap are preserved to this end. Sometimes the freezers in which the ice cores are stored don't work as they should. Ill-advised politicians may even turn off the power. Then there is a risk that the history archived in the ice cores for thousands of years, of erup-

---

10 Gísli Pálsson, "Celestial Bodies: Lucy in the Sky," in *Humans in Outer Space: Interdisciplinary Odysseys,* eds. Luca Codignola and Kai-Uwe Schrogl (New York: Springer, 2009), 69–81.
11 Fidelis T. Masao et al., "New Footprints from Laetoli (Tanzania) Provide Evidence for Marked Body Size Variation in Early Hominins," *eLife,* December 14, 2016.

tions, humanity, and variations in temperature and atmosphere, will gurgle down the drain.[12]

Volcanic Birthday

In 2003, an American artist named Ilana Halperin issued an open invitation to a 30th birthday party for herself and Eldfell, on Heimaey island. She wrote on her website: "Hello! I am writing to cordially invite you to the 30th birthday celebration of myself and Eldfell volcanic cone. […] You may be asking yourself if I am serious about this invite and the answer is absolutely yes, as let's face it, you and a landmass only turn 30 at (almost) exactly the same time once! All the best and see you at the crater!"[13]

Halperin lived and worked in Glasgow but had come to Iceland a few years previously and, thinking about how to celebrate her 30th birthday, had suddenly decided that the only thing to do was to go to the Westman Islands. She didn't know why, but the idea came to her when she visited her father in Maine in 2003. He had been diagnosed with cancer. His illness raised new and persistent questions about closeness and roots, topics frequently addressed by Ilana in her art.

Some of her friends said that they'd love to accompany her to the Westman Islands, it was a great idea, but they could not go just then. But a Scottish friend replied that she would attend and came to Halperin and Eldfell's birthday. The friends spent three days on Heimaey, hiked into the crater with a birthday cake and candles, drank a toast, and touched the ground to feel the warmth still within the lava.[14] It was a windy day and the candles struggled to stay lit up there on the mountain, but the cake tasted good. It was yellow, shaped like a banana, and made from

---

[12] Tatiana Schlossberg, "An Ice Scientist's Worst Nightmare," *New York Times*, April 1, 2017, https://www.nytimes.com/2017/04/11/climate/ice-cores-melted-freezer-alberta-canada.html.

[13] Ilana Halperin, interview, April 14, 2016.

[14] Ilana Halperin, "Ruins in Reverse (Nomadic Landmass)," lecture series at Whitney Museum of American Art, Astrup Fearnley Museum of Modern Art, Manchester Museum, Camden Arts Center, 2005–6.

EPILOGUE

Fig. 29. Ilana Halperin, *Eldfell*. Courtesy of Ilana Halperin.

several layers of cream, chocolate, and marzipan. The women studied the "tephra layers" of the cake, to the last crumb.

Some months later Halperin's birthday happening found a manifestation in her art, and her works about her connection to Eldfell and her intimacy with the Earth were shown widely (fig. 29). They are lyrical pieces that remind people of the indispensable comradeship of the Earth, of global connections and life's coincidences. Halperin returned to Heimaey to celebrate her birthday again ten years later. On that occasion she was even more aware, she says, of the companionship of "her" mountain for all those years. It was, among other things, Halperin's ideas about intimacy with the Earth that encouraged me to think about my roots in certain mountains.

Geologic intimacy is neither trivial nor an exotic, mere thing of the past. In 2017, New Zealand granted a sacred mountain, Mount Taranaki on the North Island, the same legal rights as a person. This was done in response to demands by Maori tribes for respect for their place and identity, as apology for breaches of treaties and broken promises, and as protection against the growing harms of tourism. For the Maori, Mount Taranaki, a well-formed volcano that last erupted in 1775, is close kin, a member of the family.

The Last of the Great Auks

Like the lava cooling on Heimaey, the modern holistic emphasis on the planet Earth per se has its roots in the Cold War. The Cold War arms race and its associated technologies encouraged people to view the planet in a new light, as an integrated thing. For the first time it was possible "to imagine a truly planetary crisis."[15] The attention of geoscientists was, for example, directed towards the spread of radioactive material around the world.[16] The idea of planetary crisis has undermined the prevailing consensus in many fields that the Earth is silent and stable, or that it can be totally ignored.[17] The industrial revolution brought not only new types of connections between people but also resulted in new relations with the Earth. For a long time, humanity maintained that the pollution concomitant with coal-burning factories and gas-powered engines was simply an unfortunate side effect, with an impact that would be negligible in the long term. Later it became clear that industrialization permanently affected the Earth, inside and out.

The effects of the industrial revolution on the Earth are part of the *longue durée,* on the historians' timescale. In recent years, however, industrial processes of many kinds have had a much sharper impact. Fracking, a process in which liquid is forced into the Earth to facilitate removal of oil or gas, has initiated earthquakes that would not otherwise have occurred.[18] Utilization of geothermal energy in Iceland and elsewhere has a similar effect. These and other drilling and mining processes have

---

15 Joseph Masco, "Bad Weather: On Planetary Crisis," *Social Studies of Science* 40, no. 1 (2010): 7–70, at 9.

16 Ibid., 17.

17 William L. Ellsworth, "Injection-Induced Earthquakes," *Science* 341, no. 6142 (July 12, 2013): 1225942.

18 Julia Adeney Thomas, "History and Biology in the Anthropocene: Problems of Scale, Problems of Value," *American Historical Review* (December 2014): 1587–607.

spoiled drinking water in many places, as lead and arsenic pollution is a serious problem. Mechanized agriculture can also cause the Earth's crust to move, as it exploits vulnerable water sources; for example, in California, part of the San Joaquin valley has subsided by almost five centimeters a month due to such practices.[19] The outcome in many places is drought and water shortage. Many people around the world suffer from acute water shortages, with some places' droughts that last for years and increasingly frequent disputes about access to water.

When I was a boy in the Westman Islands, rainwater was drained off roofs and piped into a cistern in the yard. When that supply failed, water had to be fetched from a communal spring. My father sometimes drove a water tanker, and I went with him on many trips around town, when he pumped water into the cisterns. Perhaps we were a bit like the *bunustokksmenn,* the flowpipe men, who years later pumped water onto the lava threatening the town. When dirt collected in the cisterns they had to be opened and cleaned. Children gazed in terror into the gaping holes. During the Surtsey eruption, our rain gutters got blocked by volcanic ash, and I was given the job of periodically clearing them. One summer Dad and I worked at laying water pipes from the Eyjafjöll mountains on the mainland, down to the coast, where they were linked up with undersea lines. These have supplied the Westman Islands with freshwater ever since. Once again, the Westman Islands is a microcosm of global problems. No community can thrive without a supply of clean water.

Nor are people the only victims of this new geologic age, the Age of Humans, even though we have named it after ourselves. One characteristic of environmental debates is a growing concern about the fate of other species. These are not new concerns, as the fires that farmers and hunters lit to make their lives easier thousands of years ago probably led to the annihilation of many

---

19 "California Drought Causing Valley Land to Sink," NASA, August 19, 2015, http://www.jpl.nasa.gov/news/news.php?feature=4693.

species, and others are known to have been hunted to extinction.[20]

Some species, like dinosaurs, leave a record of themselves in the stratigraphy of the planet, while others silently bid farewell unnoticed. American artist Julianne Warren has made an interesting work titled *Hopes Echo,* which directs attention to the fate of the huia, a peculiar bird species which was exterminated in New Zealand in the early twentieth century.[21] Sound recording was in its infancy when the last huia died, and its song was never recorded, but nevertheless it has been etched in vinyl, with that song, the heart of Warren's art installation. The Maori people had a tradition of luring these gorgeous birds by mimicking their song. These impersonations were preserved generation-to-generation, and eventually, in 1954, a recording was made of Henare Hkamana reproducing the bird's song. So now the extinct huia bird sings its swansong in the sound system of a renowned art museum, channeled through the vocal cords of a Maori man who has also sung his last song. How many species will the Age of Humans annihilate without bothering to record their sound or call sign?

Two of the last great auks were killed on Eldey, meaning "Fire Island," off southwest Iceland. The great auk, *Pinguinus impennis,* was a handsome bird resembling a penguin, the largest of the *Alcidae* family. The big eggs were sought after throughout the North Atlantic region, and the birds themselves were also hunted for meat. In Newfoundland there are pens where the birds were slaughtered en masse. Great auks were flightless, making them easy prey, but they stuck together, defended their territory, and resisted firmly when attacked. A skerry off Iceland's southwest coast was the main breeding site of the great auk, until the

---

20 Loren C. Eiseley, "The Fire-Drive and the Extinction of the Terminal Pleistocene Fauna," *American Anthropologist* 48 (1946): 54–59.

21 Julianne Warren, "echoEscapes," https://theunfallensilent.org/echoscapes/. See also Robert MacFarlane, "Generation Anthropocene: How Humans Have Altered the Planet Forever," *The Guardian,* April 1, 2016, https://www.theguardian.com/books/2016/apr/01/generation-anthropocene-altered-planet-for-ever.

rock vanished in a volcanic eruption in 1830 and the remaining birds relocated to Eldey. Foreign scientists and collectors were keen to acquire specimens of this endangered species and offered large rewards. In June 1844, farmers from Iceland's south coast sailed out to Eldey. They found a pair of great auks there, climbed up to their ledge, and wrung their necks. They were Iceland's last known great auks, though four birds are said to have been seen in Norway four years later. The Icelandic Institute of Natural History has a stuffed great auk in its collection, as well as some eggs. The bird was purchased in 1971 at auction in London, for a price equivalent to a three-room apartment in Reykjavík, the money raised by public subscription in a matter of days.[22] The slaughter of the last of the great auks signaled new times in Iceland, like the end of the dinosaurs before it. Nowadays, it seems, species are decimated unopposed.[23]

New Times, New Contract

As I began contemplating writing this memoir, I was invited to join a research project in Oslo. The anthropologist in charge of the project, Marianne Elisabeth Lien, told me it would be about the connection between humanity and nature in the northern countries, not least the domestication of animals. Most participants, she said, were likely to look at nomadic herding and fish farming. I hesitated to accept the invitation because I wanted to spend the next years writing about volcanic eruptions. At first glance I could not see how this was compatible with the Oslo project. Feeling slightly dubious, I replied to the invitation, saying that I would be interested in coming to Oslo if I could discuss what I half-jokingly called the "domestication of volcanoes." I quite expected Lien to thank me politely for considering the matter, but that volcanoes were unfortunately not on the agenda. Did volcanoes have anything in common with domestic animals? Was it possible to tame an eruption? On the contrary,

---

22 "Síðustu geirfuglarnir í Noregi," *Morgunblaðið,* March 22, 2010, 22.
23 Gísli Pálsson, *Fuglinn sem gat ekki flogið* (Reykjavík: Mál og menning, 2020).

Fig. 30. The author in the crater of Eldfell, 2016. Photo by Valdimar Leifsson.

Lien took the idea well, and there was no going back. I went to Oslo and began an unexpected and enjoyable encounter with volcanic eruptions and the people who live with them (fig. 30).

In new times we must review our traditional ideas. Our social contracts — how we resolve urgent problems such as inequality or the unequal division of wealth, and provide for people's interaction, citizens' rights, and the duties of government — are based on the work of Enlightenment thinker Jean-Jacques Rousseau and his contemporaries. Some of these eighteenth-century ideas are outdated, while others may point the way forward.[24] Nowadays, it is particularly important to avoid unilateral social contracts that ignore our relationship with the Earth. It is time, I think, to take the idea of geosociality seriously and speak of a geosocial contract, in which old and valid concepts such as solidarity and equality gain new and more down-to-earth meanings.[25]

---

24 Axel Honneth, *The Idea of Socialism: Towards a Renewal* (Oxford: Polity Press, 2017).
25 Thomas Lemke, "New Materialisms: Foucault and the 'Government of Things,'" *Theory, Culture & Society* 32, no. 4 (2015): 3–25; Jane Bennett, *Vibrant Matter: A Political Ecology of Things* (Durham: Duke University Press, 2010); Ilana Halperin, "Autobiographical Trace Fossils," in *Making*

American political scientist Jane Bennett believes there is need for a new type of politics which assumes that material things are alive. Her work aims "to articulate a vibrant materiality that runs alongside and inside humans to see how analyses of political events might change if we gave the force of things more due."[26] World politics urgently needs to view the Earth as a direct participant. Political debates wrongly revolve around the utilization of the Earth's resources, such as ores or oil, as if the Earth itself were not a political force.[27] Humanity's inventiveness and engineering have obviously achieved a great deal in many fields, as we have captured solar energy, harnessed nuclear energy, and nudged aside lava flows from erupting volcanoes. At the same time, we have created ongoing environmental problems which have no obvious solution.

The General Assembly of the Earth, if such a thing can be imagined, consists of the Earth, representatives of diverse groups of people from all over the world, and organisms of all shapes and sizes. Mass protests and general strikes may break out at any time, transcending all borders. Events are difficult to understand or control, as we see in the case of problems with international climate change conferences, but this is the world in which people and other organisms have to live, as well as one to which they must adjust.[28] We are bound up together in place and

---

the Geologic Now: Responses to Material Conditions of Contemporary Life, eds. Elizabeth Ellsworth and Jamie Kruse (Brooklyn: punctum books, 2013), 154–58; Tim Ingold and Gísli Pálsson, *Biosocial Becomings: Integrating Social and Biological Anthropology* (Cambridge: Cambridge University Press, 2013).

26 Bennett, *Vibrant Matter*, vii.

27 See Simon Dalby, "Rethinking Geopolitics: Climate Security in the Anthropocene," *Geopolicy* 5, no. 1 (2014): 1–9.

28 James C. Scott, *Seeing Like a State: How Certain Schemes to Improve the Human Condition Have Failed* (New Haven: Yale University Press, 1998); William E. Connolly, *Facing the Planetary: Entangled Humanism and the Politics of Swarming* (London: Duke University Press, 2017), 120; Bruno Latour, *Facing Gaia: Eight Lectures on the New Climatic Regime*, trans. Catherine Porter (Oxford: Polity Press, 2017); Brian Fagan, *The Attacking Ocean: The Past, Present, and Future of Rising Sea Levels* (New York: Bloomsbury Press, 2014); Anna Tsing et al., *Arts of Living on a Damaged*

time, like the seismometers that sense earthquakes and predict eruptions, in constant connection with the Earth, dancing with its movements.

The Glaciers Weep

The Earth has now begun a new dance around its axis. The melting of the glaciers is redistributing the strain in a new way.[29] I feel it is the right time to walk up onto a glacier. Late in July 2015 my wife, Guðný, and I drive to the West Fjords with some friends. We drive for two days from the city, as far as the road goes up Iceland's west coast. It snowed unusually heavily last winter, and this summer it has rained more than normal. The mountains seem to weep, tears ripping through the snow. We rest overnight and then begin our hike to Drangajökull, "Glacier of the Lone Upstanding Rock." Unlike other Icelandic ice caps, this glacier does not reach into the island's central highlands, but it is nonetheless majestic. Its history is remarkable too. For centuries farmers and seamen crossed the firn, following familiar trails to fetch provisions, lug driftwood, or deliver news.

The glacier can be seen from the main road. It pokes out tongues of ice, as if to taunt us or challenge these city-dwellers who know nothing about glaciers and their melting. We are not prepared for a long hike, as all we have with us in our rucksacks is a few water bottles and some fruit. But we are sturdily shod. My hiking boots are good quality, though, like me, getting on in years; I sometimes say that they will outlive their owner. We continue, like bulldozers, across the difficult terrain of gravel flats, crags, streams, and bogs. It is not easy going. I know that this hike is not without risk. If one of us has an accident we are in trouble. We are way off the beaten track, and there is no mobile phone coverage.

Planet: Stories from the More-than-human Anthropocene (Washington, DC: Island Press, 2016). For a discussion on the Icelandic context, see, for example, Guðni Elísson, "Nú er úti veður vont: Gróðurhúsaáhrif og íslensk umræðuhefð," *Ritið* 1 (2007): 5–44.

29 Surendra Adhikari and Erik R. Ivins, "Climate-Driven Polar Motion: 2003–2015," *Science Advances,* April 8, 2016.

Our goal is to reach the edge of the glacier. We might find it difficult to walk on the ice itself without ice crampons or ropes. We don't know which route to take or what to avoid. We feel a gentle summer breeze at the start of the hike, in the valley mouth below the glacier. It is as though the air has been locked into this sunny valley. Here, complete peace reigns and only the occasional bird song is heard. Closer to the glacier the valley narrows. Now we are aware of cool ripples of air from the ice cap, a refreshing change on an arduous hike.

The acoustics have changed too, as though powerful loudspeakers are at work all around. Amplified echoes are carried from the mountainside. Running water is everywhere, bursting from beneath the snow cover on the ice-cap. The only way to carry on a conversation is to shout over the melancholy song of the glacier. Now and again we pick our way across streams and puddles, stepping on stones or jumping over the water to keep our feet dry. We avoid the biggest streams that flow straight from under the glacier. When we look back down the slope towards the coast, we see the conspicuous light-brown smudge that these streams have painted on the surface of the sea.

On our way up to the glacier we meet a few other hikers. A young couple from Switzerland is on their second hike to the ice cap in two years. Another couple, from Germany, has come here three years ago. They are like pilgrims making their progress. I wonder to myself what makes people come all this way again and again. None of us Icelanders have been here before.

Just before we reach the glacier the heel starts to come off my boot. It follows me like a nagging presence, gently slapping at every step. The walk turns out to be much longer than we thought. We seem to be approaching the glacier, but will we get there? The hike was not supposed to take more than two hours, and we are getting tired. I'm amused to think that in the end I have outlived my hiking shoes, but the loose heel gets in my way on the difficult hike. I sit down and manage to tie the loose heel to the upper, using the long bootlace.

Finally, we reach the glacier's edge. We stop for a while at the mouth of an ice cave and rest. I notice the ice-cold wind from the glacier and the roar of flowing water. At times I am rapt, mindful only of the frozen world, but in between, many questions spring to mind. What role have the glaciers played in the past, in the lives of Icelanders and others who live in their neighborhood? What are the effects of global heating on places such as this?

No doubt it is to some extent questions like these that explain why so many people choose to visit glaciers now, whether they are locals or come from farther away.[30] Visible in the glacier margin are ash layers from volcanic eruptions, irregular horizontal stripes that time has engraved in the ice, reminiscent of the historical traces of the soot-seismometers during the Heimaey eruption. If things continue as predicted, the evidence of human actions will become ever clearer with each passing year, until the glacier is gone. But history does not vanish with the glaciers, and neither does the environmental challenge they symbolize.[31]

In times of increasing environmental awareness the term *habitat — bólstaður,* in my native language — is used for people's immediate environment, encompassing everything from their home, on the smallest scale, to the Earth itself.[32] "We are guests, and our hotel is the Earth," wrote Icelandic poet Tómas Guðmundsson in the mid-twentieth century. Not just our ho-

---

[30] Benjamin Orlove, Ellen Wiegandt, and Brian H. Luckman, *Darkening Peaks: Glacier Retreat, Science, and Society* (Berkeley: University of California Press, 2008); Helgi Björnsson, *The Glaciers of Iceland: A Historical, Cultural and Scientific Overview* (New York: Springer, 2009); Þorvarður Árnason, *Jökulsárlón: Árið um kring* (Reykjavík: Opna, 2010).

[31] Andri Snær Magnason, *On Time and Water* (London: Profile Books, 2020).

[32] Prussian polymath Alexander von Humboldt spoke of *Gäa* and *Kosmos* when discussing Earth, see Andrea Wulf, *The Invention of Nature: The Adventures of Alexander von Humboldt* (London: John Murray, 2015). See also Janet Carsten and Stephen Hugh-Jones, *About the House: Lévi-Strauss and Beyond* (Cambridge: Cambridge University Press, 1995); Christopher Morton, "Remembering the House: Memory and Materiality in Northern Botswana," *Journal of Material Culture* 12, no. 2 (2007): 157–79; David Grinspoon, *Earth in Human Hands: Shaping Our Planet's Future* (New York: Grand Central Publishing, 2016); Latour, *Facing Gaia*.

tel, comfortable for a short stay, but the only home of all life as we know it. What does that mean? Anthropologist Stephen Gudeman points out that South American farmers have long placed emphasis on caring for their habitat so that they can support themselves, which we now speak of as "sustainability."[33] For these farmers the land and *casa* are pivotal. It is necessary to look "from the door inwards," otherwise the house will collapse. Occasionally — perhaps only once in a lifetime and for a very special event — these farmers will hold a feast that is excessive, requiring more than the land they cultivate can support. They then speak of "throwing the house out the window." Such feasts mean more than normal bankruptcy, because here there is no hope of outside help.

Now people all over the world are well on their way to throwing the only house they have "out of the window." The greatest problem ever faced by humanity will not be solved in the way the Westman Islanders solved the problem of the Heimaey eruption. There is no fishing fleet to sail away with us, no "mainland" to offer for the environmental refugees of the future. It is best to be realistic about this and stay down to earth — on the only Earth we have.

As Max Frisch observed in 1979 in *Man in the Holocene*, novels are no use "on days like these, they deal with people and their relationships, […] with society, etc., as if the place for these things were assured, the earth for all time earth, the sea level fixed for all time."[34] A perceptive artist, Frisch seemed to anticipate what was coming, although he didn't name the new epoch "the Age of Humans," only "days like these." The sea level, indeed, we now know, does not remain fixed. The peninsula were I now live, an extension of Reykjavík, will become an island when all the glaciers melt.

---

33 Stephen Gudeman, "Vital Energy: The Current of Relations," *Social Analysis* 56, no. 1 (2012): 57–73; Heather Anne Swanson, Marianne Lien, and Gro B. Ween, eds., *Decentering Domestication: Stories from the Margins* (Durham: Duke University Press, 2018).
34 Max Frisch, *Man in the Holocene: A Story*, trans. Geoffrey Skleton (London: Dalkey Archive Press, 1980).

TIMELINE

About 400,000 years ago – Humans domesticate fire.
About 36,000 years ago – Oldest known pictures of volcanoes are scratched on cave walls in France.
About 14,000 years ago – Heimaey island is formed.
About 6,000 years ago – Mt. Helgafell erupts.
Around 900 – The Westman Islands are colonized by humans.
1783 – The Laki eruption in Iceland begins on June 8, and the volcanic haze spreads widely across the globe.
1815 – Mt. Tambora on the island of Sumbawa, Indonesia, begins erupting, one of the largest eruptions in history, causing global cooling, crop failure, and severe winters in both the northern and southern hemispheres; twenty thousand people die.
1883 – Krakatoa in Indonesia begins erupting. Sea flows into the volcanic crater, causing an enormous explosion. Tsunamis are triggered,

	causing devastation and killing about 36,000 people on nearby islands.
1906 –	The worker's cottage known as Bólstaður is built on Heimaey.
1918 –	Katla erupts. Volcanic ash spreads across over half of Iceland.
1934 –	*June 2*: A large earthquake shakes Dalvík, northern Iceland, and the adjacent areas. Many locals spend the summer in tents and temporary shelters while repairs are made.
1947 –	Hekla in Iceland erupts, a long intense eruption. One man dies studying it.
1949 –	The author is born at Bólstaður on the Westman Islands.
c. 1950 –	Anthropocene, the Age of Humans, begins .
1963 –	The volcanic island Surtsey is born, not far from Heimaey.
1968 –	The author's family from Bólstaður moves to Reykjavík.
1972 –	Soot-seismometers are installed at Laugarvatn and Skammadalshóll. The author begins graduate studies at the University of Manchester.
1973 –	*January 22*: Earthquake specialists in southern Iceland predict an eruption, possibly on Heimaey. *January 23*: An eruption begins on Heimaey. Westman Islanders are evacuated to the mainland in fishing boats. *February 6*: The first experiments in cooling the lava begin.

March 22: Sigurgeir Örn Sigurgeirsson dies from breathing toxic volcanic gases on Heimaey, exact time of death unknown.
April 2: Lava cooling with high-pressure hoses begins. Bólstaður, on Heimagata, is engulfed by lava and burns.
April 22: The battle for Heimaey is considered won when lava floods east of Eldfell.
July 3: The Heimaey eruption ends.
August: the author visits Heimaey.

1974 – *July*: The first End of the Eruption Festival is held.
December 20: An avalanche falls on Neskaupstaður, eastern Iceland; 12 die.

1980 – Mt. St. Helens erupts, the largest eruption in US history, devastating several hundred square kilometers of land.

2000 – *June 17*: A large earthquake, 6.5 on the Richter scale, strikes south Iceland, followed by another a few days later.

2004 – A tsunami triggered by an earthquake strikes countries around the Indian Ocean; 230,000 people die

2010 – Eyjafjallajökull in Iceland erupts. Ash clouds disrupt flights around the world.

2014 – Eldheimar Museum opens in the Westman Islands, showcasing the 1973 volcanic eruption.

BIBLIOGRAPHY

N.B. Entries are following Iceland alphabetical order, with Ð following D, Á, É, Í, Ó, Ú, and Ý following A, E, I, O, U, and Y respectively, and Þ, Æ, and Ö following Z.

PUBLISHED SOURCES

"60 hús undir hraun í nótt." *Vísir,* March 23, 1973.
"64 hús hurfu á 8 klst." *Morgunblaðið,* March 24, 1973.
"1000 sek. lítrar af sjó — á 1100 stiga heitt hraun." *Morgunblaðið,* April 3, 1973, 32.
Adeney Thomas, Julia. "History and Biology in the Anthropocene: Problems of Scale, Problems of Value." *American Historical Review* (December 2014): 1587–607. DOI: 10.1093/ahr/119.5.1587.
Adhikari, Surendra, and Erik R. Ivins. "Climate-Driven Polar Motion: 2003–2015." *Science Advances* 2, no. 4 (April 2016): e1501693. DOI: 10.1126/sciadv.1501693.
AFP. "Volcanic Eruption in Cape Verde Destroys Two Villages." *Daily Mail,* December 16, 2014. http://www.dailymail.co.uk/wires/afp/article-2876017/Volcanic-eruption-Cape-Verde-destroys-villages.html.
Anderson, Benedict R. *Imagined Communities: Reflections on the Origin and Spread of Nationalism.* London: Verso, 2010.

Ágústsson, Steinar. "Sigurgeir Sigurgeirsson – Kveðja." *Morgunblaðið*, May 8, 1973, 53.
Árnason, Þorvarður. *Jökulsárlón: Árið um kring*. Reykjavík: Opna, 2010.
Bateson, Gregory. *Steps to an Ecology of Mind*. Frogmore: Paladin, 1972.
Bennett, Jane. *Vibrant Matter: A Political Ecology of Things*. Durham: Duke University Press, 2010.
Birgisdóttir, Soffía Auður. *Ég skapa þess vegna er ég: Um skrif Þórbergs Þórðarsonar*. Reykjavík: Opna, 2015.
Björnsson, Björn Th. *Sandgreifarnir*. Reykjavík: Mál og menning, 1989.
Björnsson, Helgi. *The Glaciers of Iceland: A Historical, Cultural and Scientific Overview*. Translated by Julia Meldo D'Arcy. New York: Springer, 2017.
Borges, Jorge Luis. *Labyrinths: Selected Stories and Other Writings*. Translated by James E. Irby et al. New York: New Directions, 1962.
"Bólstaður." *Heimaslóð*. http://www.heimaslod.is/index.php/Bolstad.
Brunner, Bernd. *Moon: A Brief History*. New Haven: Yale University Press, 2011.
de la Cadena, Marisol. *Earth Beings: Ecologies of Practice across Andean Worlds*. Durham: Duke University Press, 2015.
"California Drought Causing Valley Land to Sink." NASA, August 19, 2015. http://www.jpl.nasa.gov/news/news.php?feature=4693.
Carsten, Janet, and Stephen Hugh-Jones, eds. *About the House: Lévi-Strauss and Beyond*. Cambridge: Cambridge University Press, 1995.
Chakrabarty, Dipesh. "Postcolonial Studies and the Challenge of Climate Change." *New Literary History* 43, no. 1 (2012): 1–18. DOI: 10.1353/nlh.2012.0007.
Clabby, Catherine. "Seismic Visions of Middle Earth." *American Scientist* 103, no. 2 (2015): 100–105. DOI: 10.1511/2015.113.102.

Clark, Nigel, Alexandra Gormally, and Hugh Tuffen. "Speculative Volcanology: Time, Becoming, and Violence in Encounters with Magma." *Environmental Humanities* 10, no. 1 (2018): 274–94. DOI: 10.1215/22011919-4385571.

Cohen, Jeffrey Jerome. *Stone: An Ecology of the Inhuman*. Minneapolis: University of Minnesota Press, 2015.

Colgate, Stirling A., and Þorbjörn Sigurgeirsson. "Dynamic Mixing of Water and Lava." *Nature* 244, no. 41 (1973): 552–55. DOI: 10.1038/244552a0.

Connolly, William E. *Facing the Planetary: Entangled Humanism and the Politics of Swarming*. Durham: Duke University Press, 2017.

Crutzen, Paul J., and Eugene F. Stoermer. "The Anthropocene." *Global Change Newsletter* 41 (2000): 17–18.

Dalby, Simon. "Rethinking Geopolitics: Climate Security in the Anthropocene." *Geopolicy* 5 (2014): 1–9. DOI:10.1111/1758-5899.12074.

Delanty, Gerard, and Aurea Mota. "Governing the Anthropocene: Agency, Governance, Knowledge." *European Journal of Social Theory* 20 (2017): 9–38. DOI: 10.1177/1368431016668535.

"Eigum við ekki bara að tjalda hérna." *Vísir*, July 3, 1973.

Einarsson, Einar H. "Vísindamaður í Vestur-Skaftafellssýslu." In *Séð og heyrt á Suðurlandi: 22 Sunnlendingar segja frá*, edited by Jón R. Hjálmarsson, 40–60. Selfoss: Suðurlandsútgáfan, 1979.

Einarsson, Guðmundur. "Heklugosið 1947." *Eimreiðin* 53, no. 2 (1949): 84–94.

Einarsson, Páll. "Short-Term Seismic Precursors to Icelandic Eruptions 1973–2014." *Frontiers in Earth Science*, May 8, 2018. DOI: 10.3389/feart.2018.00045.

Einarsson, Páll, and Sveinbjörn Björnsson. "Jarðskjálftamælingar á Raunvísindastofnun Háskólans." In *Í hlutarins eðli*, edited by Þorsteinn Ingi Sigfússon, 251–78. Reykjavík: Menningarsjóður, 1987.

Einarsson, Trausti. "Bergmyndunarsaga Vestmannaeyja." In *Árbók Ferðafélags Íslands*, 131–57. Reykjavík: Ferðafélag Íslands, 1948.

"Eins og Helgafell hafi hlíft byggðinni." *Morgunblaðið*, January 24, 1973, 11.

Eiseley, Loren C. "The Fire-Drive and the Extinction of the Terminal Pleistocene Fauna." *American Anthropologist* 48 (1946): 54–59. DOI: 10.1525/aa.1946.48.1.02a00060.

Elder, W.A. "Drilling into Magma and the Implications of the Icelandic Deep Drill Drilling Project (IDDP) for High-Temperature Geothermal Systems Worldwide." *Geothermics* 49 (2014): 111–18. DOI: 10.1016/j.geothermics.2013.05.001.

Elíasson, Gyrðir. *Tvífundnaland*. Reykjavík: Mal og menning, 2003.

Elísson, Guðni. "Nú er úti veður vont: Gróðurhúsaáhrif og íslensk umræðuhefð." *Ritið* 1 (2007): 5–44.

Ellsworth, Elizabeth, and Jamie Kruse. "Evidence: Making A Geologic Turn in Cultural Awareness." In *Making the Geologic Now: Responses to Material Conditions of Contemporary Life,* edited by Elizabeth Ellsworth and Jamie Kruse, 6–26. Brooklyn: punctum books, 2013.

Ellsworth, William L. "Injection-Induced Earthquakes." *Science* 341 (July 12, 2013). DOI: 10.1126/science.1225942.

Erlingsson, Steindór J. "Veirur, kjarnorka og eðlisvísindi á Íslandi." *Morgunblaðið*, October 8, 2016, 30.

"Eru náttúruöflin að kenna okkur að standa saman?" *Tíminn,* January 24, 1973.

Eyjólfsson, Guðjón Ármann. Vestmannaeyjar: Árbók Ferðafélags Íslands. Reykjavík: Ferðafélag Íslands, 2009.

———. *Vestmannaeyjar: Byggð og eldgos*. Reykjavík: Ísafoldarprentsmiðja, 1973.

Fagan, Brian. *The Attacking Ocean: The Past, Present, and Future of Rising Sea Levels*. New York: Bloomsbury Press, 2014.

Falk, Oren. "The Vanishing Volcanoes: Fragments of Fourteenth-Century Icelandic Folklore." *Folklore* 118 (2007): 1–22. DOI: 10.1080/00155870601096257.

"Fannst látinn af völdum gass." *Vísir,* April 5, 1973.
Farrier, David. "'Like a Stone': Ecology, Enargeia, and Ethical Time in Alice Oswald's Memorial." *Environmental Humanities* 4 (2014): 1–18. DOI: 10.1215/22011919-3614908.
"Flýttu þér heim, pabbi – það er gos í Helgafelli." *Tíminn,* January 26, 1973.
Frisch, Max. *Man in the Holocene: A Story.* Translated by Geoffrey Skelton. London: Dalkey Archive Press, 1980.
Glazner, Allen, John M. Bartley, and Drew S. Coleman. "We Need a New Definition of 'Magma'." *EOS: Earth and Space Science News,* September 22, 2012. https://eos.org/opinions/we-need-a-new-definition-for-magma.
Goldenberg, Suzanne. "Climate Change Is Lifting Iceland." *The Guardian,* January 30, 2015. https://www.theguardian.com/environment/2015/jan/30/climate-change-lifting-iceland-volcanic-eruptions.
Grinspoon, David. *Earth in Human Hands: Shaping Our Planet's Future.* New York: Grand Central Publishing, 2016.
———. "Why Most Planets Will Either Be Lush or Dead." *Nautilus — Cosmos,* December 2016. http://cosmos.nautil.us/short/73/why-most-planets-will-either-be-lush-or-dead.
Gudeman, Stephen. "Vital Energy: The Current of Relations." *Social Analysis* 56, no. 1 (2012): 57–73. DOI: 10.3167/sa.2012.560105.
Guðmundsson, Ari Trausti. "Annar og þriðji gosdagur í Eyjum." *Jökull* 33 (1983): 162.
———. *Íslenskar eldstöðvar.* Edited by Svala Þormóðsdóttir. Reykjavík: Vaka-Helgafell, 2001.
Guðmundsson, Ari Trausti, and Ragnar Th. Sigurðsson. *Eldgos 1913–2004.* Reykjavík: Vaka-Helgafell, 2005.
Guðnason, Haraldur. *Við Ægisdyr: Saga Vestmannaeyjabæjar I–II.* Reykjavík: Stofn, 1982–1991.
Halldórsson, Jón Berg. "Frásögn á 40 ára gosafmæli." *1973 í bátana,* March 2013. http://1973-i-batana.blogspot.is/2013/03/utbjo-essa-blogg-siu-til-i-tvennum.html.
Halperin, Ilana. "Autobiographical Trace Fossils." In *Making the Geologic Now: Responses to Material Conditions of*

Contemporary Life, edited by Elizabeth Ellsworth and Jamie Kruse, 154–58. Brooklyn: punctum books, 2013.

———. "Physical Geology (A Field Guide to the New Landmass in Three Formations)." In *Ilana Halperin: New Landmass/Neu Landmasse,* edited by Sara Barnes and Andrew Patrizio, 52–61. Berlin: Berliner Medizinhistorischen Museums der Charité/Shering Stiftung, 2012.

———. "Ruins in Reverse (Nomadic Landmass)." Lecture series at Whitney Museum of American Art, Altria; Astrup Fearnley Museum of Modern Art; Manchester Museum; Camden Arts Centre, 2005–2006.

———. "Ruins in Reverse (Nomadic Landmass)." http://www.ilanahalperin.com/new/eldhus.html.

Hamilton, James. *Volcano: Nature and Culture.* London: Reaktion Books, 2012.

Haraway, Donna. "Situated Knowledges: The Science Question in Feminism and the Privilege of Partial Perspective." *Feminist Studies* 14, no. 23 (1988): 575–99. DOI: 10.2307/3178066.

"Haroun Tazieff, 83, a Volcanist and Iconoclast on Environment." *New York Times,* February 8, 1998. https://www.nytimes.com/1998/02/08/world/haroun-tazieff-83-a-volcanist-and-iconoclast-on-environment.html.

"Heimaeyjargosið: Gosannáll." *Heimaslóð.* http://www.heimaslod.is/index.php/Heimaeyjargosið:Gosannáll.

"Heimaklettur." *Facebook.* https://www.facebook.com/groups/166156446851821/.

Helgason, Haukur. "Eldgos séð fyrir: Engin óvænt gos en kannski 'gabb'." *Vísir,* October 10, 1972, 6.

Hill, Lisa. "Life after the Volcano: The Embodiment of Small Island Memories and Efforts to Keep Montserratian Culture Alive in Preston, UK." *Area* 26, no. 2 (2014): 146–53. DOI: 10.1111/area.12084.

Hjartarson, Árni. "Alfred Wegener og samskipti hans við Íslendinga." *Náttúrufræðingurinn* 1–4 (2012): 126–34.

Holmberg, Karen. "Beyond the Catastrophe: The Volcanic Landscape of Barú, Western Panama." In *Living Under the Shadow: Cultural Impacts of Volcanic Eruptions,* edited by John Grattan and Robin Torrence, 274–97. Walnut Creek: Left Coast Press, 2007.

———. "The Cultural Nature of Tephra: 'Problematic' Ecofacts and Artifacts and the Barú Volcano, Panama." *Quaternary International* (March 2015): 1–19. DOI: 10.1016/j.quaint.2015.01.016.

Holt, Jim. "Something Faster Than Light? What Is It?" *New York Review of Books* (November 2016): 50–52. https://www.nybooks.com/articles/2016/11/10/something-faster-than-light-what-is-it/.

Honneth, Axel. *The Idea of Socialism: Towards a Renewal.* Cambridge: Polity Press, 2017.

"Hraun í höfnina." *Vísir,* April 2, 1973.

Hreinsson, Viðar. *Jón lærði: Náttúrur náttúrunnar.* Reykjavík: Forlagið, 2016.

Hrólfsdóttir, Gunnhildur. *Þær þráðinn spunnu.* Reykjavík: Frum, 2015.

Huijbens, Edward H., and Gísli Pálsson. "The Bog in Our Brain and Bowels: Social Attitudes to the Cartography of Icelandic Wetlands." *Environment and Planning D: Society and Space* 27 (2009): 296–316. DOI: 10.1068/d9508.

Hutton, James. *Theory of the Earth: Or an Investigation of the Laws Observable in the Composition, Dissolution, and Restoration of Land Upon the Globe.* Edinburgh: Transactions of the Royal Society of Edinburgh, 1788.

Höskuldsson, Ármann, Einar Kjartansson, Árni Þór Vésteinsson, Sigurður Steinþórsson, and Oddur Sigurðsson. "Eldstöðvar í sjó." In *Náttúruvá á Íslandi: Eldgos og jarðskjálftar,* edited by Júlíus Sólnes, 403–25. Reykjavík: Viðlagatrygging Íslands/Háskólaútgáfan, 2013.

Ingold, Tim, and Gísli Pálsson, eds. *Biosocial Becomings: Integrating Social and Biological Anthropology.* Cambridge: Cambridge University Press, 2013.

Irving, Dorothy J. *This Too Is Diplomacy: Stories of a Partnership*. Bloomington: AuthorHouse, 2007.

Johnsen, Hlöðver. *Bergið klifið: Minningar veiðimanns*. Reykjavík: Almenna bókafélagið, 1986.

Johnsen, Sigfús M. *Saga Vestmannaeyja*. Vol. I. Reykjavík: Fjölsýn forlag, 1946.

———. *Saga Vestmannaeyja*. Vol. II. Reykjavík: Fjölsýn forlag, 1946.

Jónsson, Björn. "Eftir tíu ár: Úr ferð um landskjálftasvæðið frá 1898." *Ísafold* 67 (1906): 266.

Jónsson, Finnur, ed. *Landnámabók I–III*. Copenhagen: Det Kongelige Nordiske Oldskrift-Selskab, 1900.

Jónsson, Stefán. *Mínir menn: Vertíðarsaga*. Reykjavík: Ægisútgáfan, 1962.

Jónsson, Valdimar K., and Matthías Matthíasson. "Hraunkæling á Heimaey: Verklegar framkvæmdir." *Tímarit Verkfræðingafélags Íslands* 59, no. 5 (1974): 70–83.

Kalman, Jón. *Eitthvað á stærð við alheiminn*. Reykjavík: Bjartur, 2015.

Kaplan, Sarah. "Climate Change, Melting Glaciers Make Iceland Spring Upward Like a Trampoline." *Washington Post*, February 2, 2015. https://www.washingtonpost.com/news/morning-mix/wp/2015/02/02/climate-change-melting-glaciers-make-iceland-spring-upward-like-a-trampoline/.

Kristinsson, Björn. *Kjarnorkuver fyrir Vestmannaeyjar: Lýsing á tilboði General Electric*. Reykjavík: Orkudeild Raforkumálastjóra, 1959.

"Kæruleysi gagnvart gaseitrun." *Vísir*, March 26, 1973.

"Landskjálptarnir." *Lögberg* 40 (October 15, 1896): 2, 6.

Latour, Bruno. *Facing Gaia: Eight Lectures on the New Climatic Regime*. Translated by Catherine Porter. Oxford: Polity Press, 2017.

Lemke, Thomas. "New Materialisms: Foucault and the 'Government of Things.'" *Theory, Culture & Society* 32, no. 4 (2015): 3–25. DOI: 10.1177/0263276413519340.

Leopold, Aldo. *A Sand County Almanac and Sketches Here and There*. New York: Oxford University Press, 1949.

Lilyblad, Christopher Marc. "Between Hope and Despair: The Community of Cha das Caldeiras after the Fogo Volcano Eruption." *Europa Archives*, January 7, 2014. http://eeas.europa.eu/archives/delegations/cape_verde/documents/press_corner/20140107_en.pdf.

"Líklegast orðið of seint að breyta hraunrennslinu." *Vísir*, February 13, 1973.

Lovelock, James E. *Gaia: A New Look at Life on Earth*. Oxford: Oxford University Press, 1979.

Lovelock, James E., and Lynn Margulis. "Atmospheric Homeostasis by and for the Biosphere: The Gaia Hypothesis." *Tellus* 26, nos. 1–2 (1974): 2–10. DOI: 10.3402/tellusa.v26i1-2.9731.

Lund, Katrín Anna, and Karl Benediktsson. "Inhabiting a Risky Earth: The Eyjafjallajökull Eruption in 2010 and Its Impacts." *Anthropology Today* 27, no. 1 (2011): 6–9. DOI: 10.1111/j.1467-8322.2011.00781.x.

MacFarlane, Robert. "Generation Anthropocene: How Humans Have Altered the Planet Forever." *The Guardian*, April 1, 2016. https://www.theguardian.com/books/2016/apr/01/generation-anthropocene-altered-planet-for-ever.

Magnason, Andri Snær. *On Time and Water*. London: Profile Books, 2020.

Margulis, Lynn, and Dorion Sagan. *What Is Life?* Berkeley: University of California Press, 1995.

Marsh, George Perkins. *Man and Nature*. Edited by David Lowenthal. Cambridge: The Belknap Press of Harvard University Press, 1864.

Masao, Fidelis T., et al. "New Footprints from Laetoli (Tanzania) Provide Evidence for Marked Body Size Variation in Early Hominins." *eLife*, December 14, 2016. DOI: 10.7554/eLife.19568.

Masco, Joseph. "Bad Weather: On Planetary Crisis." *Social Studies of Science* 40, no. 1 (2010): 7–70. DOI: 10.1177/0306312709341598.

Matter, Juerg M., et al. "Rapid Carbon Mineralization for Permanent Disposal of Anthropogenic Carbon Dioxide Emission." *Science* 352, no. 6291 (June 10, 2016): 1312–14. DOI: 10.1126/science.aad8132.

Mattsson, Hannes, and Ármann Höskuldsson. "Geology of the Heimaey Volcanic Centre, South Iceland: Early Evolution of a Central Volcano in a Propagating Rift?" *Journal of Volcanology and Geothermal Research* 127 (2003): 55–71. DOI: 10.1016/S0377-0273(03)00178-1.

McGuire, Bill. "Obituary: Haroun Tazieff." *The Independent*, February 7, 1998. https://www.independent.co.uk/news/obituaries/obituary-haroun-tazieff-1143330.html.

McPhee, John. "Cooling the Lava." In *The Control of Nature*, 95–179. New York: Farrar Straus Giroux, 1989.

Merchant, Carolyn. "The Scientific Revolution and The Death of Nature." *Isis* 97, no. 33 (2006): 513–33.

"Með rannsóknum má segja fyrir um eldgos." *Morgunblaðið*, August 21, 1965.

Minakami, Takesi. "Fundamental Research for Predicting Volcanic Eruptions." *Bulletin of the Earthquake Research Institute* 38 (1960): 497–644.

Morton, Christopher. "Remembering the House: Memory and Materiality in Northern Botswana." *Journal of Material Culture* 12, no. 2 (2007): 157–79. DOI: 10.1177/1359183507078123.

Needham, Joseph. *Science and Civilization in China, Volume 3: Mathematics and the Sciences of the Heavens and the Earth*. Cambridge: Cambridge University Press, 1959.

Nelly Ben Hayoun Studios. "The Other Volcano." http://nellyben.com/projects/the-other-volcano/.

Nomade, Sébastien, et al. "A 36,000-Year-Old Volcanic Eruption Depicted in the Chauvet-Pont d'Arc Cave (Ardèche, France)?" *Plos One*, January 8, 2016. DOI: 10.1371/journal.pone.0146621..

Oppenheimer, Clive. *Eruptions That Shook the World*. Cambridge: Cambridge University Press, 2011.

Oppenheimer, Clive, et al. "The Eldgjá Eruption: Timing, Long Range Impacts and Influence on the Christianisation of Iceland." *Climate Change* 3–4 (2018): 369–81. DOI: 10.1007/s10584-018-2171-9.

Oreskes, Naomi. "From Continental Drift to Plate Tectonics." In *Plate Tectonics: An Insider's History of the Modern Theory of the Earth,* edited by Naomi Oreskes, 3–27. Boulder: The Westview Press, 2003.

Orlove, Benjamin, Ellen Wiegandt, and Brian H. Luckman, eds. *Darkening Peaks: Glacier Retreat, Science, and Society.* Berkeley: University of California Press, 2008.

Óskarsson, Ingibergur. "1973 - Allir í bátana," https://en.1973-alliribatana.com/ingibergur.

Pagli, Carolina, and Freysteinn Sigmundsson. "Will Present Day Glacier Retreat Increase Volcanic Activity? Stress Induced by Recent Glacier Retreat and Its Effect on Magmatism at the Vatnajökull Ice Cap, Iceland." *Geophysical Research Letters* 35 (2008): 1–5. DOI: 10.1029/2008GL033510.

Pálmadóttir, Elín. "Hekla vaknaði 1947 af aldarsvefni." *Morgunblaðið,* March 27, 1997.

Pálsson, Gísli. "Celestial Bodies: Lucy in the Sky." In *Humans in Outer Space: Interdisciplinary Odysseys,* edited by Luca Codignola and Kai-Uwe Schrogl, 69–81. New York: Springer, 2009.

———. *Fuglinn sem gat ekki flogið.* Reykjavík: Mál og menning, 2020.

———. "Nature and Society in the Age of Postmodernity." In *Reimagining Political Ecology,* edited by Aletta Biersack and James Greenberg, 70–93. Durham: Duke University Press, 2006.

———. *Nature, Culture, and Society: Anthropological Perspectives on Life.* Cambridge: Cambridge University Press, 2016.

———. *The Human Age: How We Created the Anthropocene Epoch and Caused the Climate Crisis.* London: Welbeck, 2020.

Pálsson, Gísli, and Helgi Bernódusson. "Hefnd Helgafells." *Fylkir* (December 2017): 12–13, 15.

Pálsson, Gísli, and Heather Anne Swanson. "Down to Earth: Geosocialities and Geopolitics," *Environmental Humanities* 8, no. 2 (2016): 149–71. DOI: 10.1215/22011919-3664202.

Pálsson, Gísli, et al. "Reconceptualizing the 'Anthropos' in the Anthropocene: Integrating the Social Sciences and Humanities in Global Environmental Change Research." *Environmental Science and Policy* 28 (2013): 3–13. DOI: 10.1016/j.envsci.2012.11.004.

Pálsson, Sigurður Þór. *Skriðið úr skrápnum*. Reykjavík: Bókbindarinn, 1972.

Pyle, David M. *Volcanoes: Encounters through the Ages*. Oxford: Bodleian Library, 2017.

Raffles, Hugh. *The Book of Uncomformities: Speculations on Lost Time*. New York: Pantheon, 2020.

———. "Twenty-Five Years Is a Long Time." *Cultural Anthropology* 27, no. 3 (2012): 526–34. DOI: 10.1111/j.1548-1360.2012.01158.x.

Riede, Felix. "Volcanic Activity and Human Society." *Quaternary International* 294 (2016): 1–5. DOI: 10.1016/j.quaint.2015.08.090.

Rockström, Johan, et al. "A Safe Operating Space for Humanity." *Nature* 461 (2009): 472–75. DOI: 10.1038/461472a.

Roy, Eleanor Ainge. "New Zealand Gives Mount Taranaki Same Legal Rights as a Person." *The Guardian*, December 22, 2017. https://www.theguardian.com/world/2017/dec/22/new-zealand-gives-mount-taranaki-same-legal-rights-as-a-person.

Rubin, Allan M., and Dominique Gillard. "Dike-induced Earthquakes: Theoretical Considerations." *Journal of Geophysical Research* 103, no. B5 (1998): 10017–30. DOI: 10.1029/97JB03514.

Rudwick, Martin J.S. *Bursting the Limits of Time: The Reconstruction of Geohistory in the Age of Revolution*. Chicago: The University of Chicago Press, 2005.

Sacks, Oliver. "Speak, Memory." *New York Review of Books*, February 21, 2013. https://www.nybooks.com/articles/2013/02/21/speak-memory/.

———. *The Man Who Mistook His Wife for a Hat*. New York: Touchstone, 1985.

Sandomir, Richard. "Leonard Reiffel, Who Studied Lunar Nuclear Bomb, Dies at 89." *New York Times*, April 26, 2017. https://www.nytimes.com/2017/04/26/us/obituary-leonard-reiffel-nuclear-bomb-moon.html.

Sandwell, David T. "Plate Tectonics: A Martian View." In *Plate Tectonics: An Insider's History of the Modern Theory of the Earth*, edited by Naomi Oreskes, 331–45. Boulder: The Westview Press, 2003.

Schlossberg, Tatiana. "An Ice Scientist's Worst Nightmare." *New York Times*, April 1, 2017. https://www.nytimes.com/2017/04/11/climate/ice-cores-melted-freezer-alberta-canada.html.

Scott, James C. *Seeing Like a State: How Certain Schemes to Improve the Human Condition Have Failed*. New Haven: Yale University Press, 1998.

Sigmundsson, Freysteinn, et al. "Segmented Lateral Dyke Growth in a Rifting Event at Bárðarbunga Volcanic System, Iceland." *Nature* 517 (2015): 191–95. DOI: 10.1038/nature14111.

Sigurgeirsson, Þorbjörn. "Hraunkæling." *Tíminn*, January 19, 1974, 8–9, 13.

———. "Lava Cooling." In *Lava-Cooling Operations During the 1973 Eruption of Eldfell Volcano, Heimaey, Vestmannaeyjar, Iceland*, edited by Richard S. Williams, Jr., 29–30. Woods Hole: U.S. Geological Survey, 1974.

Sigurðsson, Oddur. "Jarðeldar á Heimaey 1973." *Týli* 4 (1974): 5–25.

"Síðustu geirfuglarnir í Noregi." *Morgunblaðið*, March 22, 2010, 22.

Smith, Neil. "There's No Such Thing as a Natural Disaster." *Items: Insights from the Social Sciences*, June 11, 2006. http://items.ssrc.org/understanding-katrina/theres-no-such-thing-as-a-natural-disaster/.

Stawkowski, Magdalena E. "I Am a Radioactive Mutant: Emergent Biological Subjectivities at Kazakhstan's Semipalatinsk Nuclear Test Site." *American Ethnologist* 43, no. 1 (2016): 144–57. DOI: 10.1111/amet.12269.

Steingrímsson, Jón. *Fires of the Earth: The Laki Eruption 1783–1784*. Translated by Keneva Kunz. Reykjavík: University of Iceland Press, 1998.

Sveinsson, Óttar. *Útkall: Flóttinn frá Heimaey*. Reykjavík: Útkall, 2008.

Swanson, Heather Anne, Marianne Lien, and Gro B. Ween, eds. *Decentering Domestication: Stories from the Margins*. Durham: Duke University Press, 2018.

Szerszynski, Bronislaw. "The Anthropocene Monument: On Relating Geological and Human Time." *European Journal of Social Theory* 20, no. 1 (2017): 111–31. DOI: 10.1177/1368431016666087.

Tazieff, Haroun. "La Soufrière, Volcanology and Forecasting." *Nature* 269 (1977): 96–97. DOI: 10.1007/978-3-642-73759-6_5.

Theódórsson, Páll. "Þorbjörn Sigurgeirsson." *Andvari* 114, no. 1 (1989): 5–61.

Thoroddsen, Þorvaldur. *Landfræðisaga Íslands, I–V*. Reykjavík: Ormstunga, 2003–2009.

Tower, Wells. "The Hawaii Cure: A First Trip to the Island, in a Desperate Bid to Escape the News." *New York Times Magazine*, March 21, 2017. https://www.nytimes.com/2017/03/21/magazine/hawaii-travels-escape.html.

Tómasson, Þórður. "Minning: Einar H. Einarsson Skammadalshóli." *Morgunblaðið*, October 17, 1992.

Tsing, Anna, et al., eds. *Arts of Living on a Damaged Planet: Stories from the More-than-human Anthropocene*. Washington, DC: Island Press, 2016.

van Dooren, Thom. *Flight Ways: Life and Loss at the Edge of Extinction*. New York: Columbia University Press, 2014.

Van Noorden, Richard. "X-rays Reveal Words in Vesuvius-baked Scrolls." *Nature*, January 20, 2015. DOI: 10.1038/nature.2015.16763.

"Vestmannaeyjagosið framhald af Surtsey: Kvikan beið." *Morgunblaðið*, January 17, 1997.

Vilhjálmsson, Þorsteinn. "Hver var Þorbjörn Sigurgeirsson og fyrir hvað er hann þekktastur?" *Vísindavefurinn*, April 27, 2011. http://www.visindavefur.is/svar.php?id=59464.

"'Virðist út í bláinn'." *Vísir*, March 21, 1973.

"Volcano Blast Splits Island: 5,000 Saved." *Manchester Evening News*. January 23, 1973.

Warren, Julianne. "echoEscapes." https://theunfallensilent.org/echoscapes/.

Warsini, Sri, et al. "Living Through a Volcanic Eruption: Understanding the Experience of Survivors as a Phenomenological Existential Phenomenon." *Mental Health Nursing* 25 (2016): 206–13. DOI: 10.1111/inm.12212.

Winchester, Simon. *The Map That Changed the World*. London: Penguin Books, 2001.

Worster, Donald, ed. *The Ends of the Earth: Perspectives on Environmental History*. Cambridge: Cambridge University Press, 1988.

Wulf, Andrea. *The Invention of Nature: The Adventures of Alexander von Humboldt*. London: John Murray, 2015.

Yusoff, Kathryn. "Anthropogenesis: Origins and Endings in the Anthropocene." *Theory, Culture & Society* 33, no. 2 (2015): 1–26. DOI: 10.1177/0263276415581021.

"Það eru afrek þjóðarinnar sjálfrar, sem skera úr um alla framtíð hennar." *Þjóðviljinn*, February 2, 1973, 16.

"Þjóðin í heild verður að glíma við örðugleikana." *Þjóðviljinn*, January 26, 1973, 9.

Þorgilsson, Ari. *The Book of the Icelanders: The Story of the Conversion*. Translated by Siân Grønlie. London: University College of London, 2006.

Þórarinsdóttir, Guðrún G., Magnús Freyr Ólafsson, and Þórður Örn Kristjánsson. "Lostætur landnemi." *Náttúrufræðingurinn* 75, no. 1 (2007): 33–40.

Þórarinsson, Sigurður. *Heklueldar*. Reykjavík: Sögufélagið, 1968.

———. "Náttúruvernd." *Náttúrufræðingurinn* 20 (1950): 1–12.

———. *Tefrokronologiska studier på Island*. Doctoral dissertation, University of Stockholm, 1944.

———. "Þorsteinn Magnússon og Kötlugosið 1625." *Árbók (Landsbókasafns Íslands) 1975*, no. 1 (1976): 5–9.

Þórðarson, Þórbergur. *The Stones Speak*. Translated by Julian Meldon D'Arcy. Reykjavík: Mál og menning, 2012.

"Þurfum bætur jafnt fyrir heil sem ónýt hús." *Vísir*, April 2, 1973.

Ævarsdóttir, Oddný Eir. *Land of Love and Ruins*. Translated by Philip Roughton. New York: Restless Books, 2016.

UNPUBLISHED DOCUMENTS AND ARCHIVAL MATERIALS

Bjarnason, Magnús. "Privatissimo: Eldgosið í Heimaey 1973." Unpublished manuscript, 2003.

Björnsson, Sveinbjörn. "Nýting hraunhita í Vestmannaeyjum." Radio talk, December 8, 1976. RH-77-3.

Einarsson, Einar H. "Diaries of Einars H. Einarsson," 1973. Regional Archive of Skógar.

———. "Eldgosið á Heimaey 1973: Afrit af köflum úr dagbók og aflestrarskýrslum af mæli á Skammadalshóli," 1973. Regional Archive of Skógar.

"Eldgos í Heimaey í Vestmannaeyjum." Minutes of The Science Institute, University of Iceland, January 23, 1973. Documents of Þorbjörn Sigurgeirsson. Personal collection of Sveinbjörn Björnsson.

Fasteignamat Vestmannaeyjasýslu, 1916. Westman Islands Archives.

Minutes of the Town Council of the Westman Islands, January 23, 1973. Westman Islands Archives.

"Report of Dr. Stirling Colgate and Prof. Charles B. Moore to the Science Institute, University of Iceland, in cooperation with Prof. Þorbjörn Sigurgeirsson," February 26, 1973. Documents of Þorbjörn Sigurgeirsson. Personal collection of Sveinbjörn Björnsson.

Seismographs from Laugarvatn (box ER 099), January 1973. National Archives of Iceland.

Seismographs from Skammadalshóll (box ER 144), January 1973. National Archives of Iceland.

Sigurgeirsson, Þorbjörn. Diaries from the Westman Islands, 1973. Documents of Þorbjörn Sigurgeirsson. Personal collection of Sveinbjörn Björnsson.

———. "Hraunkæling." Public talk at the Nordic House, Reykjavík, November 4, 1973. Documents of Þorbjörn Sigurgeirsson. Personal collection of Sveinbjörn Björnsson.

———. Letter to Dr. C.B. Moore, New Mexico Institute of Mining and Technology, July 26, 1973. Letters of Þorbjörn Sigurgeirsson, 1970-1974, box A/0007. National Archives of Iceland.

Zóphóníasson, Páll. "Þegar sjómenn gengu á land." Speech, Westman Islands, April 4, 1993.

Made in the USA
Monee, IL
15 November 2020